radio data
reference book

radio data reference book

FIFTH EDITION

R. S. HEWES, TEng, FSERT, G3TDR
G. R. JESSOP, CEng, MIERE, G6JP

RADIO SOCIETY OF GREAT BRITAIN

Published by the Radio Society of Great Britain, Lambda House, Cranborne Road, Potters Bar, Herts EN6 3JW.

First published 1962
Fifth edition 1985

ISBN 0 900612 67 3

Printed at The Bath Press, Avon

Contents

Preface

Radio technology, embracing a vast range of electronics, has increased rapidly in complexity in recent years. Reading through a large range of publications on radio, it is very evident that there is a need for a data book containing fundamental technical material collated under one cover for easy reference. Of necessity, the data must be aimed at a specific section of the whole subject, and this book concentrates on radio circuits and radiating systems.

The material is arranged in sections to simplify retrieval. There are, of course, subjects that might logically be in more than one section, though these may be readily identified from the index. The data is presented in the form of curves, charts and tables, with only sufficient text for effective use. In adopting this method of presentation, it has been assumed that the reader has sufficient fundamental knowledge for direct application of the data. Where theoretical information on any particular subject is needed, the reader is referred to the various handbooks and manuals published by the Society.

In compiling the data for this, the fifth edition, the aim has been to provide an increased range of appropriate material which, if sought from other published sources, could require a lengthy search. A new section on ferrite materials has been added, and the section on filters has been greatly expanded. The opportunity has also been taken to update the broadcast sound and television transmitting station frequencies agreed upon at the World Administrative Radio Conference (WARC) in 1979. At the same time, data on Band I and III television stations has been removed, as these stations ceased operation in January 1985.

It is inevitable that, in compiling a reference book of this nature, a large and varied number of sources have to be consulted. Acknowledgements are therefore made to the editors and authors of data in textbooks and journals from whom information has been obtained. Particular thanks are due to the Independent Broadcasting Authority for selected material from *Broadcasting Engineer's Pocket Book*; Neosid Ltd for information on ferrite materials; and to Toko Radio Company Ltd for information on various types of available inductors for use in small-signal lf, hf and vhf circuits. A debt of gratitude is also expressed to P.J. Hart, G3SJX, for various new charts and material used in the compilation of other charts.

It is hoped that this book will fulfill a real need in university, college and electronics company libraries, as well as helping the amateur radio enthusiast. Any suggestions that readers might have to improve the content are welcomed, and every effort will be made to include them in any subsequent edition.

R.S.H.
G.R.J.

Part 1

Units and symbols

THE INTERNATIONAL SYSTEM OF UNITS

The International System (SI) comprises six basic units which are listed below, together with the symbols assigned to them. Special names have been adopted for some of the derived SI units. The definitions of these units show the relationship between them and the basic units.

BASIC SI UNITS

Quantity	Name of unit	Unit symbol
Electric current	ampere	A
Length	metre	m
Luminous intensity	candela	cd
Mass	kilogramme	kg
Thermodynamic temperature	degree Kelvin	K
Time	second	s

SI UNITS WITH SPECIAL NAMES

Physical quantity	SI unit	Unit symbol	
Electric capacitance	farad	F	$= A s/V$
Electric charge	coulomb	C	$= A s$
Electrical potential	volt	V	$= W/A$
Electric resistance	ohm	Ω	$= V/A$
Force	newton	N	$= kg\ m/s^2$
Frequency	hertz*	Hz	$= s^{-1}$
Illumination	lux	lx	$= lm/m^2$
Inductance	henry	H	$= V s/A$
Luminous flux	lumen	lm	$= cd\ sr$
Magnetic flux	weber	Wb	$= Vs$
Magnetic flux density	tesla†	T	$= Wb/m^2$
Power	watt	W	$= J/s$
Work, energy, quantity of heat	joule	J	$= N\ m$

* equivalent to cycle per second.   † equivalent to weber per square metre.

DERIVED SI UNITS WITH COMPLEX NAMES

Physical quantity	SI unit	Unit symbol
Acceleration	metre per second squared	m/s^2
Angular acceleration	radian per second squared	rad/s^2
Angular velocity	radian per second	rad/s
Area	square metre	m^2
Density (mass density)	kilogramme per cubic metre	kg/m^3
Diffusion coefficient	metre squared per second	m^2/s
Dynamic viscosity	newton second per metre squared	Ns/m^2
Electric field strength	volt per metre	V/m
Kinematic viscosity	metre squared per second	m^2/s
Luminance	candela per square metre	cd/m^2
Magnetic field strength	ampere per metre	A/m
Pressure	newton per square metre	N/m^2
Surface tension	newton per metre	N/m
Thermal conductivity	watt per metre degree Kelvin	$W/(m\ K)$
Velocity	metre per second	m/s
Volume	cubic metre	m^3

DEFINITIONS OF DERIVED SI UNITS HAVING SPECIAL NAMES

Electric capacitance
The unit of electrical capacitance called the farad is the capacitance of a capacitor between the plates of which there appears a difference of potential of one volt when it is charged by a quantity of electricity equal to one coulomb.

Electric charge
The unit of electric charge called the coulomb is the quantity of electricity transported in one second by a current of one ampere.

Electric inductance
The unit of electric inductance called the henry is the inductance of a closed circuit in which an electromotive force of one volt is produced when the electric current in the circuit varies uniformly at the rate of one ampere per second.

Electric potential
The unit of electric potential called the volt is the difference of potential between two points of a conducting wire carrying a constant current of one ampere, when the power dissipated between these points is equal to one watt.

Electric resistance
The unit of electric resistance called the ohm is the resistance between two points of a conductor when a constant difference of potential of one volt, applied between these two points, produces in this conductor a current of one ampere, this conductor not being the source of any electromotive force.

Energy
The unit of energy called the joule is the work done when the point of application of a force of one newton is displaced through a distance of one metre in the direction of the force.

Force
The unit of force called the newton is that force which, when applied to a body having a mass of one kilogramme, gives it an acceleration of one metre per second squared.

Frequency
The unit of frequency called the hertz is the frequency of a periodic phenomenon of which the periodic time is one second.

Magnetic flux
The unit of magnetic flux called the weber is the flux which, linking a circuit of one turn, produces in it an electromotive force of one volt as it is reduced to zero at a uniform rate in one second.

Magnetic flux density
The unit of magnetic flux density called the tesla is the density of one weber of magnetic flux per square metre.

Power
The unit of power called the watt is equal to one joule per second.

Temperature
The units of Kelvin and Celsius temperature interval are identical. A temperature expressed in degrees Celsius is equal to the temperature expressed in degrees Kelvin less $273 \cdot 15$.

Luminous flux
The unit of luminous flux called the lumen is the flux emitted within unit solid angle of one steradian by a point source having intensity of one candela.

Illumination
The unit of illumination called the lux is an illumination of one lumen per square metre.

OTHER METRIC UNITS

Quantity	Unit	Symbol	Equivalent
Area	are	a	$10^2 m^2$
Electrical conductivity	siemens	S	Ω^{-1}
Energy	erg	—	$10^{-7} J$
Force	dyne	—	$10^{-5} N$
Length	angstrom	Å	$10^{-10} m$
	micron	μm	$10^{-6} m$
Luminance	nit	nt	cd/m^2
	stilb	—	$10^4 cd/m^2$
Magnetic field strength	oersted	—	$10^3/4\pi A/m$
Magnetic flux	maxwell	—	$10^{-8} Wb$
Magnetic flux density	gauss	—	$10^{-4} T$
Magnetomotive force	gilbert	—	$10/4\pi A$
Mass	tonne	t	$10^3 kg$
Pressure	pascal	Pa	N/m^2
	bar	bar	$10^5 N/m^2$
Viscosity (dynamic)	centipoise	cP	$10^{-3} Ns/m^2$
Viscosity (kinetic)	centistokes	cSt	$10^{-6} m^2/s$
Volume	litre	l	$10^{-3} m^3$

MULTIPLES AND SUB-MULTIPLES
The names of the multiples and sub-multiples of units are formed by means of the prefixes shown in this table.

Factor by which the unit is multiplied	Prefix	Symbol
$1\ 000\ 000\ 000\ 000\ 000\ 000 = 10^{18}$	exa	E
$1\ 000\ 000\ 000\ 000\ 000 = 10^{15}$	peta	P
$1\ 000\ 000\ 000\ 000 = 10^{12}$	tera	T
$1\ 000\ 000\ 000 = 10^9$	giga	G
$1\ 000\ 000 = 10^6$	mega	M
$1\ 000 = 10^3$	kilo	k
$100 = 10^2$	hecto	h
$10 = 10^1$	deca	da
$0\cdot1 = 10^{-1}$	deci	d
$0\cdot01 = 10^{-2}$	centi	c
$0\cdot001 = 10^{-3}$	milli	m
$0\cdot000\ 001 = 10^{-6}$	micro	μ
$0\cdot000\ 000\ 001 = 10^{-9}$	nano	n
$0\cdot000\ 000\ 000\ 001 = 10^{-12}$	pico	p
$0\cdot000\ 000\ 000\ 000\ 001 = 10^{-15}$	femto	f
$0\cdot000\ 000\ 000\ 000\ 000\ 001 = 10^{-18}$	atto	a

CGS AND MKS UNITS

Quantity	CGS Unit	CGS Symbol	MKS Unit	MKS Symbol	Ratio MKS / CGS
Acceleration		cm/s^2		m/s^2	10^2
Area		cm^2		m^3	10^4
Density		$g.cm^3$		$kg.m^3$	
Force	dyne	$g.cm/s^2$ (dyn)	newton	$kg.m/s^2$ (N)	10^5
Inertia (moment of)		$g.cm^2$		$kg.m^2$	10^7
Length	centimetre	cm	metre	m	10^2
Mass	gramme	g	kilo-gramme	kg	10^3
Momentum		$g.cm/s$		$kg.m/s$	10^5
Pressure, stress	barye	dyn/cm^2	pascal	N/m^2	10
Power		erg/s	watt	W $(=J/s)$	10^7
Time	second	s	second	s	1
Velocity		cm/s		m/s	10^2
Volume		cm^3		m^3	10^6
Work, energy	erg	dyn. cm	joule	J $(=Nm)$	10^7

ELECTRICAL AND MAGNETIC UNITS

Quantity	Symbol	Name	MKS Unit Defining equation	MKS Unit Symbol	Ratio of MKS / CGS
Capacitance	C	farad	$C = Q/V$	F	10^{-9}
Charge	Q	coulomb	$Q = It$	As	10^{-1}
Current	I	ampere		A	10^{-1}
Electric field	E	volt/metre	$E = V/l$	V/m	10^6
Electromotive force	E	volt	$P = IE$	V	10^8
Inductance	H	henry	$M = \phi/I$	H	10^9
Magnetic field	H	ampere/metre	$H.dl = nI$	A/m	10^{-3}
Magnetic flux	ϕ	weber	$E = d\phi/dt$	Vs	10^8
Magnetic induction	B		$B = \phi/l^2$	$V.s/m^2$	10^4
Permeability (relative)	μ		$\mu = M/M_0$		1
Potential	V		$P = I.V$		
Resistance	R	ohm	$R = V/I$	Ω	10^9

CONVERSION FACTORS

Length

1 thou (= 10^{-3} in)	= 25·40 μm
1 inch	= 2·540 cm
1 foot (= 12 in)	= 0·3048 m
1 yard (= 3 ft)	= 0·9144 m
1 fathom (= 6 ft)	= 1·829 m
1 furlong (= 220 yards)	= 0·2012 km
1 statute mile (= 5,280 ft) (= 8 furlongs)	= 1·609 km
1 UK nautical mile (= 1·15 statute miles) (= 6,080 ft)	= 1·853 km
1 international nautical mile	= 1·852 km

Area

1 square inch	= 645·2 mm^2
1 square foot	= 929 cm^2
1 square yard	= 0·8361 m^2
1 acre (= 4,840 sq yd)	= 4,047 m^2
	= 0·4047 ha
1 square mile	= 2·590 km^2

Volume

1 cubic inch	= 16·39 cm^3
1 fluid ounce	= 28·41 cm^3
1 pint	= 568·3 cm^3
1 imperial gallon	= 4·546 litres
1 US gallon	= 3·785 litres
1 cubic foot (= 6·23 imperial gallons)	= 28·32 litres
1 cubic yard	= 0·7646 m^3

Speed

1 revolution/minute	= 0·1047 rad/s
1 mile/hour (= 88/60 ft/s)	= 0·4470 m/s
1 knot (= 1 nautical mile/h)	= 0·5148 m/s

Mass

1 ounce	= 28·35 g
1 pound (lb)	= 0·4536 kg
1 slug (= 32·17 lb)	= 14·59 kg
1 hundredweight (cwt) (= 112 lb)	= 50·8 kg
1 ton (= 2,240 lb)	= 1·016 t

Density

1 lb/in^3	= 27·68 g/cm^3
1 lb/ft^3	= 16·02 kg/m^3
1 lb/gallon	= 99·78 kg/m^3
1 ton/yd^3	= 1·329 t/m^3

Moments of mass

1 lb ft	= 0·1383 kg m
1 lb ft^2	= 421·4 kg cm^2

Force

1 lb force (lbf)	= 4·448 N (standard gravity)

| 1 poundal (pdl) (= 0·0311 lbf) | = 0·1383 N |
| 1 ton force | = 9·964 kN |

Pressure (or stress)

1 lb/ft^2	= 47·88 N/m^2
1 lb/in^2 (psi)	= 6·895 kN/m^2
1 ton/ft^2	= 107·3 kN/m^2
1 ton/in^2	= 15·44 N/mm^2
1 in Hg (0°C) (= 0·491 psi)	= 3·386 kN/m^2
1 ft H$_2$O (4°C) (= 0·434 psi)	= 2·989 kN/m^2
1 atmosphere (atm)	= 1·013 bar

Energy

1 ft lbf	= 1·356 J
1 ft pdl	= 42·14 mJ
1 horse-power (= 550 ft lbf/s)	= 745·7 W
1 electron volt (eV)	= 1·602 × 10^{-19} J
1 calorie	= 4·184 J
1 BTU (= 252 cal)	= 1·055 kJ
1 CHU (= 9/5 BTU)	= 1·899 kJ
1 therm (= 10^5 BTU)	= 105·5 MJ
1 BTU/hour	= 0·293 W

PHYSICAL CONSTANTS

Acceleration due to gravity (Potsdam)	= 9·81274 m/s^2
	= 32·1940 ft/s^2
Avogadro's number, N	= 6·02252 × 10^{23} molecules/mole
Boltzmann's constant, k	= 1·38054 × 10^{-23} J/K
Charge/mass ratio for electron, e/m	= 1·7588 × 10^{11} C/kg
Density of mercury at 0°C	= 13·59508 Mg/m^3
Electronic charge, e	= 1·60210 × 10^{-19} coulombs
	= 4·80298 × 10^{-10} esu
Faraday's constant, F	= 9·6487 × 10^4 C/mole
Gas constant, R	= 8·3143 J/K/mole
	= 1·98717 calories/K/mole
Gravitational constant, G	= 6·670 × 10^{-11} Nm^2/k
Latent heat of fusion of ice	= 3·334 × 10^5 J/kg
Latent heat of vaporization of water	= 2·257 × 10^6 J/kg
Mass of electron, m	= 9·1091 × 10^{-31} kg
Mechanical equivalent of heat	= 4·1840 joules/calorie
Planck's constant, h	= 6·6256 × 10^{-34} Js
ℏ (= h/2π)	= 1·05450 × 10^{-34} Js
Radius of electron, r	= 2·81777 × 10^{-15} m
Velocity of light in vacuo, c$_0$	= 2·997925 × 10^8 m/s
Velocity of sound in dry air at normal pressure and 20°C	= 343·6 m/s (1,127·3 ft/s)

FRACTIONS OF AN INCH WITH METRIC EQUIVALENTS

Fractions of an inch	Decimals of an inch	mm	Fractions of an inch	Decimals of an inch	mm
$\frac{1}{64}$	0·0156	0·397	$\frac{33}{64}$	0·5156	13·097
$\frac{1}{32}$	0·0312	0·794	$\frac{17}{32}$	0·5313	13·494
$\frac{3}{64}$	0·0468	1·191	$\frac{35}{64}$	0·5469	13·891
$\frac{1}{16}$	0·0625	1·588	$\frac{9}{16}$	0·5625	14·287
$\frac{5}{64}$	0·0781	1·985	$\frac{37}{64}$	0·5781	14·684
$\frac{3}{32}$	0·0938	2·381	$\frac{19}{32}$	0·5938	15·081
$\frac{7}{64}$	0·1094	2·778	$\frac{39}{64}$	0·6094	15·478
$\frac{1}{8}$	0·1250	3·175	$\frac{5}{8}$	0·6250	15·875
$\frac{9}{64}$	0·1406	3·572	$\frac{41}{64}$	0·6406	16·272
$\frac{5}{32}$	0·1563	3·969	$\frac{21}{32}$	0·6563	16·668
$\frac{11}{64}$	0·1719	4·366	$\frac{43}{64}$	0·6719	17·065
$\frac{3}{16}$	0·1875	4·762	$\frac{11}{16}$	0·6875	17·462
$\frac{13}{64}$	0·2031	5·159	$\frac{45}{64}$	0·7031	17·859
$\frac{7}{32}$	0·2187	5·556	$\frac{23}{32}$	0·7188	18·256
$\frac{15}{64}$	0·2344	5·953	$\frac{47}{64}$	0·7344	18·653
$\frac{1}{4}$	0·2500	6·350	$\frac{3}{4}$	0·7500	19·050
$\frac{17}{64}$	0·2656	6·747	$\frac{49}{64}$	0·7656	19·447
$\frac{9}{32}$	0·2813	7·144	$\frac{25}{32}$	0·7813	19·843
$\frac{19}{64}$	0·2969	7·541	$\frac{51}{64}$	0·7969	20·240
$\frac{5}{16}$	0·3125	7·937	$\frac{13}{16}$	0·8125	20·637
$\frac{21}{64}$	0·3281	8·334	$\frac{53}{64}$	0·8281	21·034
$\frac{11}{32}$	0·3438	8·731	$\frac{27}{32}$	0·8438	21·431
$\frac{23}{64}$	0·3593	9·128	$\frac{55}{64}$	0·8594	21·828
$\frac{3}{8}$	0·3750	9·525	$\frac{7}{8}$	0·8750	22·225
$\frac{25}{64}$	0·3906	9·922	$\frac{57}{64}$	0·8906	22·622
$\frac{13}{32}$	0·4063	10·319	$\frac{29}{32}$	0·9062	23·019
$\frac{27}{64}$	0·4219	10·716	$\frac{59}{64}$	0·9219	23·416
$\frac{7}{16}$	0·4375	11·12	$\frac{15}{16}$	0·9375	23·812
$\frac{29}{64}$	0·4531	11·509	$\frac{61}{64}$	0·9531	24·209
$\frac{15}{32}$	0·4687	11·906	$\frac{31}{32}$	0·9688	24·606
$\frac{31}{64}$	0·4844	12·303	$\frac{63}{64}$	0·9844	25·003
$\frac{1}{2}$	0·5000	12·700		1·0000	25·400

SOME AVERAGE SOUND LEVELS

Sound pressure (mPa)	Pressure ratio		Intensity ratio	Sound level (dB)	Source or description of typical sound
0·2 (datum)	1	(= 10^0)	1	0	Sound-proof room (threshold of hearing)
0·063	3·16	(= $10^{0.5}$)	10^1	10	Rustle of leaves in a gentle breeze
0·2	10	(= 10^1)	10^2	20	A whisper
0·63	31·6	(= $10^{1.5}$)	10^3	30	Quiet conversation
2	100	(= 10^2)	10^4	40	Surburban home
6·3	316	(= $10^{2.5}$)	10^5	50	Average conversation
20	1,000	(= 10^3)	10^6	60	Large shop
63	3,160	(= $10^{3.5}$)	10^7	70	Busy city street
200	10,000	(= 10^4)	10^8	80	Noisy typing office
630	31,600	(= $10^{4.5}$)	10^9	90	Underground railway
2,000	100,000	(= 10^5)	10^{10}	100	Pneumatic drill at 10 ft
6,300	316,000	(= $10^{5.5}$)	10^{11}	110	Prop aircraft taking off
20,000	1,000,000	(= 10^6)	10^{12}	120	Jet aircraft taking off (threshold of pain)

GREEK ALPHABET

Capital letters	Small letters	Greek name	English equivalent	Capital letters	Small letters	Greek name	English equivalent
A	α	Alpha	a	N	ν	Nu	n
B	β	Beta	b	Ξ	ξ	Xi	x
Γ	γ	Gamma	g	O	o	Omicron	ŏ
Δ	δ	Delta	d	Π	π	Pi	p
E	ε	Epsilon	e	P	ρ	Rho	r
Z	ζ	Zeta	z	Σ	σ	Sigma	s
H	η	Eta	é	T	τ	Tau	t
Θ	θ	Theta	th	Υ	υ	Upsilon	u
I	ι	Iota	i	Φ	ϕ	Phi	ph
K	κ	Kappa	k	X	χ	Chi	ch
Λ	λ	Lambda	l	Ψ	ψ	Psi	ps
M	μ	Mu	m	Ω	ω	Omega	ō

CIRCUIT SYMBOLS

⊗ Indicates preferred symbol

BIPOLAR TRANSISTORS

TR collector TR c
b   base
emitter e
npn   pnp

FIELD-EFFECT TRANSISTORS (FET)

JUGFET

TR drain TR d
gate source g s
n-channel   p-channel

MOSFET

TR d   TR d
g s   g1 g2 s
Single-gate   Dual-gate
n-channel   p-channel
Depletion-type

IGFET

TR d sub   TR d sub
g1 g2 s   g s
Dual-gate   Single-gate
n-channel   p-channel
Enhancement-type

Envelope optional

a + k PN diode
D

a + k Varactor
D

a + k Zener diode
D

a + k Tunnel diode
D

D + k Thyristor
a g

+ Bridge rectifier
~

R / R ⊗	Fixed resistor	C	Fixed capacitor
RV / RV ⊗	Variable resistor	C	Variable capacitor
RV / RV ⊗	Resistor with preset adjustment	C	Capacitor with preset adjustment
RV / RV ⊗	Potentiometer	C	Feed-through capacitor
RV / RV ⊗	Preset potentiometer	C	Variable differential capacitor
L / L ⊗	Inductor winding	C	Variable split-stator capacitor
RFC / RFC ⊗	Radio-frequency choke	C	Electrolytic capacitor
L / L ⊗	Iron-cored inductor	C	Non-polarized electrolytic capacitor
L / L ⊗	Inductor with adjustable iron-core	FS / FS ⊗	Fuse
T / T ⊗	Iron-cored transformer	LP	Signal lamp
L / L ⊗	Tapped inductor	PL	Coaxial plug
-t° ⊗	Thermistor	SK	Coaxial socket
		PL	Plug
		SK	Socket
	Frame or chassis	Fe / Fe	Ferrite bead
	Earth (ground)		Wires joined
	Antenna (aerial)	⊗	Wires crossing

RL	Solenoid
	Relay
	Contacts
	Coaxial cable
+ B	Battery (single-cell)
TL	Headphones
LS	Loudspeaker
MIC	Microphone
	Morse key
V JK	Closed-circuit
	Jack sockets
V JK	Open-circuit
S	
S	Switches
XL	Piezo-electric crystal
V A mA	Meters

CIRCUIT SYMBOLS *(continued)*

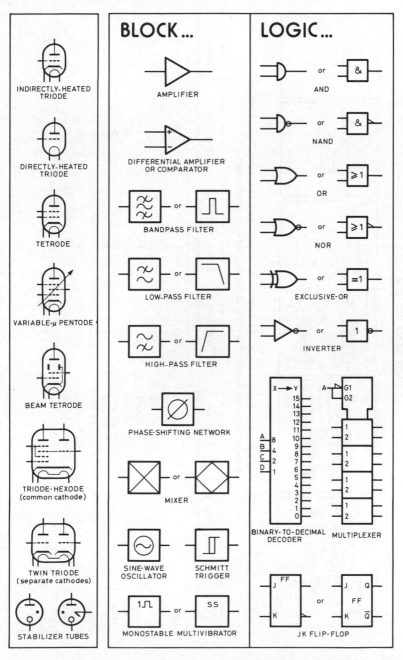

BLOCK...

AMPLIFIER

DIFFERENTIAL AMPLIFIER OR COMPARATOR

BANDPASS FILTER

LOW-PASS FILTER

HIGH-PASS FILTER

PHASE-SHIFTING NETWORK

MIXER

SINE-WAVE OSCILLATOR

SCHMITT TRIGGER

MONOSTABLE MULTIVIBRATOR

LOGIC...

or — AND

or — NAND

or — OR

or — NOR

or — EXCLUSIVE-OR

or — INVERTER

BINARY-TO-DECIMAL DECODER

MULTIPLEXER

JK FLIP-FLOP

INDIRECTLY-HEATED TRIODE

DIRECTLY-HEATED TRIODE

TETRODE

VARIABLE-μ PENTODE

BEAM TETRODE

TRIODE-HEXODE (common cathode)

TWIN TRIODE (separate cathodes)

STABILIZER TUBES

UNITS AND SYMBOLS **11**

COMPONENT COLOUR CODES

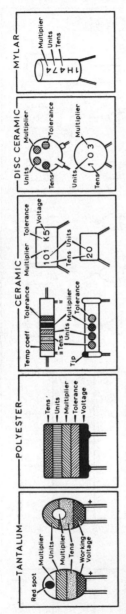

─TANTALUM─ ─POLYESTER─ ─CERAMIC─ ─DISC CERAMIC─ ─MYLAR─

Some of the many colour coding systems found on UK, American and Japanese fixed capacitors. Resistors are as per the tubular ceramic capacitors without the temperature coefficient.

Colour	Significant figure (1st, 2nd)	Decimal multiplier (M)	Tolerance (T) (per cent)	Temp coeff (TC) (parts/10^6/°C)	Voltage (V) (tantalum cap)	Voltage (V) (polyester cap)
Black	0	1	±20	0	10	—
Brown	1	10	±1	−30	—	100
Red	2	100	±2	−80	—	250
Orange	3	1,000	±3	−150	—	—
Yellow	4	10,000	+100, −0	−220	6·3	400
Green	5	100,000	±5	−330	16	—
Blue	6	1,000,000	±6	−470	20	—
Violet	7	10,000,000	—	−750	—	—
Grey	8	100,000,000	—	+30	25	—
White	9	1,000,000,000	±10	+100 to −750	3	—
Gold	—	—	±5	—	—	—
Silver	—	—	±10	—	—	—
Pink	—	—	—	—	35	—
No colour	—	—	±20	—	—	—

Units used are ohms for resistors, picofarads for ceramic and polyester capacitors, and microfarads for tantalum capacitors.

BS 1852 RESISTOR CODE

Resistor value

0·47 Ω	marked R47	100·0 Ω	marked 100R
1·00 Ω	marked 1R0	1 KΩ	marked 1K0
4·7 Ω	marked 4R7	10 KΩ	marked 10K
10·0 Ω	marked 10R	1 MΩ	marked 1M0
47·0 Ω	marked 47R	10 MΩ	marked 10M

Tolerance suffix

F = 1 per cent   K = 10 per cent
G = 2 per cent   M = 20 per cent
J = 5 per cent

Examples

R33M = 0·33 Ω ± 20 per cent   6K8F = 6·8kΩ ± 1 per cent
4R7K = 4·7 Ω ± 10 per cent   68KK = 68 kΩ ± 10 per cent
390RJ = 390 Ω ± 5 per cent   4M7M = 4·7 MΩ ± 20 per cent

PREFERRED NUMBER SERIES

The figures given in the tables below, and their decimal multiples and submultiples, are the series of preferred values for capacitors and resistors, in accordance with BS2488 and IEC publication 63.

E6:	10	15	22	33	47	68						
E12:	10	12	15	18	22	33	39	47	56	68	82	
E24:	10	11	12	13	15	16	18	20	22	24	27	30
	33	36	39	43	47	51	56	62	68	75	82	91
E96:	100	102	105	107	110	113	115	118	121	124	127	130
	133	137	140	143	147	150	154	158	162	165	169	174
	178	182	187	191	196	200	205	210	215	221	226	232
	237	243	249	255	261	267	274	280	287	294	301	309
	316	324	332	340	348	357	365	374	383	392	402	412
	422	432	442	453	464	475	487	499	511	523	536	549
	562	576	590	604	619	634	649	665	681	698	715	732
	750	768	787	806	825	845	866	887	909	931	953	976

COLOUR CODING FOR GLASS FUSES

Colour	Rating (mA)	Colour	Rating (a)
Green/yellow	10	Green	0·75
Red/turquoise	15	Blue	1·0
Eau-de-Nil	25	Light blue	1·5
Salmon pink	50	Purple	2·0
Black	60	Yellow and purple	2·5
Grey	100	White	3·0
Red	150	Black and white	5·0
Brown	250	Orange	10·0
Yellow	500		

Note that this coding does not apply to the ceramic-bodied fuse commonly found in 13A plugs etc.

COMMON SEMICONDUCTOR OUTLINES—DIODES

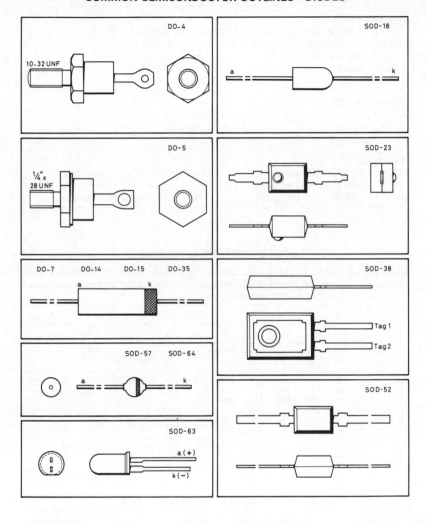

COMMON SEMICONDUCTOR OUTLINES—TRANSISTORS

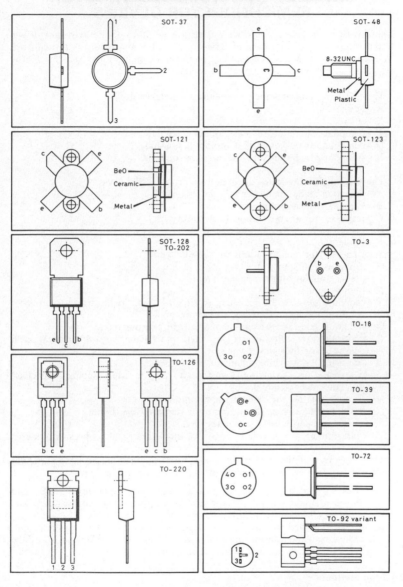

PRO ELECTRON NOMENCLATURE FOR SEMICONDUCTOR DEVICES

The Pro Electron system describes a transistor or other device by means of two letters followed by a serial number. The serial number may consist of three figures or one letter and two figures depending on the main application of the device. The system is used by many European semiconductor manufacturers.

The first letter indicates the semiconductor material used:
A—germanium
B—silicon
C—compound materials such as gallium arsenide
D—compound materials such as indium antimonide
R—compound materials such as cadmium sulphide

The second letter indicates the general function of the device:
A—detection diode, high-speed diode, mixer diode
B—variable capacitance diode
C—transistor for af applications (not power type)
D—power transistor for af applications
E—tunnel diode
F—transistor for rf applications (not power type)
G—multiple of dissimilar devices; miscellaneous devices
L—power transistor for rf applications
N—photo-coupler
P—radiation sensitive device such as a photo-diode, photo-transistor, photo-conductive cell, or a radiation detector diode
Q—radiation generating device such as a light-emitting diode
R—controlling/switching device (eg thyristor) having a specified breakdown characteristic (not power types)
S—transistor for switching applications (not power types)
T—controlling and switching power device (eg thyristor) having a specified breakdown characteristic
U—power transistor for switching applications
X—multiplier diode such as a varactor or step-recovery diode
Y—rectifier diode, booster, efficiency diode
Z—voltage reference or voltage regulator diode, transient suppressor diode

The remainder of the type number is a serial number indicating a particular design or development and is one of the following two groups:

(a) device intended primarily for use in consumer applications (radio and television, audio amplifiers, tape recorders, domestic applicances etc). The serial number consists of three figures.
(b) device intended mainly for applications other than (a), eg industrial, professional and transmitting equipments. The serial number consists of one letter (Z,Y,X,W etc) followed by two figures.

Range numbers

Where there is a range of variants of a basic type of rectifier diode, thyristor or voltage regulator diode, the type number as defined above is often used to identify the range; further letters and figures are added after a hyphen to identify individual types within the range. These additions are as follows:

(a) *Rectifier diodes and thyristors*
The group of figures indicates the rated repetitive peak reverse voltage, V_{RRM},

or the rated repetitive peak off-state voltage, V_{DRM}, whichever value is lower, in volts for each type. The final letter R is used to denote a reverse polarity version (stud anode) where applicable. The normal polarity version (stud cathode) has no special final letter.

(b) *Voltage regulator diodes, transient suppression diodes*
The first letter indicates the nominal percentage tolerance in the operating voltage V_Z.

A—±1 per cent	D—±10 per cent
B—±2 per cent	E—±15 per cent
C—±5 per cent	

The letter is omitted on transient suppressor diodes. The group of figures indicates the typical operating voltage V_Z for each type at the nominal operating current I_Z rating of the range. For transient suppressor diodes the figure indicates the maximum recommended stand-off voltage V_R. The letter V is used to denote a decimal sign. The final R is used to denote a reverse polarity version.

Examples

BF180	Silicon rf transistor intended primarily for consumer applications.
ACY17	Germanium af transistor primarily for industrial application.
BTW24–800R	Silicon thyristor for industrial applications. In BTW24 range with 800 V maximum repetitive peak voltage, reverse polarity, stud connected to anode.
BZY88–C5V6	Silicon voltage regulator diode for industrial applications. In BZY88 range with 5·6 V operating voltage ±5 per cent tolerance.
RPY71	Photo-conductive cell for industrial applications.

Old system

Some earlier semiconductor diodes and transistors have type numbers consisting of two or three letters followed by a group of one, two or three figures. The first letter is always "O", indicating a semiconductor device. The second (and third) letter(s) indicate the general class of device:

A—diode or rectifier
AP—photo-diode
AZ—voltage regulator diode
C—transistor
CP—photo-transistor

The group of figures is a serial number indicating a particular design or development.

JAPANESE INDUSTRIAL STANDARD (JIS–C–7012) TYPE DESIGNATION CODE FOR SEMICONDUCTOR DEVICES

This designation code applies to discrete transistors, diodes and rectifiers (single devices only) as set out below in the sequence shown.

First symbol—digit 0, 1, 2 or 3
Second symbol—letter S
Third symbol—letter (eg A etc)
Fourth symbol—digit (groups of two or three)
Fifth symbol—letter A, B, C etc

The *first symbol* (digit) indicates type of semiconductor:

0—Photo-transistor
1—Signal, rectifier, varactor diode
2—Bipolar, junction field-effect transistor (with single gate), silicon-controlled rectifier etc
3—as 2 but with two gates

The *second symbol* (letter) indicates that the device is diffused from semiconductor elements. The *third symbol* (letter) indicates polarity and application of the device in the following manner:

A—High-frequency pnp transistor
B—Low-frequency pnp transistor
C—High-frequency npn transistor
D—Low-frequency npn transistor
F—p-gate scr thyristor
G—n-gate scr thyristor
J—p-channel field-effect transistor (fet)
K—n-channel field-effect transistor (fet)

N.B. When the first symbol (digit) is 0 or 1, only numbers are used for the third symbol, ie photo-transistors and diodes.

The *fourth symbol* (digits) have numbers of 11 or more which are given according to the sequence of registration with JIS. The *fifth symbol* (letter) indicates a revision of the product originally introduced. For each revision A, B, C etc is added.

Part 2

Basic calculations

GENERAL FORMULAE

Capacitance

The capacitance of a parallel-plate capacitor is

$$C = \frac{0 \cdot 224 \, KA}{d} \text{ picofarads}$$

where K = dielectric constant (air = $1 \cdot 0$)
A = area of plate (sq in)
d = thickness of dielectric (in)

If A is expressed in square centimetres and d in centimetres

$$C = \frac{0 \cdot 0885 \, KA}{d} \text{ picofarads}$$

For multiplate capacitors, multiply by the number of dielectric thicknesses.

Capacitance of a coaxial cylinder

$$C = \frac{0 \cdot 242}{\log_{10} \dfrac{r_1}{r_2}} \text{ picofarads per centimetre length}$$

r_1 = radius of outer cylinder, r_2 = radius of inner cylinder.

Capacitors in series or parallel

The effective capacitance of a number of capacitors in *series* is

$$C = \frac{1}{\dfrac{1}{C_1} + \dfrac{1}{C_2} + \dfrac{1}{C_3} + \text{etc}}$$

For two capacitors only

$$C = \frac{C_1 \times C_2}{C_1 + C_2}$$

The effective capacitance of a number of capacitors in *parallel* is

$$C = C_1 + C_2 + C_3 + \text{etc}$$

Decibels

The bel is defined as the common logarithm of the ratio of two powers. Normally the decibel (one-tenth of a bel) is employed as a more convenient unit.

$$\text{Decibels (dB)} = 10 \times \log_{10} \frac{P_1}{P_2}$$

where P_1 and P_2 are the two power levels. The dBW is a reference unit usually applied to rf power. $0 \, \text{dBW} = 1 \, \text{W}$.

If equal impedances are employed:

$$\text{Decibels} = 20 \times \log_{10} \frac{V_1}{V_2} = 20 \times \log_{10} \frac{I_1}{I_2}$$

where V_1, V_2 are the voltage levels and I_1, I_2 the two current levels.

Dynamic resistance

In a parallel-tuned circuit at resonance the dynamic resistance is

$$R_d = \frac{L}{Cr} = Q\omega L = \frac{Q}{\omega C} \text{ ohms}$$

where L = inductance (henrys)
C = capacitance (farads)
r = effective series resistance (ohms)
Q = Q-value of coil
$\omega = 2\pi \times$ frequency (hertz)

Frequency—wavelength—velocity

The velocity of propagation of a wave is

$$v = f\lambda \text{ centimetres per second}$$

where f = frequency (hertz)
λ = wavelength (centimetres)

For electromagnetic waves in free space the velocity of propagation v is approximately 3×10^{10} cm/s, and if f is expressed in kilohertz and λ in metres

$$f = \frac{300,000}{\lambda} \text{ kilohertz} \qquad\qquad f = \frac{300}{\lambda} \text{ megahertz}$$

or

$$\lambda = \frac{300,000}{f} \text{ metres} \qquad\qquad \lambda = \frac{300}{f} \text{ metres}$$
$$\text{where } f \text{ is in megahertz}$$

Impedance

The impedance of a circuit comprising inductance, capacitance and resistance in series is

$$Z = \sqrt{R^2 + \left(\omega L - \frac{1}{\omega C}\right)^2}$$

where R = resistance (ohms) $\qquad\qquad L$ = inductance (henrys)
$\omega = 2\pi \times$ frequency (hertz) $\qquad\quad C$ = capacitance (farads)

The characteristic impedance Z_0 of a feeder or transmission line depends on its cross-sectional dimensions.

(i) Open-wire line:

$$Z_0 = 276 \log_{10} \frac{2D}{d} \text{ ohms}$$

where D = centre-to-centre spacing of wires$\Big\}$ expressed in the same units
d = *wire diameter*

(ii) Coaxial line:

$$Z_0 = \frac{138}{\sqrt{K}} \log_{10} \frac{d_o}{d_i}$$

(iii) Cut-off frequency of a coaxial cable:

$$F_c(MHz) = \frac{7,520}{d_i + d_o \sqrt{K}}$$

where K = dielectric constant of insulation between the conductors (eg 2·3 for polythene, 1·0 for air)
d_i = inside diameter of outer conductor (in)
d_o = outside diameter of inner conductor (in)

Inductances in series or parallel

The total effective value of a number of inductances connected in *series* (assuming that there is no mutual coupling) is given by

$$L = L_1 + L_2 + L_3 + etc$$

If they are connected in *parallel*, the total effective value is

$$L = \frac{1}{\dfrac{1}{L_1} + \dfrac{1}{L_2} + \dfrac{1}{L_3} + etc}$$

When there is mutual coupling M, the total effective value of two inductances connected in series is

$$L = L_1 + L_2 + 2M \text{ (windings aiding)}$$
$$\text{or } L = L_1 + L_2 - 2M \text{ (windings opposing)}$$

Self-inductance of a straight wire

At radio frequencies, the self-inductance of a straight round wire is given by

$$L = 0·0021 \left(2·303 \log_{10} \frac{4l}{d} - 1\right) \text{ microhenrys}$$

where l = length in cm
d = dia in cm

Inductance of single-layer coils

$$L \text{ (in microhenrys)} = \frac{a^2 N^2}{9a + 10l} \text{ approximately}$$

If the desired inductance is known, the number of turns required may be determined by the formula:

$$N = \frac{5L}{na^2} \left[1 + \sqrt{\left(1 + \frac{0·36n^2 a^3}{L}\right)}\right]$$

where N = number of turns
a = radius of coil in inches
n = number of turns per inch
L = inductance in microhenrys (μH)
l = length of coil in inches

Slug tuning. The variation in inductance obtainable with adjustable slugs depends on the winding length and the size and composition of the core, and no universal correction factor can be given. For coils wound on Aladdin type F804 formers and having a winding length of 0·3–0·8 in a dust-iron core will *increase* the inductance to about twice the air-core value: a brass core will *reduce* the inductance to a minimum of about 0·8 times the air-core value.

Ohm's Law

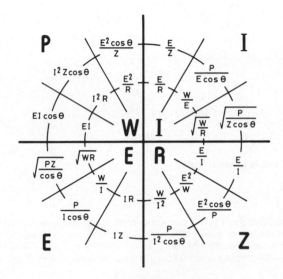

For a undirectional dc current of constant magnitude flowing in a metallic conductor

$$I = E/R \qquad E = IR \qquad R = E/I$$

where I is current (A), E is voltage (V) and R is resistance (Ω).

$$\text{Power} = W = EI = E^2/R = I^2R$$

For an alternating ac current of constant magnitude, the above relationships become

$$I = E/Z \qquad E = IZ \qquad Z = E/I$$

where Z = impedance (Ω)

$$\text{Power} = P = EI \cos\theta = \frac{E^2 \cos\theta}{Z} = I^2Z \cos\theta$$

where θ is phase angle between voltage and current dependent on the difference of impendance (Z) to resistance R. Note that $\theta = 0$ ($\cos\theta = 1$) where Z is purely resistive.

Admittance (Y) is the reciprocal of impedance

$$Y = \frac{I}{Z} \text{ (dc)} \qquad \text{or} \qquad \frac{I}{\sqrt{R^2 + X^2}} \text{ (ac) mhos}$$

In solid-state circuits admittance is frequently known as the Y *parameter*.

Conductance (G) is the reciprocal of resistance

$$G = \frac{I}{R} \text{ (dc)} \qquad \text{or} \qquad \frac{R}{R^2 + X^2} \text{ (ac) mhos}$$

Susceptance (B) is the reciprocal of reactance

$$B = \frac{I}{X} \qquad \text{or} \qquad \frac{-X}{R^2 + X^2} \text{ mhos}$$

Q

The Q value of an inductance is given by

$$Q = \frac{\omega L}{R}$$

where $\omega = 2\pi \times$ frequency (hertz)
L = inductance (henrys)
R = effective series resistance (ohms)

Q factor of single tuned circuit

$$Q = \frac{f_0}{f_1 - f_2}$$

where f_0 is the frequency giving maximum response, f_1 and f_2 the frequencies either side of f_0 where the response falls to 0·71 of maximum. All frequency measurements must be expressed in the same units.
Q factors of between 50 and 200 are typical for modern coils.

Reactance

The reactance of an inductor and a capacitor respectively is given by

$$X_L = \omega L \text{ ohms} \qquad\qquad X_c = \frac{1}{\omega C} \text{ ohms}$$

where $\omega = 2\pi \times$ frequency (hertz)
L = inductance (henrys)
C = capacitance (farads)

The total reactance of an inductance and a capacitance in series is $X_L - X_C$.

Resistors in series or parallel

The effective value of several resistors connected in series is

$$R = R_1 + R_2 + R_3 + \text{etc}$$

When several resistors are connected in parallel the effective total resistance is

$$R = \frac{1}{\dfrac{1}{R_1} + \dfrac{1}{R_2} + \dfrac{1}{R_3} + \text{etc}}$$

for two resistors

$$R = \frac{R_1 \times R_2}{R_1 + R_2}$$

Resonance

The resonant frequency of a tuned circuit is given by

$$f = \frac{1}{2\pi\sqrt{LC}} \text{ hertz}$$

where L = inductance (henrys)
C = capacitance (farads)

If L is in microhenrys (μH) and C is in picofarads (pF) this formula becomes

$$f = \frac{10^6}{2\pi\sqrt{LC}} \text{ kilohertz}$$

This basic formula can be rearranged thus:

$$L = \frac{1}{4\pi^2 f^2 C} \text{ henrys} \qquad C = \frac{1}{4\pi^2 f^2 L} \text{ farads}$$

Since $2\pi f$ is commonly represented by ω, these expressions can be written as

$$L = \frac{1}{\omega^2 C} \text{ henrys} \qquad C = \frac{1}{\omega^2 L} \text{ farads}$$

Time constant

For a combination of inductance and resistance in series the time constant (ie the time required for the current to reach $1/\varepsilon$ or 63 per cent of its final value) is given by

$$t = \frac{L}{R} \text{ seconds}$$

where L = inductance (henrys)
R = resistance (ohms)

For a combination of capacitance and resistance in series the time constant (ie the time required for the voltage across the capacitance to reach $1/\varepsilon$ or 63 per cent of its final value) is given by

$t = CR$ seconds where C = capacitance (farads), R = resistance (ohms)
(see also p 36)

Toroidal cores

Ferrite ring cores are suitable for use in pulse transformers, i.f. transformers, dc-to-dc converter transformers, wideband and impedance matching transformers, filter coils, rf coils and delay line coils.

The inductance of a coil wound on a ferrite ring is:

$$L = 0\!\cdot\!0046 \; \mu N^2 h \; \log_{10} \frac{OD}{ID} \text{ microhenrys}$$

where μ = permeability of the core material
N = number of turns
OD = outside diameter of core
ID = inside diameter of core
h = height of core

Magnetizing force

$$H = \frac{0 \cdot 4\, NI}{l} \text{ oersteds}$$

where NI = ampere turns
l = mean magnetic path length

Peak flux density

$$B = \frac{E.10^8}{4 \cdot 4\, f.N.A} \text{ gauss}$$

where E = rms value of the sinusoidal magnetizing voltage in volts
f = frequency
N = number of turns
A = cross-sectional area of the core (cm^2)
$$u = \frac{B}{H}$$

Transformer ratios
The ratio of a transformer refers to the ratio of the number of turns in one winding to the number of turns in the other winding. To avoid confusion it is always desirable to state in which sense the ratio is being expressed: eg the "primary-to-secondary" ratio n_p/n_s. The turns ratio is related to the impedance ratio thus

$$\frac{n_p}{n_s} = \sqrt{\frac{Z_p}{Z_s}}$$

where n_p = number of primary turns
n_s = number of secondary turns
Z_p = impedance of primary (ohms)
Z_s = impedance of secondary (ohms)

NOISE

A resistance R at temperature T generates across its open-circuited terminals a voltage resulting from the random motion of free electrons, thermally agitated.

$$e_n^2 = 4KTRB$$

where e_n = noise voltage
K = Boltzmann's constant ($1{\cdot}38054 \times 10^{-23}$ J/K)
T = absolute temperature (K)
R = resistance (Ω)
B = bandwidth (Hz)

If this resistor is connected to a matched load, $R_L = R$, maximum transfer of noise power will occur. This available noise power (P_n) is independent of the value of R.

$$P_n = KTB$$

For a bandwidth of 1 Hz at room temperature (290 K)

$$P_n = KT = 3{\cdot}98 \times 10^{-21} \text{ W} = -174 \text{ dBm}$$

An ideal amplifier, generating no noise, connected to a resistive source will amplify the available noise power by the gain (G) of the amplifier to give a noise power output $= KTBG$.

A practical amplifier will generate internal noise and give a higher noise power output, N_o. The ratio of actual noise power output to that produced by an ideal amplifier is the noise factor.

$$F = \frac{N_o}{KTBG}$$

Noise factor is also the degradation in signal-to-noise ratio between input and output

$$F = \frac{\dfrac{S_i}{N_i}}{\dfrac{S_o}{N_o}}$$

Noise figure (F_{dB}) is the noise factor expressed logarithmically

Hence $F_{dB} = 10 \log_{10}F$ $N_o = FKTBG$
$N_0(\text{dBm}) = F_{dB} + G_{dB} + KT(\text{dBm}) + 10 \log_{10}B$

In a 1 Hz bandwidth at room temperature

$$N_o(\text{dBm}) = F_{dB} + G_{dB} - 174$$

Consider a cascaded network as below

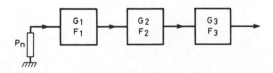

G_1, G_2, G_3 are the gains expressed as a ratio (not decibels) of the individual networks. F_1, F_2, F_3, are the noise factors of the individual networks. If a network consists of an attenuator, $F_n = 1/G_n$. For example, a 6 dB attenuator has $G = \frac{1}{4}$ and $F = 4$.

The total gain
$$G_{tot} = G_1 \times G_2 \times G_3$$

The total noise factor
$$F_{tot} = F_1 + \frac{(F_2 - 1)}{G_1} + \frac{(F_3 - 1)}{G_1 G_2}$$

In general for n cascaded networks
$$F_{tot} = F_1 + \frac{(F_2 - 1)}{G_1} + \ldots + \frac{(F_n - 1)}{G_1 G_2 \ldots G_{n-1}}$$

CHARTS AND TABLES

OHM'S LAW CHART

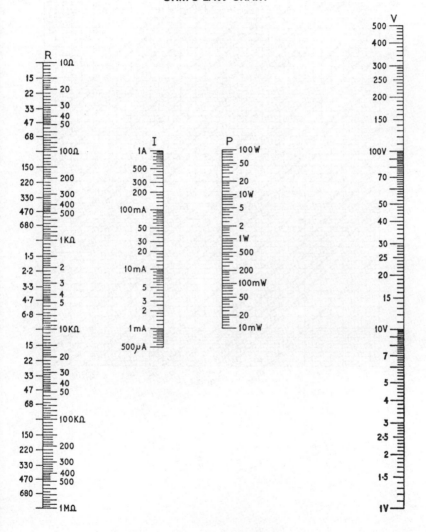

POWER, VOLTAGE, CURRENT, RESISTANCE ABAC

To use the abac, select known points on any two of the vertical scales and lay a ruler across these points so as to cut the other two scales. The points where the ruler cuts these latter scales will give the values required

REACTANCE CHART
CAPACITANCE

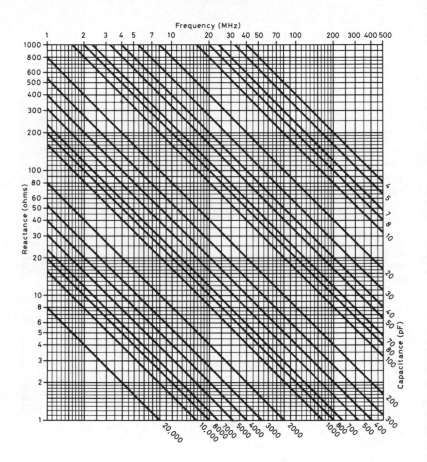

REACTANCE CHART
INDUCTANCE

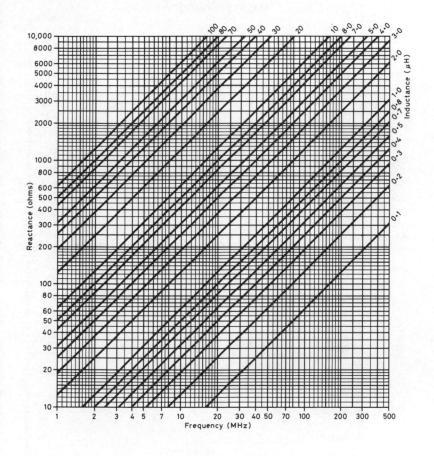

REACTANCE AND RESONANCE CHART

AUDIO FREQUENCY

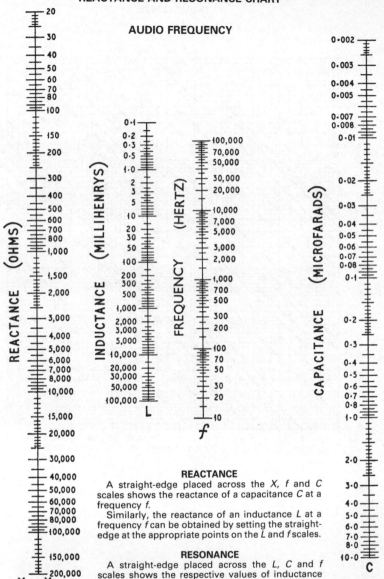

REACTANCE (OHMS)

20
30
40
50
60
70
80
100
150
200
300
400
500
600
700
800
1,000
1,500
2,000
3,000
4,000
5,000
6,000
7,000
8,000
10,000
15,000
20,000
30,000
40,000
50,000
60,000
70,000
80,000
100,000
150,000
200,000

X_C or X_L

INDUCTANCE (MILLIHENRYS)

0·1
0·2
0·3
0·5
1·0
2
3
5
10
20
30
50
100
200
300
500
1,000
2,000
3,000
5,000
10,000
20,000
30,000
50,000
100,000

L

FREQUENCY (HERTZ)

100,000
70,000
50,000
30,000
20,000
10,000
7,000
5,000
3,000
2,000
1,000
700
500
300
200
100
70
50
30
20
10

f

CAPACITANCE (MICROFARADS)

0·002
0·003
0·004
0·005
0·007
0·008
0·01
0·02
0·03
0·04
0·05
0·06
0·07
0·08
0·1
0·2
0·3
0·4
0·5
0·6
0·7
0·8
1·0
2·0
3·0
4·0
5·0
6·0
7·0
8·0
10·0

C

REACTANCE

A straight-edge placed across the *X*, *f* and *C* scales shows the reactance of a capacitance *C* at a frequency *f*.

Similarly, the reactance of an inductance *L* at a frequency *f* can be obtained by setting the straight-edge at the appropriate points on the *L* and *f* scales.

RESONANCE

A straight-edge placed across the *L*, *C* and *f* scales shows the respective values of inductance and capacitance which will resonate at a specific frequency.

REACTANCE AND RESONANCE CHART

RADIO FREQUENCY

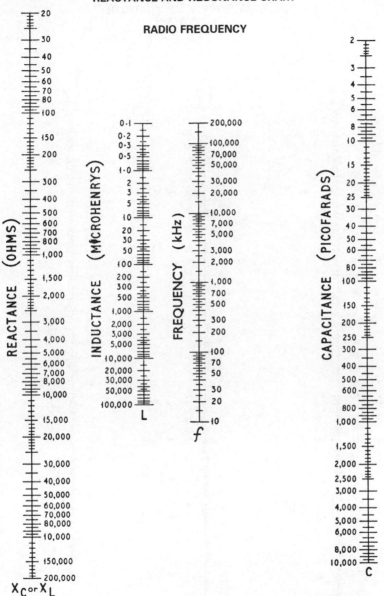

UK Amateur Allocations 1
FREQUENCY V. WAVELENGTH
1–1,000 MHz

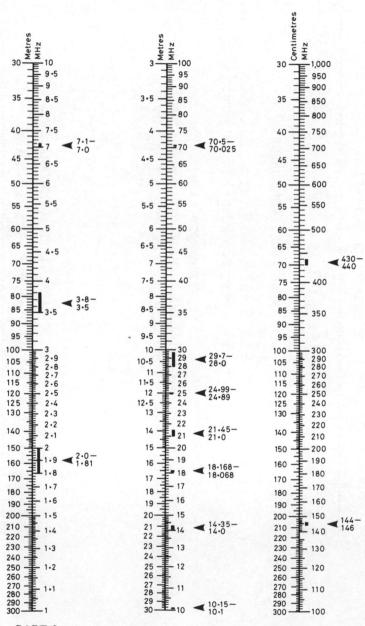

UK Amateur Allocations 2
FREQUENCY V. WAVELENGTH
1–1,000 GHz

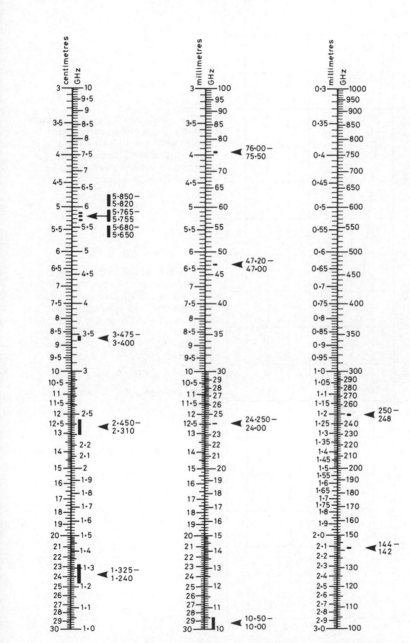

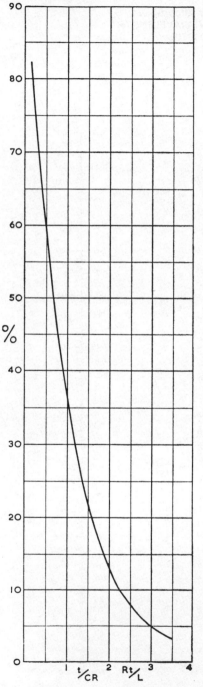

The time constant of a circuit having a capacitor or inductor in series with a resistor $t = CR$ or L/R and is the time required for the current or voltage to reach 63·2 per cent of its maximum value.

$$i = \frac{E}{R}\,e^{-tC/R}$$

$$i = \frac{E}{R}\,e^{-tR/L}$$

The graph enables either time or percentage of maximum voltage (or current) to be found. Example: a capacitor and a resistor have a time constant CR of 4 s. If initially charged, what percentage of the charge-voltage will be retained after 8 s?

$$t/CR = 8/4 = 2$$

from the curve 2 = 14 per cent.

DECIBEL TABLE

Voltage ratio (equal impedance)	Power ratio	← − dB + →	Voltage ratio (equal impedance)	Power ratio
1·000	1·000	0	1·000	1·000
0·989	0·977	0·1	1·012	1·023
0·977	0·955	0·2	1·023	1·047
0·966	0·933	0·3	1·035	1·072
0·955	0·912	0·4	1·047	1·096
0·944	0·891	0·5	1·059	1·122
0·933	0·871	0·6	1·072	1·148
0·923	0·851	0·7	1·084	1·175
0·912	0·832	0·8	1·096	1·202
0·902	0·813	0·9	1·109	1·230
0·891	0·794	1·0	1·122	1·259
0·841	0·708	1·5	1·189	1·413
0·794	0·631	2·0	1·259	1·585
0·750	0·562	2·5	1·334	1·778
0·708	0·501	3·0	1·413	1·995
0·668	0·447	3·5	1·496	2·239
0·631	0·398	4·0	1·585	2·512
0·596	0·355	4·5	1·679	2·818
0·562	0·316	5·0	1·779	3·162
0·531	0·282	5·5	1·884	3·548
0·501	0·251	6·0	1·995	3·981
0·473	0·224	6·5	2·113	4·467
0·447	0·200	7·0	2·239	5·012
0·422	0·178	7·5	2·371	5·623
0·398	0·159	8·0	2·512	6·310
0·376	0·141	8·5	2·661	7·079
0·355	0·126	9·0	2·818	7·943
0·335	0·112	9·5	2·985	8·913
0·316	0·100	10	3·162	10·00
0·282	0·0794	11	3·55	12·6
0·251	0·0631	12	3·98	15·9
0·224	0·0501	13	4·47	20·0
0·200	0·0398	14	5·01	25·1
0·178	0·0316	15	5·62	31·6
0·159	0·0251	16	6·31	39·8
0·141	0·0200	17	7·08	50·1
0·126	0·0159	18	7·94	63·1
0·112	0·0126	19	8·91	79·4
0·100	0·0100	20	10·00	100·0
$3·16 \times 10^{-2}$	10^{-3}	30	$3·16 \times 10$	10^3
10^{-2}	10^{-4}	40	10^2	10^4
$3·16 \times 10^{-3}$	10^{-5}	50	$3·16 \times 10^2$	10^5
10^{-3}	10^{-6}	60	10^3	10^6
$3·16 \times 10^{-4}$	10^{-7}	70	$3·16 \times 10^3$	10^7
10^{-4}	10^{-8}	80	10^4	10^8
$3·16 \times 10^{-5}$	10^{-9}	90	$3·16 \times 10^4$	10^9
10^{-5}	10^{-10}	100	10^5	10^{10}
$3·16 \times 10^{-6}$	10^{-11}	110	$3·16 \times 10^5$	10^{11}
10^{-6}	10^{-12}	120	10^6	10^{12}

RELATIONSHIP BETWEEN dBm AND VOLTAGE

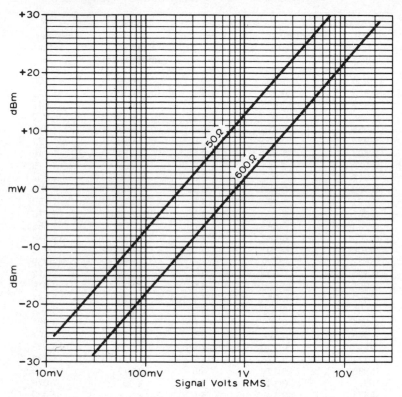

A power level of 1 mW into a 600 or 50 Ω resistance has become a standard for comparative purposes; it is the datum 0 dBm. Signal levels above and below this datum are expressed in ±dBm. They correspond to finite voltage (or current) levels—not ratios. 0 dBm into a 600 Ω resistance corresponds to 0·775 V whereas 0 dBm into a 50 Ω resistance corresponds to 0·225 V.

dBm—VOLTS CONVERSION

dBm	μV	dBm	mV
−130	0·071	−40	2·24
−120	0·224	−30	7·07
−110	0·707	−15	39·8
−100	2·24	−10	70·7
−90	7·07	−5	126·0
−80	22·4	0	224
−70	70·7	+5	398
−60	224	+10	707
−50	707	+15	1,257

SIGNAL VOLTAGE—dBm—WATTS CONVERSION

μV	dBm	W
1	−127	2×10^{-16}
5	−113	5×10^{-15}
10	−87	2×10^{-12}
20	−81	8×10^{-12}
30	−77·5	$1·8 \times 10^{-11}$
40	−75	$3·2 \times 10^{-11}$
50	−73	5×10^{-11}
100	−67	2×10^{-10}
200	−61	8×10^{-10}
300	−57·5	$1·8 \times 10^{-9}$
400	−55	$3·2 \times 10^{-9}$
500	−53	$5·0 \times 10^{-9}$
1 mV	−47	2×10^{-8}
10 mV	−27	2×10^{-6}
100 mV	−7	2×10^{-4}
500 mV	−7	0·005
1 V	+13	0·02
5 V	+27	0·5

RELATIONSHIP BETWEEN NOISE FIGURE AND NOISE TEMPERATURE

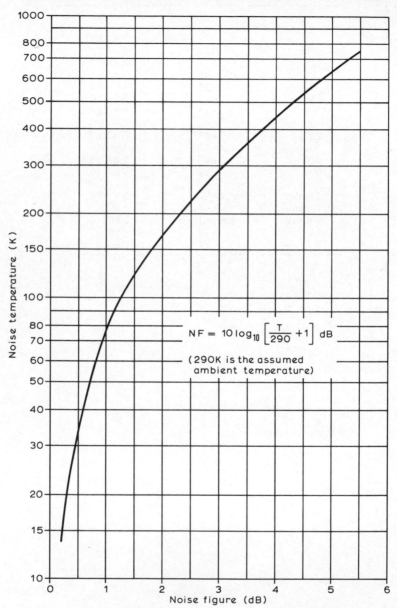

$$NF = 10 \log_{10} \left[\frac{T}{290} + 1 \right] dB$$

(290K is the assumed ambient temperature)

Noise temperature (K)

Noise figure (dB)

Part 3

Resonant circuits and filters

TIME CONSTANTS FOR SERIES CIRCUITS

The two charts provide data for finding the time constant of a network for a series circuit. Time constants for either resistance-capacitance series networks or inductance-resistance series networks can be found. The example below gives the method of using the charts.

Example: Given a resistance of $0 \cdot 1$ MΩ in series with a capacitance $0 \cdot 25$ μF, find the time constant of the network. Placing a straight edge through these respective values (using resistance scale No 2 and capacitance scale No 2), the time constant scale is intersected at $0 \cdot 025$ s and the frequency scale at 40 Hz.

The time constant scale gives the interval of time necessary for the current to rise, or decay, to within $1/e$ of the steady state value (approximately 63 per cent of its final value). The frequency scale reads the highest frequency at which $63 \cdot 2$ per cent of the exciting voltage can be developed across the network.

In a resistance-capacitance series network, the time constant is defined by:

$$T \text{ (seconds)} = R \text{ (ohms)} \times C \text{ (farads)}$$

In an inductance-resistance series network, the time constant is defined by:

$$T \text{ (seconds)} = \frac{L \text{ (henrys)}}{R \text{ (ohms)}}$$

CHART 1—0·1 Hz–100 kHz

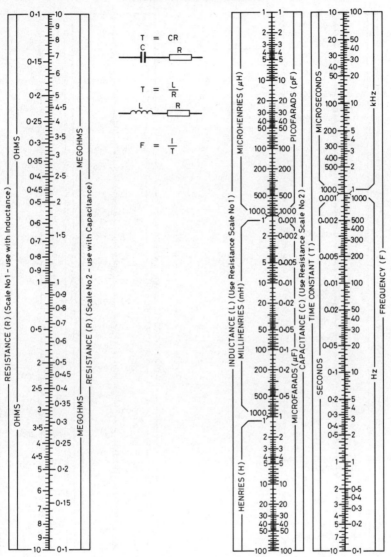

$$T = CR$$

$$T = \frac{L}{R}$$

$$F = \frac{I}{T}$$

CHART 2—10 Hz–10 MHz

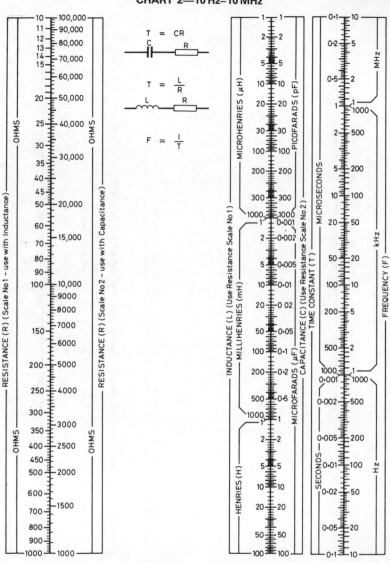

$$T = CR$$

$$T = \frac{L}{R}$$

$$F = \frac{I}{T}$$

SMALL INDUCTORS

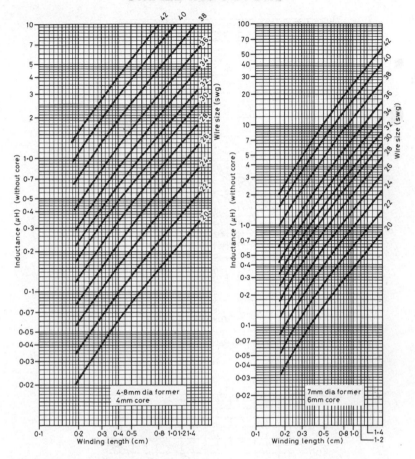

Small inductances such as those required for receivers or exciters may be designed using the charts shown above which give details of coils wound on small standard formers, using 4 and 6 mm cores. The charts give data for close-wound coils without a core. The increase of inductance will be dependent on the actual type of core used.

The curves are given as inductance and winding length in centimetres (a more convenient measurement of winding length than inches). Individual curves are given for wire 20 to 42 swg.

Conversion of length to turns for enamelled wire

Wire size (swg)	20	22	24	26	28	30	32	34	36	38	40
Turns per inch	26	33	41·6	51·2	61·7	72·4	81·9	97	116	145	178
Turns per cm	10·2	13	16·4	20·2	24·3	28·5	32·2	38·2	45·7	57·1	70·1

The range of inductance covered is 0·1 to 50 μH. Below 0·1 μH the lead length will have a significant effect on the total value of the inductor.

RESONANT CIRCUITS AND FILTERS   **45**

VHF INDUCTORS

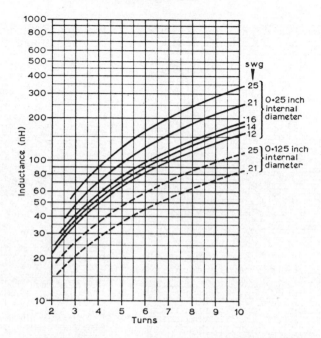

The inductance of 0·125 and 0·25 in internal diameter coils with turns spaced one diameter apart

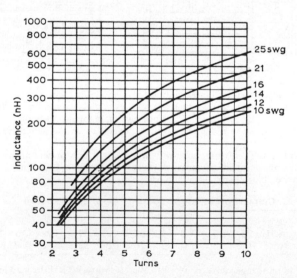

The inductance of 0·375 in internal diameter coils with turns spaced one diameter apart

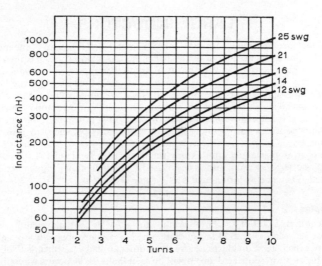

The inductance of 0·5 in internal diameter coils with turns spaced one diameter apart

SELF-RESONANT FREQUENCIES OF TYPICAL CAPACITORS

Capaci-tance (pF)	Frequency (MHz) with		ERIE Type	Capaci-tance (pF)	Frequency (MHz) with		ERIE Type
	¼ in leads	½ in leads			¼ in leads	½ in leads	
330	85	62					
220	120	82					
100	145	120					
47	240	180		10,000	14	12	
33	250	210	A				
22	280	235					811
15	400	300					
10	530	390					
6·8	600	470		1,000 (feed through) (18 swg single lead)	—	40	701B
			831				
1,000	75	42		1,000 (discoidal) (18 swg single lead)	200	125	CDFT 100-107

LARGE INDUCTORS

The inductance of a coil is proportional to diameter $\times$ F $\times$ square of the number of turns, F being a function of the *shape*. If F is plotted against shape it is then possible to find the inductance of any given coil. F would then represent the inductance of a coil of unity diameter if all its turns were connected in parallel to make one turn.

In the inverse process of finding the turns for a required value of inductance the shape is not fixed till the turns are known, and the "one-turn coil" conception is useful, but it is better to work in terms of one turn per inch and plot a new curve, the points of which can be multiplied by n^2 (n turns per inch) to give the true inductance.

The chart opposite gives in this way the inductance L_0 of coils of various shapes wound one turn per inch, and may be used for finding either inductance or turns required. The chart is for circular section one-layer coils.

Examples

(a) Required: a coil of 15 μH inductance for a 7 MHz pa tank circuit, which it is proposed to wind on a $2\frac{3}{4}$ in *inside* diameter, $\frac{1}{8}$ in copper tube with a pitch of four turns per inch. First divide 15 μH by 4^2 in order to find L_0, which is 0·94. On the curve for $D = 3$ in (outside diam) it will be seen that L_0 0·94 occurs when the length is 5 in. The number of turns is therefore 20.

(b) A coil former of diameter $1\frac{1}{2}$ in is threaded 16 turns per inch, and wound with 24 turns. What is the inductance? The length is 24/16 which equals $1\frac{1}{2}$ in, and the chart gives L_0 as 0·060. n is equal to 16, therefore $L = 0·060 \times 16^2 = 15·3 \mu$H.

Alternatively, if it is desired to fill a given winding space and produce a certain inductance, then this inductance is divided by the L_0 value given on the chart to find n^2, the square root of which is the turns per inch. The coil may then be wound to this pitch, or a suitable type of wire selected to fit this pitch.

Note.—In coils of heavy conductor such as those made from tubing, rf currents flow on the outside. For that reason, therefore it is the overall diameter which must be taken. If the former is of hexagonal section, the *effective* diameter is only 90 per cent of the diameter across opposite corners.

INDUCTANCE DESIGN CHART

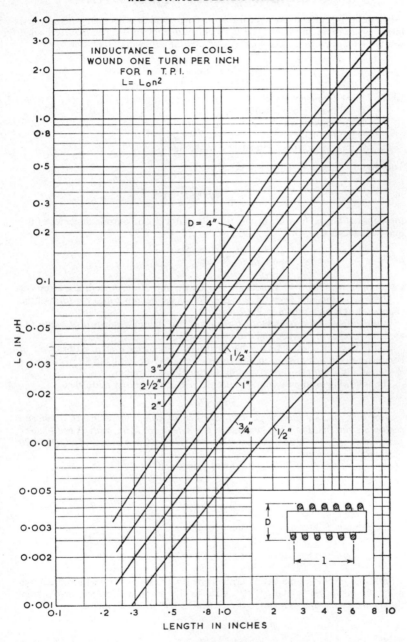

INDUCTANCE L_o OF COILS
WOUND ONE TURN PER INCH
FOR n T.P.I.
$L = L_o n^2$

D = 4"

1½"

3"

2½"

1"

2"

¾"

½"

L_o IN μH

LENGTH IN INCHES

D

1

TRANSMISSION LINE RESONATORS

When designing a resonator to be used as a tank circuit it is necessary to know first how long to make the lines. The resonant frequency of a capacitatively loaded shorted line, open-wire or coaxial, is given by the following expression:

$$\frac{1}{2\pi fC} = Z_0 \tan \frac{2\pi l}{\lambda}$$

where f is the frequency
  C is the loading capacitance
  λ is the wavelength
  l is the line length
  Z_0 is the characteristic impedance of the line.

The characteristic impedance is given by

$$Z_0 = 138 \log_{10} \frac{d_0}{d_1}$$

for a coaxial line with inside diameter of the outer d_0 and outside diameter of the inner conductor d_1

or
$$Z_0 = 276 \log_{10} \frac{2D}{d}$$

for an open-wire line with conductor diameter d and centre-to-centre spacing D.

The results obtained from these expressions have been put into the form of the simple set of curves shown in Fig 2 on p 52.

In the graphs, fl has been plotted against fC for different values of Z_0, with f in megahertz, C in picofarads and l in centimetres.

In the case of coaxial lines (the right-hand set of curves), r is the ratio of conductor diameters or radii and for open-wire lines (the left-hand set of curves), r is the ratio of centre-to-centre spacing to conductor diameter.

The following examples should make the use of the graphs quite clear:

Example 1
How long must a shorted parallel-wire line of conductor diameter 0·3 in and centre-to-centre spacing 1·5 in be made to resonate at 435 MHz, with an end-loading capacitance of 2 pF (the approximate output capacitance, in practice, of a QQV03-20 push-pull arrangement)
First, work out $f \times C$, in megahertz and picofarads.

$$fC = 435 \times 2$$
$$= 870$$
$$= 8·7 \times 10^2.$$

The ratio, r, of line spacing to diameter is:

$$r = \frac{1·5}{0·3} = 5·0.$$

Then, from the curves marked "parallel-wire lines", $r = 5·0$ project upwards from $8·7 \times 10^2$ on the horizontal "$f \times C$" scale to the graph and project across from the point on the graph so found to the vertical "$f \times l$" scale, obtaining:

$$fl = 2,800$$

therefore
$$l = \frac{2,800}{435} = 6·45 \text{ cm approximately.}$$

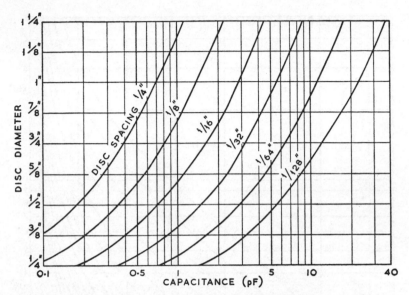

Fig 1. Parallel lines or concentric tuned circuits are conveniently tuned by means of a variable air capacitor comprising two parallel discs. This chart shows the capacitance between two parallel discs of various diameters

The anode pins would obviously absorb quite a good deal of this line length but, if the lines were made 6 cm long, with an adjustable shorting-bar they would be certain to be long enough.

Example 2

A transmission line consisting of a pair of 10 swg copper wires spaced 1 in apart and 10 cm long is to be used as part of the anode tank circuit of a TT15 or QQV06-40 pa at 145 MHz. How much extra capacitance must be added at the valve end of the line to accomplish this?

For a pair of wires approximately $\frac{1}{8}$ in diameter spaced 1 in r is about 8. Also $f \times l$ is equal to 145×10, ie 1,450. Estimating the position of the "$r = 8$" curve for a parallel-wire line between "$r = 10$" and "$r = 7$," $f \times C$ is found to be about $1 \cdot 55 \times 10^2$, ie 1,550. Hence the total capacitance C required is given by

$$145 \times C = 1,550$$
$$C = 1,550 \div 145$$
$$= 10 \cdot 7 \, \text{pF}.$$

Now the output capacitance of a TT15 or QQV06-40 push-pull stage is around 4 pF in practice, so about 7 pF is required in addition. A 25 + 25 pF split stator capacitor should therefore be quite satisfactory, giving 12 to 15 pF extra at maximum capacitance.

Example 3

A coaxial line with outer and inner radii of $5 \cdot 0$ and $2 \cdot 0$ cm, respectively, is to be used as the resonant tank circuit (short-circuited at one end of course) for a 4X150A power amplifier on the 70 cm amateur band. What length of line is required?

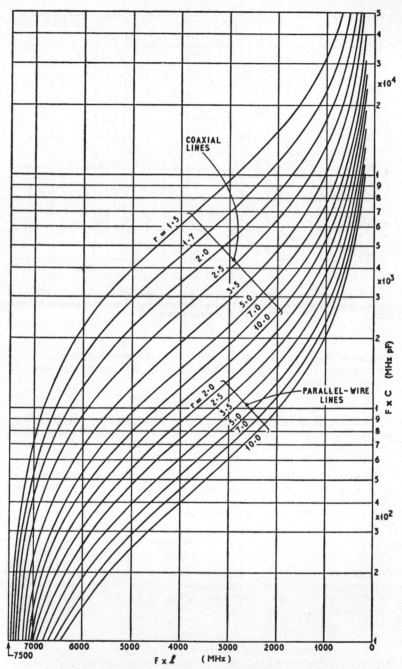

Fig 2. Resonance curves for capacitively loaded transmission line resonators

COAXIAL RESONATORS

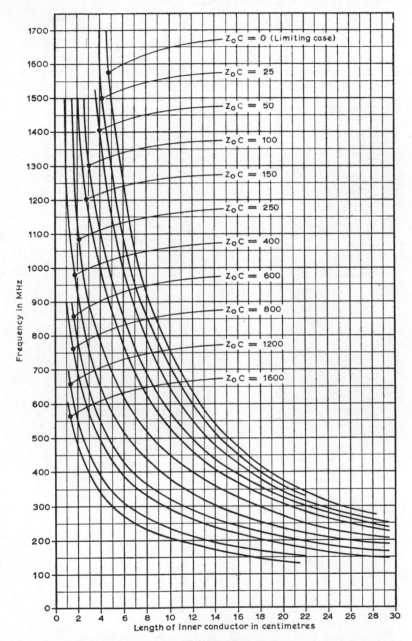

Fig 3. Chart plotting frequency against length of inner line for various values of the characteristic impedance multiplied by the total capacitance. C is in picofarads and Z_0 in ohms

In this case: $f \times C = 435 \times 4 \cdot 6 = 2{,}001$.
Using the "$r = 2 \cdot 5$" curve for coaxial lines,

$$f \times l = 4{,}620$$

Hence $\qquad l = 4{,}620 \div 435 = 10 \cdot 6 \text{ cm}$ approximately.

This length includes the length of the anode and cooler but, as in Example 1, a line 10 cm long would be long enough, as the output capacitance used in the calculations is that quoted by the valve manufacturers, the effective capacitance being somewhat greater in practical circuits. A shorting bridge is the best method of tuning the line to resonance.

UHF RESONATORS

The table shows the inductance (nH) self-capacitance (pF) and self-resonance of the system shown for various values of *D, H* and *L*.

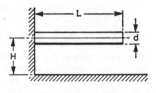

Height H above ground plane (in)	Diameter D (in)	Length L (in)								
		1·0	1·5	2	2·5	3·0	3·5	4·0	4·5	5·0
$\frac{1}{4}$	$\frac{1}{4}$	5	9	12	15	19	22	26	29	33 nH
		0·7	1·1	1·5	1·8	2·2	2·5	2·9	3·3	3·6 pF
		2·4	1·5	1·1	0·9	0·7	0·6	0·5	0·45	0·4 GHz
	$\frac{1}{8}$	9	14	19	24	29	34	40	45	50
		0·4	0·6	0·8	1	1·2	1·4	1·6	1·8	2·0
		2·5	1·6	1·2	0·95	0·8	0·7	0·6	0·55	0·5
	$\frac{1}{16}$	12	19	26	33	40	47	54	61	67
		0·3	0·4	0·6	0·7	0·9	1	1·1	1·3	1·4
		2·5	1·6	1·2	1	0·8	0·7	0·6	0·55	0·5
$\frac{1}{2}$	$\frac{1}{4}$	7	12	17	22	27	32	38	43	48
		0·4	0·6	0·8	1	1·2	1·4	1·6	1·8	2·0
		2·7	1·7	1·3	1	0·8	0·7	0·6	0·55	0·5
	$\frac{1}{8}$	10	17	24	31	37	44	51	58	65
		0·3	0·4	0·5	0·6	0·7	0·9	1·1	1·2	1·3
		2·7	1·7	1·3	1	0·8	0·7	0·6	0·55	0·5
	$\frac{1}{16}$	14	22	31	39	48	57	65	74	83
		0·2	0·3	0·5	0·6	0·7	0·8	0·9	1	1·1
		2·6	1·7	1·2	1	0·8	0·7	0·6	0·55	0·5
1	$\frac{1}{4}$	8	14	21	27	34	41	47	54	61
		0·3	0·4	0·6	0·7	0·9	1	1·1	1·3	1·4
		3	1·9	1·3	1	0·9	0·7	0·65	0·6	0·5
	$\frac{1}{8}$	11	19	27	36	44	63	61	70	78
		0·2	0·3	0·5	0·6	0·7	0·8	0·9	1	1·1
		2·9	1·8	1·3	1	0·8	0·7	0·6	0·55	0·5
	$\frac{1}{16}$	15	24	34	44	55	65	75	86	96
		0·2	0·3	0·4	0·5	0·6	0·7	0·7	0·8	0·9
		2·8	1·8	1·3	1	0·8	0·7	0·6	0·55	0·5

WIDEBAND COUPLERS

Most wideband couplers consist of two tuned circuits, individually resonant at the same frequency and coupled together. The coupling is usually inductive, but the general characteristics are the same with any type. From Fig 1, it can be seen that as the coupling is increased from zero, the single-peaked response rises to a maximum, flattens out, then divides into two peaks. Further increase in coupling results in greater separation and sharpness of the peaks. Note that the twin peaks are not caused by detuning, but by close coupling of two circuits tuned to the same frequency. The coupling coefficient is the ratio of the mutual inductance between windings to the inductance of one winding. This is true where the primary and secondary are identical; for simplicity, this is taken to be the case.

When the peak of the response is flat and on the point of splitting, the coupling is as its critical value, which is given by:

$$k_c = \frac{1}{Q} \ (Q_p = Q_s)$$

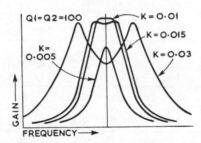

Fig 1. Effect of varying the coupling between the coils in a wideband coupler
(after Terman)

Hence, the higher the Q, the lower the coupling required. In a normal i.f. transformer, the coupling is set at the critical value; however, for use in wideband couplers, it is convenient to have it slightly higher. The design formulae and practical values given below are based on a coupling/critical coupling ratio of 1·86, corresponding to a peak-to-trough ratio of 1·2:1, or a response flat within 2 dB over the band.

The most convenient way of introducing variable coupling between two tuned circuits is with a small trimmer between the "hot" ends of the coils (see Fig 2). This is equivalent, except where phase relationships are concerned, to a mutual inductance of the value:

$$M = \frac{C_1}{C_1 + C} L$$

Hence the coupling coefficient is:

$$k = \frac{C_1}{C_1 + C}$$

The purpose of the damping resistors shown in Fig 2 is to obtain correct circuit Q; they should not be omitted. The secondary damping resistors are also the resistors of the next stage, and should never be omitted. In Class A amplifiers, they may be simply shunted across the secondary with no blocking capacitor. In wideband multipliers, R should be the same for all bands, so that the output stage resistor will

TABLE 1
AMATEUR BAND COUPLER DATA

Lowest frequency (MHz)	Centre frequency (MHz)	Highest frequency (MHz)	Coupling (pF)	Parallel capacitance (pF)	L (μH)	Winding details
3·5	3·65	3·8	6	78	24	60 t 32 swg close-wound
7	7·25	7·5	3	47	10	40 t 28 swg close-wound
14	14·5	15	1·5	24	5	27 t 24 swg close-wound
21	21·225	21·45	1	52	1	12 t 20 swg spaced to ⅜ in
28	29	30	0·6	10 pri.	3	21 t 24 swg spaced to ⅜ in
				30 sec.	1	12 t 20 swg

The formers used are all ⅜ in dia and the winding lengths of the coils ¾ in. The use of slugged formers is not recommended. On all bands except 28 MHz, primary and secondary are identical. Each coupler should be adjusted to cover the frequency range shown. Damping resistors are 15 kΩ on all bands.

be correct for each coupler. Primary and secondary coils should be as near identical as possible, and tuning done with trimmers only. This does not apply to the 28 MHz coupler as strays necessitate the use of dissimilar Qs.

Given set values of damping resistance, passband, and centre frequency, all values may be calculated from the following formulae:

$$k = 0.84 \, \frac{\text{Bandwidth (kHz)}}{\text{Centre frequency (kHz)}}$$

$$Q = \frac{1·86}{k} \qquad L = \frac{R}{2\pi f Q} \qquad C = \frac{1}{L}\left(\frac{1}{2\pi f}\right)^2$$

where C is in microfarads, L is in microhenrys and f is the centre frequency in megahertz. R is in ohms.

Note that C includes all strays; if the calculated value of C is less than the estimated strays on any band, a lower value of R should be used. The bandswitch can increase the strays to 20 pF (0·00002 μF) or more.

Coupling capacitance, C_1, is given by:

$$C_1 = \frac{k}{1-k} C$$

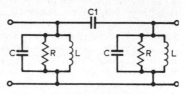

Fig 2. Basic coupler circuit

As the percentage bandwidth on 21 MHz is so low, this band could be covered adequately by a single low-Q tuned circuit such as a self-resonant coil. However, values for this band are given in Table 1, which is based on a value for R of 15 kΩ on all bands. The coverage of some of the couplers is greater than the band limits, as they are needed to multiply up to 30 MHz. The 28 MHz coupler was specially designed with different primary and secondary Qs, as the strays were greater on the output side than the identical-Q coupler tuning capacitance. This coupler allows 30 pF total capacitance, which should be ample for most layouts. The anode side strays are covered adequately by 10 pF, as there is no switch and only 2 pF anode-to-cathode capacitance and wiring strays. The coil data is for ⅜ in diameter formers, and a total winding length of ¾ in.

RESONANT CIRCUITS AND FILTERS   57

PI AND L-PI NETWORK COUPLERS

IMPROVED DESIGN METHODS

The purpose of the pi-network coupler is to present at its input terminals an impedance R_a in order to load a valve or transistor amplifier correctly when the actual load connected to the output terminals of the coupler is a resistance R_2, as shown in Fig 1.

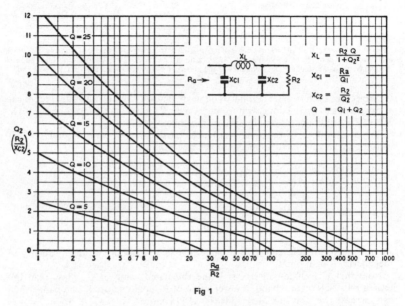

Fig 1

Earlier design formulae and curves have assumed X_L to be resonated by X_{C1} and X_{C2} in series, but this assumption is correct only if r_2 is much larger than X_{C2}; this condition is only approached for large ratios of R_a to R_2. For ratios of less than 10, the error becomes quite large and this has become obvious when using the existing formulae for designing transistor matching networks.

To analyse the behaviour of the circuit correctly, it is necessary to convert the parallel components X_{C2}, R_2 into their series equivalent, to add the value of X_L and then reconvert into parallel components. To do this, the following standard conversion formulae are needed; in Fig 2, the parallel circuit X_p and R_p is equivalent to the series circuit X_s and R_2, if

$$R_s = \frac{R_p \cdot X_p^2}{R_p^2 + X_p^2} \qquad (1)$$

Fig 2

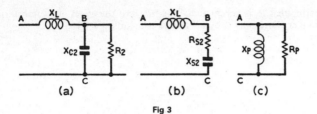

Fig 3

$$X_s = \frac{R_p^2 \cdot X_p}{R_p^2 + X_p^2} \tag{2}$$

$$R_p = \frac{R_s^2 + X_s^2}{R_s} \tag{3}$$

$$X_p = \frac{R_s^2 + X_s^2}{X_s} \tag{4}$$

The pi-network omitting X_{C1} is shown in Fig 3(a). The impedance between B and C consists of X_{C2} and R_2 in parallel and is equivalent to R_{s2} and X_{s2} in series as shown in Fig 3(b) where

$$R_{s2} = \frac{R_2 \cdot X_{C2}^2}{R_2^2 + X_{C2}^2} \tag{5}$$

$$X_{s2} = \frac{R_2^2 \cdot X_{C2}}{R_2^2 + X_{C2}^2} = R_{s2} \cdot \frac{R_2}{X_{C2}} \tag{6}$$

The coil reactance X_L is in series with these and X_L must be greater than X_{s2} because the total impedance between A and C must be inductive in order to tune with a capacitive X_{C1}. In Fig 3(b) we have a resistance R_{s2} in series with an inductive reactance $(X_L - X_{s2})$; this combination may be converted to the parallel combination of X_p and R_p shown in Fig 3(c), where

$$R_p = \frac{R_{s2}^2 + (X_L - X_{s2})^2}{R_{s2}} \tag{7}$$

$$X_p = \frac{R_{s2}^2 + (X_L - X_{s2})^2}{X_L - X_{s2}} \tag{8}$$

The resistive part R_p is clearly our wanted load resistance R_1, while the input capacitance to the pi-coupler X_{C1} must tune out X_p. Hence, numerically $R_1 = R_p$ and $X_{C1} = X_p$.

The loaded Q of the whole circuit is given by

$$Q = \frac{X_L}{R_{s2}} \tag{9}$$

provided that the impedance of the source is large compared with R_a. Let us designate

$$\frac{R_2}{X_{C2}} = Q_2 \quad \text{and} \quad \frac{R_1}{X_c} = Q_1$$

RESONANT CIRCUITS AND FILTERS   **59**

remembering that R_1 is not an actual resistor, but the effect of R_2 transformed by the pi-coupler. Dividing (8) by (7) and rearranging, we have

$$X_{C1} = \frac{R_a \cdot R_{s2}}{X_L - X_{s2}}$$

Therefore

$$\frac{X_{C1}}{R_a} = \frac{R_{s2}}{X_L - X_{s2}}$$

$$\frac{R_a}{X_{C1}} = \frac{X_L}{R_{s2}} - \frac{X_{s2}}{R_{s2}}$$

But

$$\frac{X_{s2}}{R_{s2}} = \frac{R_2}{X_{C2}} \text{ (from equation (6))}.$$

therefore

$$\frac{X_L}{R_{s2}} = \frac{R_a}{X_{C1}} + \frac{R_2}{X_{C2}}$$

ie

$$Q = Q_1 + Q_2. \tag{10}$$

Dividing equation (7) by R_{s2}

$$\frac{R_a}{R_{s2}} = 1 + \left(\frac{X_L - X_{s2}}{R_{s2}}\right)^2 = 1 + (Q - Q_2)^2$$

But from equation (5)

$$R_{s2} = \frac{R_2}{1 + \left(\dfrac{R_2}{X_{C2}}\right)^2} = \frac{R_2}{1 + Q_s^2}$$

therefore

$$\frac{R_a}{R_2}(1 + Q_2^2) = 1 + (Q - Q_2)^2$$

$$\frac{R_a}{R_2} = \frac{1 + (Q - Q_2)^2}{1 + Q_2^2} = \frac{1 + Q_1^2}{1 + Q_2^2} \tag{11}$$

Now from equation (9)

$$\frac{X_L}{R_2} = \frac{Q \cdot R_{s2}}{R_2}$$

and since from equation (5)

$$R_{s2} = \frac{R_2}{1 + Q_2^2}$$

therefore

$$\frac{X_L}{R_2} = \frac{Q}{1 + Q_2^2} \tag{12}$$

We can now prepare design curves for pi-couplers for any chosen value of Q, by selecting combinations of Q_1 and Q_2 and calculating R_a/R_2 from

60   PART 3

$$\frac{1 + Q_1^2}{1 + Q_2^2}$$

Thus for $Q = 15$

Q_1	15	14	13	10	7·5	5	2	1	0
Q_2	0	1	2	5	7·5	10	13	14	15
$\dfrac{R_a}{R_2}$	226	98·5	34	3·88	1	0·257	0·0294	0·0102	0·0044

If Q_2 (ie R_2/X_{C2}) is plotted against R_a/R_2 the appropriate value can be read on the chart for any transformation ratio. It is unnecessary to plot values of R_a/R_2 less than 1, since the coupler is reversible.

The chart, Fig 1, gives the curves for $Q = 5, 10, 15, 20$ and 25. Having found Q_2 from the curves then

$$X_{C2} = \frac{R_2}{Q_2}$$

$$X_{C1} = \frac{R_a}{Q - Q_2}$$

$$X_L = \frac{R_2 \cdot Q}{1 + Q_2^2}$$

It should be noted that the ratio R_a/R_2 which corresponds to $Q_2 = 0$, is a theoretical maximum ratio for the value of Q assumed. In fact X_{C2} is infinity at this ratio (that is, C_2 has disappeared) and the practical limit is a somewhat smaller ratio.

Worked example

An amplifier requiring an anode load of 500 Ω is required to match a 50 Ω antenna feeder.

$$\frac{R_a}{R_2} = \frac{500}{50} = 10$$

Let us select a loaded Q of 15. From Fig 1, $Q_2 = 3·5$, hence $Q_1 = 15 - 3·5 = 11·5$

from equation 12,

$$\frac{X_L}{R_2} = \frac{15}{1 + 3·5^2} = 1·132$$

Hence

$$X_{C2} = \frac{50}{3·5} = 14·3\,\Omega$$

$$X_{C1} = \frac{500}{11·5} = 43·5\,\Omega$$

$$X_L = 1·132 \times 50 = 56·6\,\Omega$$

so that for any given frequency, the values of C_1, C_2 and L can now be calculated.

RESONANT CIRCUITS AND FILTERS   61

Design for the I-pi network

The I-pi network can readily be designed by this method if it is regarded as two pi networks, back to back, in which the input capacitance is provided wholly by the output capacitance of the transistor.

The circuit then becomes Fig 4:

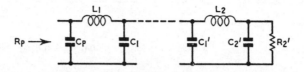

Fig 4

The following is an example where it is needed to match a 2N3632 transistor of output capacitance = 22 pF and requiring a load of 29 Ω, into a final load of 72 Ω. Q values of 10 for the first network and 15 for the second network were assumed and the design is for use at 144 MHz where the reactance of 22 pF is 50 Ω.

Now
$$\frac{R_p}{X_p} = \frac{29}{50} = 0{\cdot}58$$

Let us call this Q_2 as the transformation in the first section is from low to high impedance. From Fig 1, R_a/R_2 can be seen to be 66 for $Q_2 = 0{\cdot}58$ and $Q = 10$. Hence the effective load across the output of the first section is $66 \times 29 = 1{,}920\,\Omega$. Since

$$Q_1 = 10 - 0{\cdot}58 = 9{\cdot}42$$

$$X_{C1} = \frac{1{,}920}{9{\cdot}42} = 204\,\Omega$$

also
$$\frac{X_{L1}}{R_2} = \frac{10}{1 + 0{\cdot}58^2} = 7{\cdot}49$$

$$X_{L1} = 29 \times 7{\cdot}49 = 218\,\Omega$$

The second network must now match $1{,}920\,\Omega$ to the $72\,\Omega$ (antenna feeder),

hence
$$\frac{R_a{}^1}{R_2{}^1} = 26{\cdot}6 \text{ and for } Q = 15$$

Fig 1 shows
$$Q_2 = 2{\cdot}3$$

hence
$$X_{C2}{}^1 = \frac{72}{2{\cdot}3} = 31{\cdot}3\,\Omega$$

now
$$Q_1 = 15 - 2{\cdot}3 = 12{\cdot}7$$

hence
$$X_{C1}{}^1 = \frac{1{,}920}{12{\cdot}7} = 151\,\Omega$$

from equation 12,
$$\frac{X_{L2}}{R_2{}^1} = \frac{15}{1 + 2{\cdot}3^3} = 2{\cdot}38$$

$$X_{L2} = 2{\cdot}38 \times 72 = 172\,\Omega$$

Network	**Simplified formulae and comments**
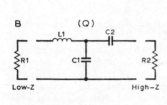 A (Q) Low-Z High-Z	$X_{L1} = QR_1$ $X_{C1} = X_{L1} = \dfrac{R_1^2 + X_{L1}^2}{X_{L1}}$ $R_2 = R_1(1 + Q^2)$ Simple L network often lacks flexibility. Will only match between unequal impedances.
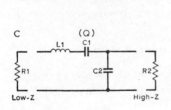 B (Q) Low-Z High-Z Suitable for transistor input/output tuning networks. Will only match between unequal impedances.	$X_{L1} = QR_1$ $X_{C2} = AR_2$ $X_{C1} = \dfrac{B}{Q - A}$ $A = \sqrt{\left[\dfrac{R_1(1 + Q^2)}{R_2}\right] - 1}$ $B = R_1(1 + Q^2)$
C (Q) Low-Z High-Z	$X_{L1} = X_{C1} + \dfrac{R_1 R_2}{X_{C2}}$ $X_{C1} = QR_1$ $X_{C2} = R_2\sqrt{\dfrac{R_1}{R_2 - R_1}}$ Suitable for transistor input/output tuning networks. Will only match between unequal impedances.
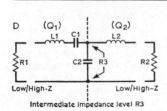 D (Q_1) (Q_2) Low/High-Z Low/High-Z Intermediate impedance level R3 Q_1 and Q_2 need not be the same. Intermediate impedance level higher than R_1 or R_2. Ideal for matching between near equal impedances.	$C_2 = C_A + C_B$ $R_3 = R_2(1 + Q_2^2)$ $X_{CA} = R_3\sqrt{\dfrac{R_1}{R_3 - R_1}}$ $X_{CB} = \dfrac{R_2^2 + X_{L2}^2}{X_{L2}}$ $X_{C1} = Q_1 R_1$ $X_{L1} = X_{C1} + \dfrac{R_1 R_3}{X_{C2}}$ $X_{L2} = Q_2 R_2$

RESONANT CIRCUITS AND FILTERS   63

FILTERS

There are many applications for which multi-element filters are necessary; the types in general use are elliptic (Cauer-Chebyshev), Butterworth and Chebyshev filters. Their salient features may be briefly described as follows.

Butterworth filters have a maximally flat response in the passband. Chebyshev filters exhibit a sharper roll-off in the stopband but exhibit ripples in the passband, the number depending on the number of filter sections. Cauer-Chebyshev or elliptic function filters have the sharpest roll-off in the stopband of all three types but exhibit ripples in the stopband (zeroes) as well as ripples in the passband (poles). Chebyshev and elliptical filters have a higher group delay and overshoot, particularly at frequencies close to the cut-off frequency and should be avoided in applications where pulse distortion is critical, eg rtty filters. The cut-off frequency is generally defined as the frequency at which the response is 3 dB down.

ELLIPTIC (CAUER-CHEBYSHEV) FILTERS

Using modern design procedure, a "normalized" filter having the desired performance is chosen from a series of precalculated designs. The following presentation, originally due to W3NQN, uses normalization to a cut-off frequency of 1 Hz and termination resistances of 1 Ω, and all that is required to ascertain the constants of a practical filter is to specify the actual cut-off frequency and termination resistance required and to scale the normalized filter data to these parameters.

In these curves, the following abbreviations are used:

A = attenuation (dB)
A_p = maximum attenuation in pass-band,
f_4 = first attenuation peak,
f_2 = second attenuation peak with two-section filter or third attenuation peak with three-section filter.
f_6 = second attenuation peak with three-section filter,
f_{co} = frequency where the attenuation first exceeds that in the pass-band,
A_s = minimum attenuation in stop-band,
f_s = frequency where minimum stop-band attenuation is first reached.

The attenuation peaks f_4, f_6 or f_2 are associated with the resonant circuits L4/C4, L6/C6 and L2/C2 on the respective diagrams.

Applications

Because of their low values of reflection coefficient (P) and vswr, Tables 1–1, 1–2 and 1–3, and Tables 2–1 to 2–6 inclusive, are best suited for rf applications where power must be transmitted through the filter. The two-section filter has a relatively gradual attenuation slope and the stop-band attenuation level (A_s) is not achieved until a frequency (f_s) is reached, which is two to three times the cut-off frequency. If a more abrupt attenuation slope is desired, then one of the three-section filters (Tables 2–1 to 2–6) should be used. In these cases the stop-band attenuation level may be reached at a frequency only 1·25 to 2 times f_{co}.

Tables 1–4, 1–5 and 1–6 are intended for af applications where transmission of appreciable power is not required, and consequently the filter response may have a much higher value of vswr and pass-band ripple without adversely affecting the filter performance. If the higher pass-band ripple is acceptable, a more abrupt attenuation slope is possible. This can be seen by comparing the different values of f_s at 50 dB in Tables 1–4, 1–5 and 1–6 which have pass-band ripple peaks of 0·28, 0·50 and 1·0 dB respectively. The values of A_s for the audio filters were selected to be between 35 and 55 dB, as this range of stop-band attenuation was believed to be optimum for most audio filtering requirements.

It should be noted that *all* C and L tabular data *must be multiplied by a factor of 10^{-3}*.

With one exception, all the C and L tabulated data of each table have a consistent but unequal increase or decrease in value, a characteristic of most computer-derived filter tables. An exception will be noted in Table 1–5, $A_s = 50$, column C1. The original author points out that this is not an error but arose from a minor change necessitated in the original computer program to eliminate unrealizable component values.

How to use the filter tables

After the desired cut-off frequency has been chosen, the frequencies of f_s and the attenuation peaks may be calculated by multiplying their corresponding tabular values by the required cut-off frequency (f_{co}). The component values of the desired filter are then found by multiplying C and L values in the tables by $1/Rf_{co}$ and R/f_{co} respectively.

Example 1

A low-pass audio filter to attenuate speech frequencies above 3 kHz with a minimum attenuation of 40 dB for all frequencies above 3·8 kHz, and to be terminated in resistive loads of 1·63 kΩ. (This odd value has been chosen merely for convenience in demonstrating the design procedure).

The circuit of Fig 1 is chosen because this has the minimum number of inductors, which are both more expensive and have higher losses than do capacitors.

The parameters are:

$A_s = 40$ dB
$f_{co} = 3$ kHz
$R = 1·63$ kΩ.

From Table 1–5, $A_s = 40$ dB, calculate f'_s, f'_4 and f'_2. (Numbers with the prime (') are the frequency and component values of the final design: numbers *without* the prime are from the filter catalogue).

(1) $f'_s = f_s(f_{co}) = 1·270 \times 3 = 3·81$ kHz.
$f'_4 = f_4(f_{co}) = 1·308 \times 3 = 3·92$ kHz.
$f'_2 = f_2(f_{co}) = 1·878 \times 3 = 5·63$ kHz.

(2) Calculate factors $1/Rf_{co}$ and R/f_{co} to determine the capacitor and inductor values.

$$1/Rf_{co} = 1/(1·63 \times 10^3)(3 \times 10^3)$$
$$= 1/(4·89 \times 10^6)$$
$$= 0·2045 \times 10^{-6}$$
$$R/f_{co} = (1·63 \times 10^3)/(3 \times 10^3) = 0·543.$$

(3) Calculate the component values of the desired filter by multiplying all the catalogue tabular values of C by $1/Rf_{co}$ and L by R/f_{co} as shown below:

$$C'1 = C1(1/Rf_{co}) = (238 \times 10^{-3})(0·2045)10^{-6}$$
$$= 0·0487 \, \mu F$$
$$C'3 = C3(1/Rf_{co}) = (299 \times 10^{-3})(0·2045)10^{-6}$$
$$= 0·0612 \, \mu F$$
$$C'5 = C5(1/Rf_{co}) = (177·3 \times 10^{-3})(0·2045)10^{-6}$$
$$= 0·0363 \, \mu F$$
$$C'2 = C2(1/Rf_{co}) = (44·4 \times 10^{-3})(0·2045)10^{-6}$$
$$= 0·00908 \, \mu F$$

REFLECTION COEFFICIENT, VSWR & Ap	As dB	fs Hz	f4 Hz	f2 Hz	C1 Farad	C3 Farad	C5 Farad	C2 Farad	L2 Henry	C4 Farad	L4 Henry
Table 1—1 p = 4% VSWR = 1·08 Ap = 0·0069 dB	70	3·24	3·39	5·42	110·4	235	103·5	4·34	199·0	11·72	187·5
	65	2·92	3·07	4·88	109·6	233	101·0	5·39	197·9	14·67	183·7
	60	2·56	2·68	4·24	108·2	229	96·9	7·20	195·8	19·88	177·3
	55	2·37	2·48	3·90	107·2	227	93·8	8·57	194·3	23·9	172·7
	50	2·13	2·23	3·48	105·5	223	88·6	10·88	192·0	31·0	164·7
Table 1—2 p = 5% VSWR = 1·11 Ap = 0·011 dB	70	3·07	3·22	5·13	118·3	243	110·8	4·73	203	12·78	191·0
	65	2·79	2·92	4·64	117·4	241	108·3	5·82	202	15·82	187·2
	60	2·46	2·57	4·06	116·0	237	104·0	7·67	200	21·2	180·7
	55	2·28	2·39	3·75	115·0	234	100·8	9·07	198·5	25·3	175·9
	50	2·06	2·16	3·36	113·2	230	95·6	11·43	196·0	32·4	168·1
Table 1—3 p = 8% VSWR = 1·17 Ap = 0·028 dB	70	2·79	2·92	4·24	138·4	262	129·6	5·59	210	15·09	196·4
	65	2·56	2·68	4·24	137·4	259	126·9	6·75	208	18·32	192·4
	60	2·28	2·39	3·75	135·9	255	122·4	8·72	206	23·9	185·7
	55	2·06	2·16	3·36	134·2	251	117·4	10·98	204	30·6	178·4
	50	1·887	1·970	3·05	132·2	245	111·8	13·55	201	38·4	170·3
Table 1—4 p = 25% VSWR = 1·67 Ap = 0·28 dB	55	1·701	1·773	2·71	217	317	190·8	18·03	191·5	49·7	162·3
	50	1·556	1·617	2·44	213	306	181·3	22·8	187·3	63·8	151·9
	45	1·440	1·493	2·22	209	295	170·6	28·3	182·7	80·9	140·5
	40	1·325	1·369	1·988	203	279	155·8	36·4	176·0	108·0	125·1
	35	1·236	1·273	1·802	195·9	262	139·2	46·4	168·2	144·3	108·3
Table 1—5 p = 33% VSWR = 2·00 Ap = 0·50 dB	55	1·618	1·690	2·56	248	348	214	21·3	181·4	58·7	151·0
	50	1·481	1·540	2·30	249	336	210	27·4	174·9	76·7	139·3
	45	1·369	1·416	2·08	244	318	197·5	34·7	169·2	99·8	126·5
	40	1·270	1·308	1·878	238	299	177·3	44·4	161·7	133·7	110·8
	35	1·186	1·222	1·700	229	280	163·3	57·0	153·9	177·6	95·5
Table 1—6 p = 45% VSWR = 2·67 Ap = 1·00 dB	55	1·528	1·591	2·39	314	401	276	28·3	156·9	77·5	129·1
	50	1·407	1·459	2·16	308	381	260	35·5	153·3	99·6	119·4
	45	1·245	1·313	1·898	306	365	247	46·6	150·7	135·0	108·9
	40	1·217	1·250	1·755	296	341	227	59·2	138·9	176·2	92·0
	35	1·145	1·174	1·597	284	315	203	75·4	131·6	237	77·7
	As dB	fs Hz	f4 Hz	f2 Hz	L1 Henry	L3 Henry	L5 Henry	L2 Henry	C2 Farad	L4 Henry	C4 Farad

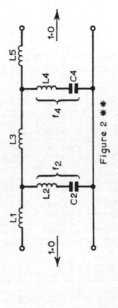

Figure 1 **

Figure 2 **

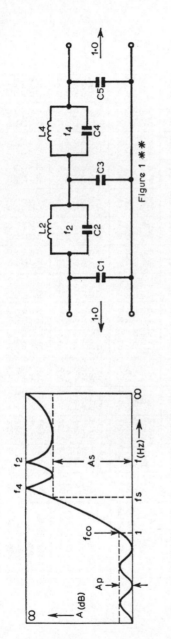

* All tabulated data of C and L must be multiplied by 10^{-3}; for example, in Table 1-1, the normalized value of C1 is $110·4 \times 10^{-3}$, for As = 70dB

** In the above tabulation, the top column headings pertain to Figure 1 while the bottom column headings pertain to Figure 2

Table 1. Two-section elliptic-function filters normalized for a cut-off frequency of 1 Hz and terminations of 1Ω

RESONANT CIRCUITS AND FILTERS 67

REFLECTION COEFFICIENT, VSWR & Ap	As dB	fs Hz	f4 Hz	f6 Hz	f2 Hz	C1 Farad	C3 Farad	C5 Farad	C7 Farad	C2 Farad	L2 Henry	C4 Farad	L4 Henry	C6 Farad	L6 Henry
	As dB	fs Hz	f4 Hz	f6 Hz	f2 Hz	L1 Henry	L3 Henry	L5 Henry	L7 Henry	L2 Henry	C2 Farad	L4 Henry	C4 Farad	L6 Henry	C6 Farad
Table 2–1 p = 1% VSWR = 1·02 Ap=0·43$\times 10^{-3}$dB	70	2·00	2·04	2·49	4·35	79·6	209	201	63·1	7·42	180·2	30·9	196·4	26·3	155·2
	64	1·836	1·876	2·27	3·95	78·3	204	194·8	58·5	9·10	178·4	38·4	187·6	33·0	148·3
	60	1·743	1·780	2·15	3·72	77·3	200	190·3	54·5	10·35	177·1	44·1	181·4	38·2	143·5
	55	1·624	1·657	1·990	3·41	75·8	194·2	183·5	48·5	12·42	175·2	53·8	171·4	47·2	135·6
	50	1·524	1·554	1·854	3·15	74·1	187·8	176·3	41·8	14·75	172·8	65·3	160·7	58·0	127·1
Table 2–2 p = 2% VSWR = 1·04 Ap=1·7$\times 10^{-3}$dB	70	1·836	1·876	2·27	3·95	93·8	222	212	75·7	8·34	194·8	35·8	201	29·4	167·0
	64	1·701	1·737	2·09	3·61	92·5	216	205	70·7	10·08	193·1	43·8	191·6	36·2	160·0
	60	1·624	1·657	1·990	3·41	91·5	212	200	67·1	11·35	191·6	49·8	185·1	41·3	154·8
	55	1·524	1·554	1·854	3·15	89·9	206	192·7	61·1	13·47	189·4	60·0	174·8	50·2	146·7
	50	1·414	1·440	1·702	2·86	87·5	196·9	182·1	52·2	16·70	186·1	76·4	160·0	64·8	135·0
Table 2–3 p = 3% VSWR = 1·06 Ap=3·9$\times 10^{-3}$dB	70	1·743	1·780	2·15	3·72	104·2	230	219	84·7	9·06	203	39·7	201	31·8	172·5
	65	1·624	1·657	1·990	3·41	102·8	224	211	79·7	10·84	201	48·1	191·8	38·7	165·4
	60	1·524	1·554	1·854	3·15	101·2	217	203	74·1	12·86	198·3	57·8	181·6	46·8	157·5
	55	1·440	1·466	1·737	2·92	99·5	211	194·8	67·9	15·12	195·9	69·0	170·8	56·3	149·1
	50	1·367	1·391	1·636	2·73	97·6	203	186·2	61·2	17·65	193·1	82·2	159·2	67·5	140·1
Table 2–4 p = 4% VSWR = 1·08 Ap=6·9$\times 10^{-3}$dB	70	1·701	1·737	2·09	3·61	113·0	236	224	93·0	9·37	208	41·6	202	32·7	177·0
	65	1·589	1·621	1·942	3·32	111·6	230	217	88·0	11·18	205	50·2	192·3	39·6	170·0
	60	1·494	1·523	1·813	3·07	110·0	224	208	82·4	13·20	203	60·0	181·9	47·6	161·9
	55	1·414	1·440	1·702	2·86	108·3	217	199·6	76·3	15·47	201	71·4	171·1	57·0	153·4
	50	1·325	1·347	1·576	2·61	105·6	206	187·5	67·3	18·94	196·9	89·7	155·6	72·2	141·3
Table 2–5 p = 5% VSWR = 1·11 Ap=11$\times 10^{-3}$dB	70	1·662	1·696	2·04	3·51	120·6	242	229	99·9	9·77	211	43·9	201	33·9	179·4
	65	1·556	1·586	1·897	3·23	119·2	235	221	94·9	11·61	209	52·7	191·1	40·9	172·0
	60	1·466	1·494	1·774	3·00	117·6	228	212	89·3	13·67	206	62·8	180·8	49·0	164·1
	55	1·367	1·391	1·636	2·73	115·2	219	199·7	81·0	16·81	203	78·8	166·2	61·9	152·7
	51·5	1·325	1·347	1·576	2·61	113·8	213	193·4	76·5	18·57	201	88·2	158·3	69·5	146·6
	50	1·305	1·327	1·548	2·55	113·1	211	190·2	74·1	19·51	199·7	93·2	154·4	73·7	143·5
Table 2–6 p = 8% VSWR = 1·17 Ap=28$\times 10^{-3}$dB	70	1·556	1·586	1·897	3·23	139·7	252	237	116·2	11·30	214	52·0	193·4	39·1	180·0
	65	1·466	1·494	1·774	3·00	138·1	245	228	110·9	13·30	212	61·9	183·5	46·6	172·5
	60	1·390	1·415	1·668	2·79	136·3	238	218	105·0	15·54	210	73·2	173·0	55·3	164·4
	55	1·325	1·347	1·576	2·61	134·4	230	208	98·6	18·05	207	86·5	161·9	65·4	155·8
	50	1·252	1·271	1·471	2·39	131·4	218	193·9	89·2	21·9	202	107·3	146·1	81·6	143·4

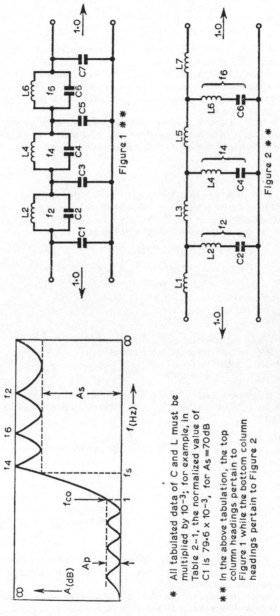

Figure 1 **

Figure 2 **

Table 2. Three-section elliptic-function filters normalized for a cut-off frequency of 1 Hz and terminations of 1Ω

* All tabulated data of C and L must be multiplied by 10^{-3}; for example, in Table 2–1, the normalized value of C1 is 79.6×10^{-3}, for As=70dB

** In the above tabulation, the top column headings pertain to Figure 1 while the bottom column headings pertain to Figure 2

RESONANT CIRCUITS AND FILTERS   69

$$C'4 = C4(1/Rf_{co}) = (133\cdot7 \times 10^{-3})(0\cdot2045)10^{-6}$$
$$= 0\cdot0273\,\mu F$$
$$L'2 = L2(R/f_{co}) = (161\cdot7 \times 10^{-3})(0\cdot543)$$
$$= 87\cdot8\,mH$$
$$L'4 = L4(R/f_{co}) = (110\cdot8 \times 10^{-3})(0\cdot543)$$
$$= 60\cdot1\,mH$$

These calculations, which may conveniently be performed with a pocket calculator, complete the design of the filter.

It should be noted that all the elliptic-function filter tabular data is based on the use of lossless components and purely resistive terminations. Therefore, components of the highest possible Q should be used and precautions taken to insure that the filter is properly terminated.

It will be noticed that some rather curious values of both capacitance and inductance may emerge from the calculations, but these may be rationalized to the extent that the tolerance on the values of components need not be closer than some ±3 per cent.

Example 2
A three-section low-pass filter to suppress harmonics at the output of a transmitter covering the hf bands up to a frequency of 30 MHz with a matching impedance of 50 Ω and a minimum attenuation in the stop-band of 50 dB.

The parameters are, from Table 2–2 (circuit Fig 2):

$$A_s = 50\,dB \qquad f_{co} = 30\,MHz \qquad R = 50\,\Omega$$

From Table 2–2 (bottom line) calculate f'_s, f'_4, f'_6, f'_2.

(1) $f'_s = f_s(f_{co}) = 1\cdot414 \times 30 = 42\cdot4\,MHz$
  $f'_4 = f_4(f_{co}) = 1\cdot440 \times 30 = 43\cdot2\,MHz$
  $f'_6 = f_6(f_{co}) = 1\cdot702 \times 30 = 51\,MHz$
  $f'_2 = f_2(f_{co}) = 2\cdot860 \times 30 = 85\cdot8\,MHz.$

(2) Calculate $1/Rf_{co}$ to determine capacitor values.
  Calculate R/f_{co} to determine inductor values.
  $1/Rf_{co} = 1/50(30 \times 10^{-6}) = 66 \times 11^{-11}$
  $R/f_{co} = 50/30 \times 10^6 = 1\cdot67 \times 10^{-6}.$

(3) Calculate component values of the desired filter by multiplying all tabular values of C by $1/Rf_{co}$ and L by R/f_{co}, remembering to multiply *all* values in the tables by 10^{-3}.

$C'2 = C2(66 \times 10^{-11})$ $L'1 = L1(1\cdot67 \times 10^{-6})$
  $= (186\cdot1 \times 10^{-3})(66 \times 10^{-11})$ $= (87\cdot5 \times 10^{-3})(1\cdot67 \times 10^{-6})$
  $= 12{,}282\cdot6 \times 10^{-14}\,F$ $= 146\cdot1 \times 10^{-9}\,H$
  $= 12{,}282\cdot6 \times 10^{-2}\,pF$ $= 0\cdot15\,\mu H$
  $= 122\cdot8\,pF$
$C'4 = (160 \times 10^{-3})(66 \times 10^{-11})$ $L'2 = 0\cdot03\,\mu H$ $L'3 = 0\cdot33\,\mu H$
  $= 105\cdot6\,pF$ $L'4 = 0\cdot13\,\mu H$ $L'5 = 0\cdot30\,\mu H$
$C'6 = 89\cdot1\,pF$ $L'6 = 0\cdot11\,\mu H$ $L'7 = 0\cdot09\,\mu H$

As a check, it will be found that the combination C4, L4 tunes to 43·2 MHz and that the other two series-tuned circuits tune to the other two points of maximum attenuation previously specified.

In order to convert the values in the filter just designed to match an impedance of 75 Ω it is only necessary to multiply all values of capacitance by 2/3 and all values of inductance by 3/2. Thus C6 and L6 in a 75 Ω filter become approximately 59·4 pF and 0·17 μH respectively.

BUTTERWORTH FILTERS

Frequency response curve

$$A = 10 \log_{10}\left[1 + \left(\frac{f}{f_c}\right)^{2K}\right]$$

where A is the attenuation, f is the frequency for insertion loss of 3·01 dB, and K is the number of circuit elements.

Low- and high-pass filters

Table 3 is for normalized element values of K from 1 to 10 (no of sections) reduced to 1 Ω source and load resistance (zero reactance) and a 3·01 dB cut-off frequency of 1 radian/s (0·1592 Hz).

Low-pass filters

$$L = \frac{R}{2\pi f_c} = L(1\,\text{ohm/radian}) \quad C = \frac{1}{2\pi f_c R} = C(1\,\text{ohm/radian})$$

High-pass filters

$$L = \frac{R}{2\pi f_c} = L(1\,\text{ohm/radian}) \quad C = \frac{1}{2\pi f_c R} = C(1\,\text{ohm/radian})$$

where R is the load resistance in ohms and f_c is the desired 3·01 dB frequency (Hz).

An example of a Butterworth low-pass filter is given in Fig 1 (see Table 3 for element values). In these examples of five-element filters (a) has a shunt element next to the load and (b) has a series element next to the load. Either filter will have the same response. In the examples of five-element filters given in Fig 2, (a) has a series element next to the load and (b) has a shunt element next to the load. Either filter will have the same response.

Butterworth band-pass filters

Centre frequency $f_o = \sqrt{f_1 f_2}$

Bandwidth $BW = f_2 - f_1$

TABLE 3

K	C_1 / L_1	C_2 / L_2	C_3 / L_3	C_4 / L_4	C_5 / L_5	C_6 / L_6	C_7 / L_7	C_8 / L_8	C_9 / L_9	C_{10} / L_{10}
1	2·000	—	—	—	—	—	—	—	—	—
2	1·4142	1·4142	—	—	—	—	—	—	—	—
3	1·000	2·000	1·000	—	—	—	—	—	—	—
4	0·7654	1·8478	1·8478	0·7654	—	—	—	—	—	—
5	0·6180	1·6180	2·000	1·6180	0·6180	—	—	—	—	—
6	0·5176	1·4142	1·9319	1·9319	1·4142	0·5176	—	—	—	—
7	0·4450	1·2470	1·8019	2·000	1·8019	1·2470	0·4450	—	—	—
8	0·3902	1·1111	1·6629	1·9616	1·9616	1·6629	1·1111	0·3902	—	—
9	0·3473	1·000	1·5321	1·8794	2·000	1·8794	1·5321	1·000	0·3473	—
10	0·3129	0·9080	1·4142	1·7820	1·9754	1·9754	1·7820	1·4142	0·9080	0·3129

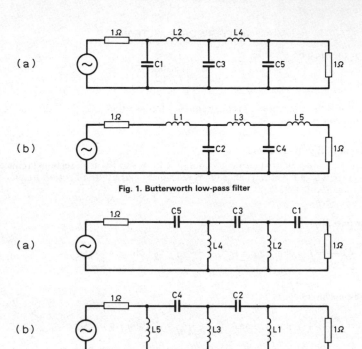

Fig. 1. Butterworth low-pass filter

Fig. 2. Butterworth high-pass filter

If the bandwidth specified is not the 3·01 dB bandwidth (BW_c) the latter can be determined from

$$BW_c = \frac{BW}{(10^{0.1A} - 1)/2K}$$

where A = required attenuation at cut-off frequencies.

Lower cut-off frequency

$$f_{cl} = \frac{-BW_c + \sqrt{(BW_c)^2 + 4f_o^2}}{2}$$

Upper cut-off frequency $\qquad f_{cu} = f_{cl} + BW_c$

An alternative more-convenient method is to choose a 3·01 dB bandwidth (as wide as possible) around the desired centre frequency and compute the attenuation at other frequencies of interest by using the transformation

$$\frac{f}{f_c} = \left[\left(\frac{f}{f_o} - \frac{f_o}{f} \right) \frac{f_o}{BW_c} \right]$$

CHEBYSHEV FILTERS

Tables 4 to 7 provide the essential information for both high- and low-pass filters of T and π form. Figures are given for pass-band ripples of 1, 0·1, 0·01 and 0·001 dB which respectively correspond to vswr of 2·66, 1·36, 1·10 and 1·03.

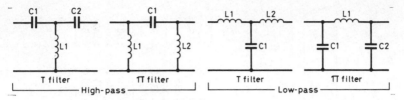

| T filter | ππ filter | T filter | ππ filter |
| High-pass | | Low-pass | |

Fig. 3. Single-section three-pole fiter elements

The filters in this case are normalized to a frequency of 1 MHz and an input and output impedance of 50 Ω. This means that for any particular desired frequency the component values simply have to be divided by the required frequency in megahertz.

The 1 MHz is the cut-off frequency; attenuation increases rapidly above the frequency for a low-pass filter and correspondingly below for a high-pass type.

The filter data is also dependent on the impedance which as given is for 50 Ω. For other impedances the component values need to be modified by the following

$$\frac{Z_n}{50} \text{ for inductors} \qquad \frac{50}{Z_n} \text{ for capacitors}$$

where Z_n is the required impedance.

There is an advantage in using toroidal-form inductors due to their self-screening (confined-field) properties. Mica or silver mica capacitors are superior to other types for filter applications.

Practical filters for the amateur hf bands are given in Table 8.

SIMPLE HF HALF-WAVE FILTERS

Filters of this type are extremely effective when used on the band for which they are designed. The minor disadvantage that a filter is required for each band is largely offset by the simplicity of construction from readily available components. In the table below, all capacitors are disc ceramic* type and should be rated at a minimum of 1,000 V working for use with a.m. transmitters running inputs of up to 150 W. The inductances are all wound with 12 swg tinned copper wire, eight turns per inch. Allowance has been made for leads of $\frac{1}{2}$ in. The values are for filters suitable for cables having impedances between 50 and 75 Ω.

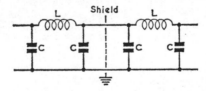

Capacitors and inductors for half-wave filters

3·5 MHz	C, 800 pF	L, 2·3 μH	(11$\frac{1}{2}$t, 1 in long, 1 in inside diameter).
7 MHz	C, 500 pF	L, 1·0 μH	(10$\frac{1}{2}$t, $\frac{3}{4}$ in inside diameter).
14 MHz	C, 220 pF	L, 0·55 μH	(6$\frac{1}{4}$t, $\frac{3}{4}$ in inside diameter).
21 MHz	C, 150 pF	L, 0·37 μH	(7$\frac{1}{2}$t, $\frac{1}{2}$ in inside diameter).
28 MHz	C, 110 pF	L, 0·28 μH	(6 t, $\frac{1}{2}$ in inside diameter).

* High grade mica also suitable.

TABLE 4. CHEBYSHEV LOW-PASS FILTER ("T" CONFIGURATION)

Ripple (dB)	L_1	L_2	L_3	L_4	L_5	C_1	C_2	C_3	C_4
Single section (3 pole)									
1	16·10	16·10	—	—	—	3,164·3	—	—	—
0·1	8·209	8·209	—	—	—	3,652·3	—	—	—
0·01	5·007	5·007	—	—	—	3,088·5	—	—	—
0·001	3·253	3·253	—	—	—	2,312·6	—	—	—
Two section (5 pole)									
1	16·99	23·88	16·99	—	—	3,473·1	3,473·1	—	—
0·1	9·126	15·72	9·126	—	—	4,364·7	4,364·7	—	—
0·01	6·019	12·55	6·019	—	—	4,153·7	4,153·7	—	—
0·001	4·318	10·43	4·318	—	—	3,571·1	3,571·1	—	—
Three section (7 pole)									
1	17·24	24·62	24·62	17·24	—	3,538·0	3,735·4	3,538·0	—
0·1	9·40	16·68	16·68	9·40	—	4,528·9	5,008·3	4,528·9	—
0·01	6·342	13·91	13·91	6·342	—	4,432·2	5,198·4	4,432·2	—
0·001	4·69	12·19	12·19	4·69	—	3,951·5	4,924·1	3,981·5	—
Four section (9 pole)									
1	17·35	24·84	25·26	24·84	17·35	3,562·5	3,786·9	3,786·9	3,562·5
0·1	9·515	16·99	17·55	16·99	9·515	4,591·9	5,146·2	5,146·2	4,591·9
0·01	6·481	14·36	15·17	14·36	6·481	4,542·5	5,451·2	5,451·2	4,542·5
0·001	4·854	12·81	13·88	12·81	4·854	4,108·2	5,299·0	5,299·0	4,108·2

Inductance in microhenrys, capacitance in picofarads. Component values normalized to 1 MHz and 50Ω.

TABLE 5. CHEBYSHEV LOW-PASS FILTER (PI CONFIGURATION)

	Ripple (dB)	C_1	C_2	C_3	C_4	C_5	L_1	L_2	L_3	L_4
Single section (3 pole)	1	6,441.3	6,441.3	—	—	—	7·911	—	—	—
	0·1	3,283.6	3,283.6	—	—	—	9·131	—	—	—
	0·01	2,007.7	2,002.7	—	—	—	7·721	—	—	—
	0·001	1,301.2	1,301.2	—	—	—	5·781	—	—	—
Two section (5 pole)	1	6,795.5	9,552.2	6,795.5	—	—	8·683	8·683	—	—
	0·1	3,650.4	6,286.6	3,650.4	—	—	10·91	10·91	—	—
	0·01	2,407.5	5,020.7	2,407.5	—	—	10·38	10·38	—	—
	0·001	1,727.3	4,170.5	1,727.3	—	—	8·928	8·928	—	—
Three section (7 pole)	1	3,538	5,052	5,052	3,538	—	17·24	18·20	17·24	—
	0·1	3,759.8	6,673.9	6,673.9	3,759.8	—	11·32	12·52	11·32	—
	0·01	2,536.8	5,564.5	5,564.5	2,536.8	—	11·08	13·00	11·08	—
	0·001	1,875.7	4,875.9	4,875.9	1,875.7	—	9·879	12·31	9·879	—
Four section (9 pole)	1	6,938.3	9,935.8	10,105	9,935.8	6,938.3	8·906	9·467	9·467	8·906
	0·1	3,805.9	6,794.5	7,019.9	6,794.5	3,805.9	11·48	12·87	12·87	11·48
	0·01	2,592.5	5,743.5	6,066.3	5,743.5	2,592.5	11·36	13·63	13·63	11·36
	0·001	1,941.7	5,124.6	5,553.2	5,124.6	1,941.7	10·27	13·25	13·25	10·27

Inductance in microhenrys, capacitance in picofarads. Component values normalized to 1 MHz and 50Ω

TABLE 6. CHEBYSHEV LOW-PASS FILTER ("T" CONFIGURATION)

	Ripple (dB)	C_1	C_2	C_3	C_4	C_5	L_1	L_2	L_3	L_4
Single section (3 pole)	1	1,573	1,573	—	—	—	8·005	—	—	—
	0·1	3,085·7	3,085·7	—	—	—	6·935	—	—	—
	0·01	5,059·1	5,059·1	—	—	—	8·201	—	—	—
	0·001	7,786·9	7,786·9	—	—	—	10·95	—	—	—
Two section (5 pole)	1	1,491	1,060·7	1,491	—	—	7·293	7·293	—	—
	0·1	2,775·6	1,611·7	2,775·6	—	—	5·803	5·803	—	—
	0·01	4,208·6	2,018·6	4,208·6	—	—	6·098	6·098	—	—
	0·001	5,865·7	2,429·5	5,865·7	—	—	7·093	7·093	—	—
Three section (7 pole)	1	1,469·2	1,028·9	1,028·9	1,469·2	—	7·160	6·781	7·160	—
	0·1	2,694·9	1,518·2	1,518·2	2,694·9	—	5·593	5·058	5·593	—
	0·01	3,994·1	1,820·9	1,820·9	3,994·1	—	5·715	4·873	5·715	—
	0·001	5,401·7	2,078	2,078	5,401·7	—	6·410	5·144	6·410	—
Three section (9 pole)	1	1,460·3	1,019·8	1,002·7	1,019·8	1,460·3	7·110	6·689	6·689	7·110
	0·1	2,662·2	1,491·2	1,443·3	1,491·2	2,662·2	5·516	4·922	4·922	5·516
	0·01	3,908·2	1,764·1	1,670·2	1,764·1	3,908·2	5·578	4·647	4·647	5·578
	0·001	5,216·3	1,977·1	1,824·6	1,977·1	5,216·3	6·657	4·780	4·780	6·657

Inductance in microhenrys, capacitance in picofarads. Component values normalized to 1 Mhz and 50Ω

TABLE 7. CHEBYSHEV HIGH-PASS FILTER (PI CONFIGURATION)

	Ripple (dB)	L_1	L_2	L_3	L_4	L_5	C_1	C_2	C_3	C_4
Single section (3 pole)	1	3·932	3·932	—	—	—	3,201·7	—	—	—
	0·1	7·714	7·714	—	—	—	2,774·2	—	—	—
	0·01	12·65	12·65	—	—	—	3,280·5	—	—	—
	0·001	19·47	19·47	—	—	—	4,381·4	—	—	—
Two section (5 pole)	1	3·727	2·652	3·727	—	—	2,917·3	2,917·3	—	—
	0·1	6·939	4·029	6·939	—	—	2,321·4	2,321·4	—	—
	0·01	10·52	5·045	10·52	—	—	2,439·3	2,439·3	—	—
	0·001	19·66	6·074	14·66	—	—	2,837·3	2,837·3	—	—
Three section (7 pole)	1	7·159	5·014	5·014	7·159	—	1,469·2	1,391·6	1,469·2	—
	0·1	8·737	3·795	3·795	8·737	—	2,237·2	2,023·1	2,237·2	—
	0·01	9·985	4·552	4·552	9·985	—	2,286·0	1,949·1	2,286	—
	0·001	13·50	5·195	5·195	13·50	—	2,584·1	2,057·7	2,057·7	2,584·1
Four section (9 pole)	1	3·651	2·549	2·507	2·549	3·651	2,844·1	2,675·6	2,675·6	2,844·1
	0·1	6·656	3·728	3·608	3·728	6·656	2,206·5	1,968·9	1,968·9	2,206·5
	0·01	9·772	4·410	4·176	4·410	9·772	2,230·5	1,858·7	1,858·7	2,230·5
	0·001	13·05	4·943	4·561	4·943	13·05	2,466·3	1,911·8	1,911·8	2,466·3

Inductance in microhenrys, capacitance in picofarads. Component values normalized to 1 MHz and 50Ω.

TABLE 8. PRACTICAL CHEBYSHEV LOW-PASS FILTERS (3 SECTION, 7 POLE)

Amateur band	28	21	14	7	3·5	1·75	MHz
F_c	36·85	21·69	15·16	7·98	4·11	2·05	MHz
VSWR	1·10	1·06	1·09	1·08	1·07	1·09	
C1, C4	68	100	160	300	560	1,200	pF
C2, C3	150	240	360	680	1,300	2,700	pF
L1, L3	0·3	0·49	0·72	1·37	2·62	5·42	µH
L4	0·36	0·59	0·85	1·62	3·13	6·41	µH

Inductance in microhenrys, capacitance in picofarads. Component values normalized to 1 MHz and 50Ω

CONSTANT-K AND m-DERIVED FILTER NETWORKS

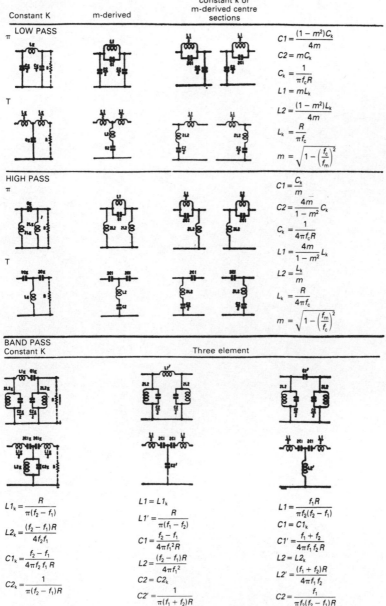

Constant K	m-derived	m-derived end sections for use with constant k or m-derived centre sections	

LOW PASS

$$C1 = \frac{(1 - m^2)C_k}{4m}$$

$$C2 = mC_k$$

$$C_k = \frac{1}{\pi f_c R}$$

$$L1 = mL_k$$

$$L2 = \frac{(1 - m^2)L_k}{4m}$$

$$L_k = \frac{R}{\pi f_c}$$

$$m = \sqrt{1 - \left(\frac{f_c}{f_m}\right)^2}$$

HIGH PASS

$$C1 = \frac{C_k}{m}$$

$$C2 = \frac{4m}{1 - m^2}C_k$$

$$C_k = \frac{1}{4\pi f_c R}$$

$$L1 = \frac{4m}{1 - m^2}L_k$$

$$L2 = \frac{L_k}{m}$$

$$L_k = \frac{R}{4\pi f_c}$$

$$m = \sqrt{1 - \left(\frac{f_m}{f_c}\right)^2}$$

BAND PASS
Constant K   Three element

$$L1_k = \frac{R}{\pi(f_2 - f_1)}$$

$$L2_k = \frac{(f_2 - f_1)R}{4f_2 f_1}$$

$$C1_k = \frac{f_2 - f_1}{4\pi f_2 f_1 R}$$

$$C2_k = \frac{1}{\pi(f_2 - f_1)R}$$

$$L1 = L1_k$$

$$L1' = \frac{R}{\pi(f_1 - f_2)}$$

$$C1 = \frac{f_2 - f_1}{4\pi f_1^2 R}$$

$$L2 = \frac{(f_2 - f_1)R}{4\pi f_1^2}$$

$$C2 = C2_k$$

$$C2' = \frac{1}{\pi(f_1 + f_2)R}$$

$$L1 = \frac{f_1 R}{\pi f_2(f_2 - f_1)}$$

$$C1 = C1_k$$

$$C1' = \frac{f_1 + f_2}{4\pi f_1 f_2 R}$$

$$L2 = L2_k$$

$$L2' = \frac{(f_1 + f_2)R}{4\pi f_1 f_2}$$

$$C2 = \frac{f_1}{\pi f_2(f_2 - f_1)R}$$

C in farads. L in henrys. R in ohms. F_c (cut-off frequency), f_m (frequency of maximum attenuation), f_1 (lower cut-off frequency) and f_2 (upper cut-off frequency) in hertz

RESONANT CIRCUITS AND FILTERS   79

Part 4

Circuit design

BIPOLAR TRANSISTORS

BIASING CIRCUITS

The transistor should be biased by a method which prevents excessive shift of the dc working point with changes in device or temperature. Insufficient dc stabilization can give rise to the following effects:

(a) wide spread in input and output impedances.
(b) risk of overloading ("saturating") at high temperatures.
(c) possibility of thermal runaway.

The biasing circuits which follow are drawn as grounded emitter but this description applies to the dc conditions only. Any electrode can be grounded to ac by means of a large capacitance, or open-circuited to ac by means of inductance, without affecting the dc conditions.

Single resistor method

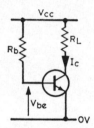

Fig 1. Single resistor bias

This is the simplest arrangement (Fig 1) and requires only one resistor but unfortunately the dc stability is poor.

$$I_c = I_{co} + h_{FE}I_b$$

$$I_b = \frac{V_{cc} - V_{be}}{R_b}$$

The leakage current for silicon transistors, I_{co}, is fairly small and also V_{be} is small in comparison with V_{cc}.

Therefore
$$I_c \simeq \frac{h_{FE}V_{cc}}{R_b}$$

The collector current is very dependent on h_{FE} (sometimes called β) which has a wide spread over a batch of transistors and increases with temperature. Unless the application is extremely uncritical of these effects, this method of biasing is generally unsuitable.

Feedback resistor method

A collector-base feedback resistor (Fig 2a) is the simplest method of including some dc stabilization in a grounded emitter circuit. The value of R_b is roughly equal to V_c/I_b. Any increase in collector current causes a drop in collector voltage and hence reduces the current flowing through R_b to the base, so compensating partly for the original change.

$$I_c = \frac{V_c h_{FE}}{R_b} \qquad V_c = V_{cc} - R_c I_c$$

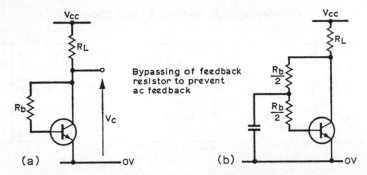

Fig 2. (a) Feedback resistor bias. (b) Bypassing of feedback resistor to prevent ac feedback

The resistor R_b also provides ac feedback which will reduce the gain of the stage. This problem can be overcome by splitting R_b into two resistors of approximately equal values and decoupling the centre point (Fig 2b).

Emitter resistor and potential divider circuit

In the emitter resistor and potential divider circuit (Fig 3a) the emitter resistor introduces negative dc feedback. The current through the device is determined by the emitter resistor R_e and potential divider R_1, R_2.

$$I_c = \frac{\left(\dfrac{V_{cc}R_2}{R_1+R_2}\right) - V_{be}}{R_e}$$

Any increase in emitter current causes a large voltage drop across the emitter resistor and reduces the base-emitter voltage. The base current is reduced and, due to the exponential shape of the input characteristic, there is a large degree of compensation for the original change.

The feedback depends on R_e; a high value gives better stabilization. The feedback also depends on how constant the base potential can be maintained during changes in base current; low values of R_1 and R_2 improve stabilization.

Resistor R_e is often decoupled with a capacitor to remove the ac negative feedback. If the resistor R_L is omitted, the collector connected direct to the supply, and the output taken from the emitter the stage becomes an emitter follower (Fig 3b).

There are other methods of biasing transistor stages, especially direct-coupled amplifiers, but these are nearly all variations of the above.

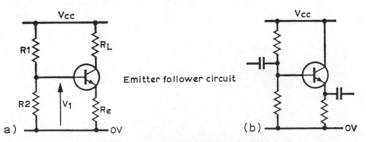

Fig 3. (a) Emitter resistor bias. (b) Emitter follower circuit

CIRCUIT DESIGN   83

COMPARISON OF BIASING ARRANGEMENTS

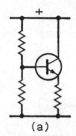

(a)

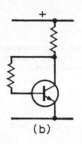

(b)

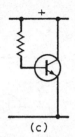

(c)

Nominal values of parameters:

$V_s = 7\,\text{V}$ $V_{be} = 0\cdot7\,\text{V}$ $h_{FE}(\beta) = 100$ $I_e = 1\,\text{mA}$ (approximately)

Parameter variation (per cent)	I_e Variation (per cent)		
	(a)	(b)	(c)
$h_{FE}(\beta) \pm 50$	$+1, -1\cdot6$	$+23, -35$	±49
$V_{be} \pm 7$	$\pm1\cdot7$	$\pm0\cdot95$	$\pm0\cdot86$
$V_s - 50$	-62	-55	-56

NOISE

For a bipolar transistor,

$$R_{eq} = r_{bb}' + \frac{r_e}{2}$$

where r_{bb}' is the extrinsic base resistance and r_e is the intrinsic emitter resistance

$$r_e = \frac{1}{g_m} \simeq \frac{25}{\text{emitter current (mA)}}\text{ohms}$$

SIMPLE GAIN AND IMPEDANCE CALCULATIONS

These formulae are only suitable for low-frequency "rule of thumb" type calculations. However, they will often be sufficiently accurate for a quick check to see if a stage is working correctly.

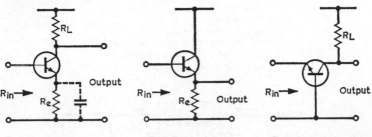

Fig 4. Common-emitter stage   Fig 5. Emitter follower   Fig 6. Common-base stage

Common-emitter stage

Input resistance

$$R_{in} = \beta \left(R_e + \frac{25}{i_e} \right)$$

where i_e is emitter current in milliamps. If R_e is decoupled to ac as shown dotted then

$$R_{in} = \beta \left(\frac{25}{i_e} \right)$$

Voltage gain

$$G_v = \frac{R_L}{R_e + (25/i_e)}$$

or if R_e is decoupled, $\quad G_v = \dfrac{R_L i_e}{25}$

Note: R_L is made up of the collector load resistor in parallel with the input impedance of the following stage.

$$\text{Current gain } G_i = \beta$$

Emitter follower stage

For an emitter follower, input resistance is the same as above but normally R_e is not decoupled and $R_e \simeq 25/i_e$, therefore

$R_{in} = \beta R_e$ Current gain $G_i = \beta$
Voltage gain $G_v \simeq 1$ Output resistance $= 25/i_e$

Common-base stage

For a common-base stage:

Input resistance $R_{in} = 25/i_e$ Current gain $G_i \simeq 1$

Voltage gain

$$G_v = \frac{R_L i_e}{25}$$

y-PARAMETERS

Short-circuit or y-parameters are the most common type of variables used to describe the performance of transistors at radio frequencies. The generalized equations for the input and output current of the black box (Fig 7) are:

$$i_1 = v_1 y_{11} + v_2 y_{12}$$
$$i_2 = v_1 y_{21} + v_2 y_{22}$$
$$y_{11} = i_1/v_1 = \text{input admittance}$$
$$y_{21} = i_2/v_1 = \text{forward transfer admittance}$$
$$y_{12} = i_1/v_2 = \text{reverse transfer admittance}$$
$$y_{22} = i_2/v_2 = \text{output admittance}$$

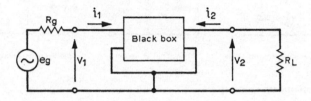

Fig 7. Four-terminal linear network representation of a transistor

Any admittance y can be resolved into components, conductance g and susceptance b, in the following format:

$$y = g + jb$$

Hence in common emitter:

$$y_{11} = y_{ie} = g_{ie} + jb_{ie}$$
$$y_{21} = y_{fe} = g_{fe} + jb_{fe}$$
$$y_{12} = y_{re} = g_{re} + jb_{re}$$
$$y_{22} = y_{oe} = g_{oe} + jb_{oe}$$

Manufacturers' specifications usually give graphs of the real and imaginary components of these parameters over a range of frequencies for different biases. These can be used to calculate the performance of transistor amplifiers using the following formulae:

Input admittance $(y_{in} = 1/z_{in})$.

$$y_{in} = y_{ie} - \frac{y_{fe} y_{re}}{y_{oe} + y_L}$$

where y_L is the load admittance $(1/z_L)$.

Highest power gain is obtained with a conjugate match condition (ie the generator is the complex conjugate, equal magnitude, opposite sign or phase, of its input impedance and the load is the complex conjugate of its output impedance.) Let

$$b_{oe} = -b_L$$

then

$$y_{ine} = y_{ie} - \frac{y_{fe} y_{re}}{g_{oe} + g_L}$$

Output admittance (*common emitter*)

$y_s = $ source admittance, if $(g_{ie} + g_s) \gg (b_{ie} + b_s)$

86 PART 4

then
$$y_{\text{oute}} = y_{\text{oe}} - \frac{y_{\text{fe}} y_{\text{re}}}{g_{\text{ie}} + g_{\text{s}}}$$

Gain

$$\text{Current gain} = \frac{y_{\text{fe}} y_{\text{L}}}{y_{\text{ie}}(y_{\text{oe}} + y_{\text{L}}) - y_{\text{fe}} y_{\text{re}}}$$

$$\text{Voltage gain} = \frac{-y_{\text{fe}}}{y_{\text{L}} + y_{\text{oe}}}$$

$$\text{Power gain} \;\; = \left(\frac{y_{\text{fe}}}{y_{\text{oe}} + y_{\text{L}}}\right)^2 \frac{g_{\text{L}}}{g_{\text{in}}}$$

TRANSISTOR RF POWER AMPLIFIERS

Transistor rf power amplifiers differ considerably in circuit techniques from valve amplifiers due mainly to the much lower impedances involved. Both input and output impedances are usually in the range 1 to 50 Ω for amplifiers delivering more than a few watts, and conventional single pi-network designs give rise to impractical components.

$$\text{Required collector load impedance } R_L = \frac{V_o^2}{2P_o}$$

P_o is the output power from the transistor, V_o is the fundamental component of the collector voltage swing, $V_o = V_{cc} - V_{ce}$ and is typically 10·5 V for devices operating from a 12 V rail or 25 V for devices operating from a 28 V rail. For push-pull amplifiers, V_o is double that for a single ended amplifier, R_L is collector-to-collector load impedance and P_o is the total power output from both devices.

Figures for input and output impedance are usually presented in published data as a series or parallel combination of a resistance and reactance. It is often necessary to convert from series form to parallel and vice versa (see p 58).

Typical circuit of vhf power amplifier

(1) The input network is required to match from 50 Ω into the input impedance of the device $(R_i + X_i)$. Component values can be calculated from the table on p 63. X_{L1} should be reduced by an amount X_i if X_i is inductive or increased by an amount X_i if X_i is capacitive.

(2) The output network is required to match from the calculated value R_L to the load impedance of 50 Ω.

(3) L3 resonates with the parallel output capacitance of the transistor

$$\omega L_3 = \frac{1}{\omega \, C_{out}}$$

(4) A suitable Q value for the networks must be selected. High Q values give good harmonic rejection but poorer efficiency, higher circuit losses and make tuning difficult. A suitable Q for a 144 MHz amplifier is 8–12.

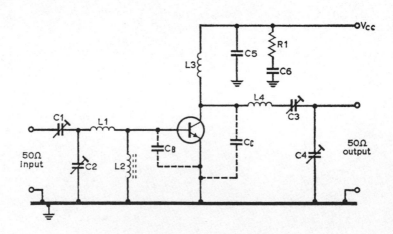

Fig 1. Typical circuit of vhf power amplifier

(5) L2 can be a small low-Q ferrite choke. Additional parallel resistive damping may be necessary with high-gain devices.

(6) C_C may be necessary for stable operation with a high-gain transistor if large harmonic collector voltage swings are present.

(7) C_B may be necessary for stable operation if operating a high-gain transistor at a frequency well below f_T.

(8) C5 should provide effective decoupling at the operating frequency.

(9) C6 and R1 ensure low-frequency stability. R1 should be a few ohms and the reactance of C6 a few ohms at a frequency of several hundred kilohertz.

(10) Emitter lead length *must* be kept *very* short, similarly the leads to C_B and C5.

Example

Mullard BLY89A operating as a 25 W fm amplifier at 144 MHz used in the circuit described and operating between 50 Ω source and loads. Supply voltage 12·5 V.

From published data $Z_i = 1·7 + j1·4\,\Omega$; $C_L = 65\,pF$; $V_{cc} = 12·5\,V$; V_o typically 11 V;

$$R_L = \frac{V_o^2}{2P_o}\ R_L = 2·4\Omega$$

Select $Q = 10$ for both input and output networks. Output network must match 2·4 Ω to 50 Ω.

From table C on p 63,

$X_{C3} = 24\,\Omega$; $X_{L4} = 34·7\,\Omega$; $X_{C4} = 11·2\,\Omega$.

L3 must resonate with $C_L = 65\,pF$ at 144 MHz.

$X_{L3} = 17\,\Omega$.

The input network must match 50 Ω to $1·7 + j1·4\,\Omega$. This corresponds to a resistor of 1·7 Ω in series with an inductive reactance of 1·4 Ω.

From table B on p 63, to match 1·7 Ω to 50 Ω

$X_{C1} = 78\,\Omega$; $X_{C2} = 20·3\,\Omega$; $X_{L1}' = 17\,\Omega$

To account for the 1·4 Ω series inductance seen at the transistor base terminal, this value must be subtracted from $X_{L1}' = 17\,\Omega$ to give $X_{L1} = 15·6\,\Omega$. Inductance and capacitance values can be found from

$$L = \frac{X}{\omega}\quad \text{and} \quad C = \frac{1}{\omega X}\quad (\omega = 2\pi f)$$

Components list

C1 14 pF; C2 54 pF; C3 46 pF; C4 98 pF; C5 1,000 pF feedthrough; C6 100 nF; R1 5 Ω; L1 17 nH; L2 1·5 turns through FX1115 ferrite bead; L3 19 nH; L4 38 nH.

FIELD-EFFECT TRANSISTORS

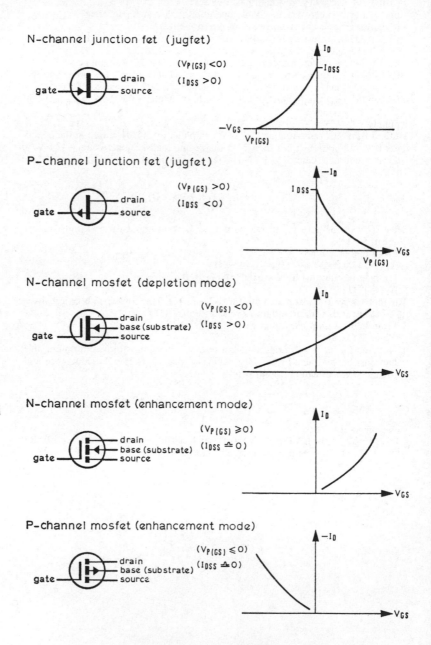

N-channel junction fet (jugfet)

gate ——— drain, source

$(V_{P(GS)} < 0)$

$(I_{DSS} > 0)$

P-channel junction fet (jugfet)

gate ——— drain, source

$(V_{P(GS)} > 0)$

$(I_{DSS} < 0)$

N-channel mosfet (depletion mode)

gate ——— drain, base (substrate), source

$(V_{P(GS)} < 0)$

$(I_{DSS} > 0)$

N-channel mosfet (enhancement mode)

gate ——— drain, base (substrate), source

$(V_{P(GS)} \geqslant 0)$

$(I_{DSS} \doteq 0)$

P-channel mosfet (enhancement mode)

gate ——— drain, base (substrate), source

$(V_{P(GS)} \leqslant 0)$

$(I_{DSS} \doteq 0)$

Fig 1. Comparison of symbols and characteristics of devices

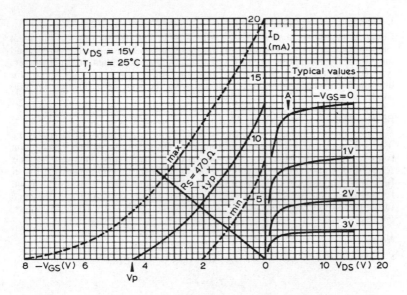

Fig 2. Typical characteristic curve for a junction fet

A typical characteristic for a junction fet is shown in more detail in Fig 2. In the region to the right of point A (pinch-off region) the device obeys the equation

$$I_d = I_{DSS} \left(1 - \frac{V_{GS}}{V_P}\right)^n \tag{1}$$

where I_{DSS} is the drain current at $V_{GS} = 0$ and $V_{DS} > |V_P|$, and the exponent $n \simeq 2$.

Transconductance (g_m)

The transconductance (g_m) of a field-effect transistor working in the pinch-off region can be found by differentiating equation (1), putting $n = 2$ and assuming $V_{DS} > V_{GS} - V_P$, giving

$$g_m = \left(\frac{2}{V_P}\right) \left[I_D I_{DSS}\right]^{\frac{1}{2}} \tag{2}$$

Voltage gain

$$\text{Voltage gain} = g_m R_L \tag{3}$$

From equations (1), (2) and (3) it can be seen that the voltage gain is proportional to the square root of the current and not the current as in a bipolar device.

Biasing

Typical spreads are shown in Fig 1 for an I_{DSS} range of 6 to 20 mA. For best signal handling bias the device at $V_{GS} = \frac{1}{2}V_p$. The load line shown is for a source resistance of 470 Ω. Under these conditions the maximum current is 7 mA and the minimum is 2·5 mA with a typical value of 4 mA. Take care that any resistance in the drain does not drop V_{DS} below 5 V.

Linearity

Equation (1) shows that $I_D \propto V_{GS}^2$ when $n = 2$. For a mixer this is the ideal characteristic in that it produces mixing products but little cross-modulation and intermodulation which are produced by third-order terms in the transfer characteristic. Biasing at $V_P/2$ is the optimum position for linearity in a mixer. Make sure that the peak oscillator swing does not drive the gate of a junction fet into conduction.

RF use of fets

For the highest frequency range (up to 900 MHz) the common-gate circuit is the most stable and offers the best signal handling. The gain is lower than the common source configuration, which may however require neutralization if maximum gain is required. The common-drain configuration offers high input impedance at low rf (up to 30 MHz) but at vhf the input impedance may go negative unless the load on the source is quite low (300 Ω or less). Dual-gate mosfet devices obviate the need for neutralization in the common-source mode due to their low feedback capacitance.

Noise

$$R_{eq} \simeq \frac{0 \cdot 7}{g_m}$$

where g_m is the device mutual conductance in milliamps per volt.

HEAT SINKS FOR SEMICONDUCTORS

Thermal resistance

By analogy with electrical resistance, thermal resistance is a measure of the temperature difference arising from a flow of heat energy along a path. Ohm's law can be applied to thermal resistance and Fig 1 represents a practical example.

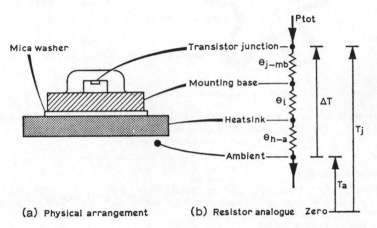

(a) Physical arrangement   (b) Resistor analogue

Fig 1. Application of Ohm's law to transistor-heat sink combination. (a) Physical arrangement, (b) resistor analogue

θ_{j-mb} = thermal resistance between semiconductor junction and mounting base (deg C/W)

θ_i = thermal resistance of washer or interface between transistor and heat sink (deg C/W)

θ_{h-a} = thermal resistance of heat sink

$$= \frac{\text{temperature rise at mounting site of transistor (deg C)}}{\text{power lost to ambient (W)}}$$

θ_{j-a} = thermal resistance between junction and ambient

Δ_T = temperature rise of junction with respect to ambient (deg C)

T_a = ambient temperature

T_j = junction temperature

θ_{j-case} = thermal resistance between junction and case (usually the cylindrical outer surface of a plastic or small metal-cased transistor)

Where a push-on heat sink is used, as with TO-5 transistors, θ_{j-case} is used, together with the θ_{h-a} of the heat sink (see Fig 2).

With small plastic devices and some rectifier diodes, θ_{j-a} is quoted for a specified form of connection to a circuit board. In this case the device leads and printed circuit board all form part of the heat radiating system and the manufacturer's wiring recommendations should be followed.

In general:

$$T_j - T_a = P_{tot}(\theta_{j-mb} + \theta_i + \theta_{h-a}) \qquad (1)$$

$$\text{or} \quad T_j - T_a = P_{tot}(\theta_{j-case} + \theta_{h-a}) \qquad (2)$$

$$\text{or} \quad T_j - T_a = P_{tot} \times \theta_{j-a} \qquad (3)$$

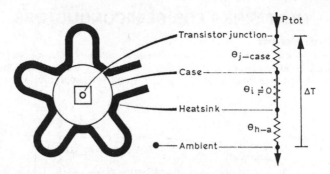

Fig 2. Equivalent circuit for push-on type heat sinks

where P_{tot} = total continuous dc power dissipated in the device, including collector-base and base-emitter dissipations

= $V_{CE}I_C + V_{BE}I_B$ under steady state conditions

Heat sink design

From equation (1) or (2), or from the manufacturer's data (Fig 3), a suitable value of θ_{h-a} may be obtained and used to select a commercially made heat sink, or a fabricated heat sink using sheet metal.

Thus from equation (1):

$$\theta_{h-a} = \frac{T_j - T_a}{P_{tot}} - (\theta_{j-mb} + \theta_i) \qquad (4)$$

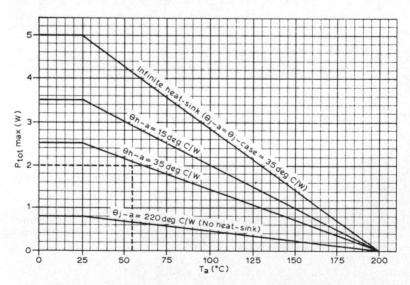

Fig 3. With this form of curve, often found in manufacturers' data, suitable values of θ_{h-a} may often be found directly. In this example (for a BFY50) the permissible area of operation is below the appropriate curve. Therefore for 2 W at 55°C ambient, a 35 deg C/W heat sink is adequate

and for a flat sheet:

$$\theta_{h-a} = \frac{6 \cdot 55 \sqrt[4]{K}}{\sqrt{\lambda e}} + \frac{100\,K}{S} \tag{5}$$

assuming natural convection both sides of the sheet,
where:

e = material thickness (in)
S = area of *one* side of heat sink (in^2)
λ = 380 for copper; 210 for aluminium; 110 for brass; and 46 for steel (units omitted)
K = 1 for horizontal, bright finish; 0·5 for horizontal, blackened finish; 0·85 for vertical, bright finish; and 0·45 for vertical, blackened finish (units omitted)
(1 in = 25·4 mm, 1 in^2 = 645·16 mm^2)

The table has been derived from equation (5) for values of thermal resistance between 2 and 10 deg C/W. The values refer to vertical, blackened heat sinks, and bright horizontal heat sinks need between two and three times the area for the same results.

HEAT SINK SIZES FOR NATURAL CONVECTION COOLING
(both sides effective)

Gauge of metal (swg)				Area (one side) (sq in) of vertical blackened heat sink for values of θ_{h-a} (deg C/W)								
Copper	Aluminium	Brass	Steel	2	3	4	5	6	7	8	9	10
16	12	—	—	53	24	16	12	9	8	7	6	5
18	14	—	—	64	26	17	12	10	8	7	6	5
20	16	10	—	87	30	18	13	10	8	7	6	5
22	18	12	—	145	34	19	14	10	9	7	6	5
24	20	14	—	—	44	22	15	11	9	8	7	6
26	22	16	10	—	56	25	16	12	9	8	7	6
28	24	18	12	—	100	31	18	13	10	8	7	6
—	26	20	14	—	—	38	20	14	11	9	7	6
—	28	22	16	—	—	51	24	16	12	9	8	7
—	—	24	18	—	—	112	32	19	13	10	8	7
—	—	26	20	—	—	—	48	23	15	11	9	8
—	—	28	22	—	—	—	150	35	20	14	10	8
—	—	—	24	—	—	—	—	50	24	16	12	9
—	—	—	26	—	—	—	—	—	41	21	15	11

COMPARISON BETWEEN LOGIC IC TYPES

Type	Example	Features	Speed (MHz)	Supply voltage	Common applications
RTL (resistor-transistor logic)	Norbit	Early form of discrete logic	Slow	—	Mainly obsolete but still used in some slow automation applications.
DTL (diode transistor logic)	800 Series	First type of integrated logic	≃1	+3·6	Obsolete.
TTL (transistor-transistor logic)	74 Series	Development of dtl and is most popular logic family. Used for small (ssi) and medium (msi) ics.	10–40	+5 (12)	Large range of standard circuit functions available.
	74L	Low-power version	10	+5	Used where low current consumption or heat dissipation is needed.
	74H	High-power/speed	60	+5	
Schottky ttl	74S	Faster than standard ttl. Schottky diodes used to prevent transistors from saturating.	150	+5	Frequency counter prescalers. Synthesizers.
ECL (emitter coupled logic)	10k Series 95 Series GH Series pecl	Non-saturating current mode logic (cml). Faster than ttl but lower logic level swing (≃1 V), therefore reduced noise immunity.	250–1,000	−5·2	Computer mainframes, prescalers for counters, frequency synthesizers. Also used for memories and programmable read-only memories.
I²L (integrated injection logic).	—	Bipolar logic. Very high density possible with low supply voltage. Linear circuits can be incorporated on same ic.	—	—	At present used mainly for custom circuits.
P-channel silicon gate	—	First type of mosfet logic. Low power consumption, easy to manufacture, high circuit density possible. Can be damaged by static.	—	−10 to −20	Random access memories (ram). Read-only memories (rom), lsi devices, eg clock chips, microprocessors, etc.
Aluminium gate	—	Faster version of above.	—	—	—
N-channel	—	MOSFET logic compatible with ttl, slightly faster than P-channel.	—	+5 to 20	As above.
CMOS (complementary metal oxide silicon)	4000 Series Mcmos Locmos	Works over a wide range of supply voltages. Takes virtually no quiescent current (supply current is proportional to speed). Early types could be damaged by static, now incorporate protection diodes.	5–10 (20 possible)	3–12	Large range of standard functions now available. Also msi, lsi circuits. Can replace ttl in many circuits.

VALVES

Amplification factor (μ) = valve anode resistance (R_a) × mutual conductance (g_m), R_a being measured in thousands of ohms and g_m measured in milliamps per volt.
Alternatively

$$g_m = \frac{\mu}{R_a} \qquad R_a = \frac{\mu}{g_m}$$

Stage gain

$$\text{Amplification } (A) = \frac{\mu \times R_1}{R_1 + R_a}$$

where R_1 is the anode load measured in the same units as R_a. If R_1 is small compared with R_a

$$A = g_m \times R_1 \text{ (approximately)}$$

Cathode follower

$$\text{Voltage gain} \qquad \frac{V_{out}}{V_{sig}} = \frac{\mu R_k}{r_a + R_k(1 + \mu)}$$

where μ = amplification factor of the valve
$\quad r_a$ = anode impedance
$\quad R_k$ = cathode resistor
The stage gain of a cathode follower will always be less than unity. When μ is large and R_k is large compared with r_a the gain will be near unity.

Stage gain in resistance coupled af amplifier

Medium frequencies $\qquad G_m = \dfrac{\mu R}{R + R_a}$

High frequencies $\qquad G_h = \dfrac{G_m}{\sqrt{(1 + \omega^2 C_1^2 r^2)}}$

Low frequencies $\qquad G_l = \dfrac{G_m}{\sqrt{\left(1 + \dfrac{1}{\omega^2 C_2^2 \rho^2}\right)}}$

where $R = \dfrac{R_1 R_2}{R_1 + R_2} \qquad r = \dfrac{R R_a}{R + R_a} \qquad \rho = R_2 + \dfrac{R_1 R_a}{R_1 + R_a}$

μ = amplification factor of valve
ω = 2π × frequency
R_1 = anode load resistor
R_2 = grid leak
R_a = valve anode resistance
C_1 = total shunt capacitance
C_2 = coupling capacitor

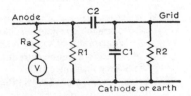

Input $V = \mu.e_g$

Given C_1, C_2, R_2 and x = fractional response required.

At highest frequency $\quad r = \dfrac{\sqrt{(1 - x^2)}}{\omega C_1 x}$, $\quad R = \dfrac{r\,R_a}{R_a - r}$, $\quad R_1 = \dfrac{R\,R_2}{R_2 - R}$

At lowest frequency $\quad C_2 = \dfrac{x}{\omega \rho \sqrt{(1 - x^2)}}$

Note the gain will be affected by the cathode and screen bypass capacitors.

Negative feedback

Voltage feedback

$$\text{Gain with feedback} = \frac{A}{1 + Ab}$$

where A is the original gain of the amplifier section over which feedback is applied (including the output transformer if included) and b is the fraction of the output voltage fed back.

$$\text{Distortion with feedback} = \frac{d}{1 + Ab} \text{ approximately}$$

where d is the original distortion of the amplifier.

$$\text{Effective output impedance} = \frac{R_a}{1 + \mu b}$$

where μ is the amplification factor of the output valve and R_a its anode resistance.

Current feedback
This form of feedback may be obtained by omitting the bypass capacitor across the cathode bias resistor. Current feedback results in an increase of effective output impedance and is not recommended for output stages.

Equivalent rf noise resistance

Saturated diode $\quad R_{eq} = \dfrac{0 \cdot 05}{I_a}\ \Omega \quad$ Space charge limited diode $\quad R_{eq} = \dfrac{0 \cdot 0333}{I_a}\ \Omega$

Triode $\quad\quad\quad\quad\quad\quad\quad R_{eq} = \dfrac{2 \cdot 5}{g_m}\ \Omega$

Pentode $\quad\quad\quad\quad\quad\quad R_{eq} = \dfrac{I_a}{I_a + I_{g2}}\left(\dfrac{2 \cdot 5}{g_m} + \dfrac{20\,I_{g2}}{g_m^{\,2}}\right)\ \Omega$

Triode mixer $\quad\quad\quad\quad R_{eq} = \dfrac{4 \cdot 0}{g_c}\ \Omega$

$\left.\begin{array}{l}\text{Pentode mixer}\\ \text{and multigrid mixer}\end{array}\right\}\quad R_{eq} = \dfrac{I_a}{I_a + I_{g2}}\left(\dfrac{4 \cdot 0}{g_c} + \dfrac{20\,I_{g2}}{g_c^{\,2}}\right)\ \Omega$

I_a and I_{g2} are measured in amps, g_m and g_c are in amps per volt.

Noise factor

Noise factor may be calculated from $\quad\quad F = \dfrac{e}{2kT}\,I_d\,R_s$

where e electron charge = $1 \cdot 59 \times 10^{-19}$ coulomb
     k Boltzman's constant = $1 \cdot 38054 \times 10^{-23}$ joules per degree K)
     T Temperature of source resistance
     I_d Noise diode anode current (amps) to double receiver noise output power
     R_s Source resistance (Ω)

At normal temperature (290 K) the above formula becomes

(*a*) as a ratio $\quad F = 20\,I_d\,R_s$
(*b*) in decibels $F = 10 \log(20\,I_d\,R_s)$

NOISE DIODE CURVES

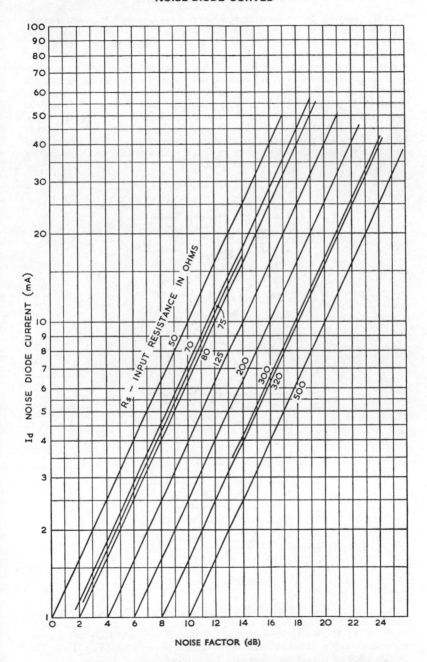

Noise diode current—noise factor curve for various diode noise generator source resistors

VALVE RF POWER AMPLIFIERS

In a tuned amplifier the anode and grid voltages are of sine-wave form and in-phase opposition. The anode current does not flow continuously, but in a series of pulses whose duration varies from 40° to more than 180° of each complete cycle of 360°.

The grid current flows for a shorter duration, since this only occurs when the grid is positive relative to the cathode. Figs 1 and 2 show the basic circuit and phase relationships, respectively. It will be seen that the peak values of anode and grid currents occur when the anode voltage is at a low voltage and the grid voltage is at its maximum positive value. The design methods given here are based on the location of this point on the valve characteristic curves and the translation of the peak values into rms and mean values, by applying factors derived from a Fourier analysis of sine and sine squared pulses of appropriate angles of flow. This method is very much quicker and only slightly less accurate than the alternative of plotting load lines on constant current characteristics.

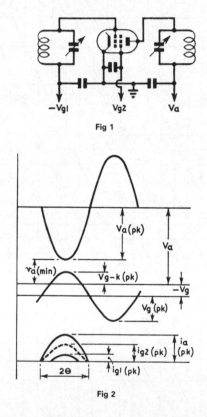

Fig 1

Fig 2

The method is best illustrated by a typical example; in this case a transmitting tetrode type TT21 (7623) has been used. The valve has a rated continuous anode dissipation of 37·5 W. Its characteristics measured at $I_a = 140$ mA are: mutual conductance $(g_m) = 11$ mA/V, and inner amplification factor $(\mu_{g1-g2}) = 8$. The relevant valve curves are shown in Figs 3, 4, 5 and 6.

100   PART 4

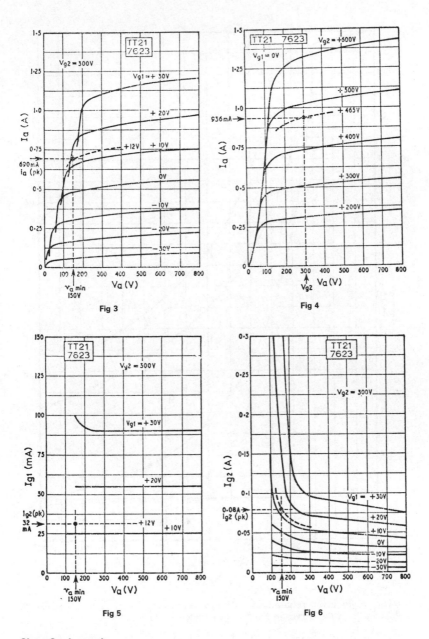

Fig 3

Fig 4

Fig 5

Fig 6

Class C telegraphy

A typical angle of anode current flow (2θ) for Class C telegraphy is 120°. Smaller angles give increased efficiency, but at the expense of increased peak emission demand, greater driving power and possibly shorter valve life. Larger angles are sometimes used when power output is more important than efficiency.

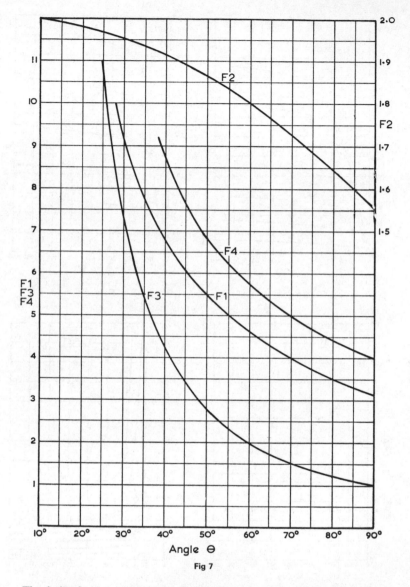

Fig 7

The design factors required for calculations are F_1, F_2, F_3, and F_4. These can be obtained from the curves in Fig 7 for an angle of θ of 60°. These are:

$$F_1 = 4{\cdot}6 \qquad F_3 = 2{\cdot}0$$
$$F_2 = 1{\cdot}8 \qquad F_4 = 5{\cdot}8$$

The design formulae are:

Peak anode current $\quad i_{a(pk)} = F_1 \times I_a$ \hfill (1)

Peak anode voltage $\quad v_{a(pk)} = V_a - v_{a(min)}$ \hfill (2)

Power output	$P_{out} = \dfrac{F_2}{2} \times I_a \times v_{a(pk)}$	(3)

Grid voltage (triodes)

$$-V_g = V_a + \left(V_{g-k(pk)} + \frac{v_{a\,min}}{\mu}\right)(F_3 - 1) \tag{4a}$$

Grid voltage (tetrodes)

$$-V_g = \frac{V_{g2} \times F_3}{\mu_{(g1-g2)}} + (v_{g1-k(pk)}) \times (F_3 - 1) \tag{4b}$$

Peak grid voltage $\quad v_{g1(pk)} = V_{g1} + (v_{g1-k(pk)}) \tag{5}$

Calculate ratio

$$\frac{V_g}{V_{g(pk)}}$$

and from curve in Fig 8 read F_5 and F_6

Grid current $\quad I_g = \dfrac{i_{g(pk)}}{F_5} \tag{6}$

Grid dissipation $\quad p_{g1} = \dfrac{I_g \times F_6 \times (V_{g1} - k_{(pk)})}{2} \tag{7}$

Driving power $\quad P_{dr} = p_{g1} + (V_g \times I_g) \tag{8}$

Screen current $\quad I_{g2} = \dfrac{i_{g2(pk)}}{F_4} \tag{9}$

Screen dissipation $\quad P_{g2} = V_{g2} \times I_{g2} \tag{10}$

Output impedance $\quad R_a = \dfrac{v_{a(pk)}}{F_3 I_a} \tag{11}$

In order to choose a value for anode input which will exploit the ratings of a chosen valve, an estimated efficiency may be assumed. Alternatively, the input may be fixed by other considerations, such as available power supplies or licence regulations.

A reasonable efficiency for a Class C amplifier, at frequencies up to 30 MHz, is 75 per cent. Hence, for the valve chosen, which has an anode dissipation rating of 37·5 W:

$$\text{Anode input} = \frac{37·5}{1 - 0·75} = 150 \text{ W}$$

At an anode voltage of 1,000 this corresponds to a dc anode current of 150 mA.

From equation (1) calculate $I_{a(pk)} = 4·6 \times 150 = 690$ mA. Next locate the current on the valves' anode current (I_a) anode voltage (V_a) characteristic (Fig 3) at a low value of anode voltage, just inside the knee of the curve; this corresponds to an anode voltage of 150 V and a grid voltage of +12 V.

From equation (2), calculate $v_{a(pk)} = 1,000 - 150 = 850$ V.

From equation (3), calculate

$$P_{out} = \frac{1·8}{2} \times 0·15 \times 850 = 115 \text{ W}.$$

The anode dissipation is the difference between anode input and power output.

$$p_a(\text{dissipation}) = 150 - 115 = 35 \text{ W}.$$

This dissipation is sufficiently close to the maximum rating and can be accepted

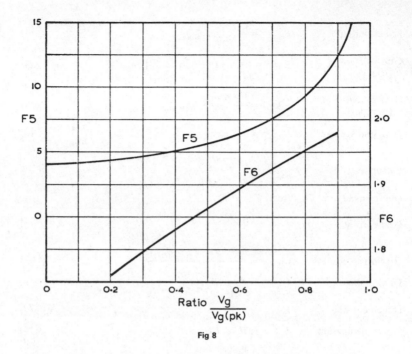

Fig 8

for the rest of the calculation. If the figure had been greater or considerably lower than the rated maximum, a new design should be made using a different power input, angle of flow or minimum anode voltage $V_{a(min)}$.

The chosen valve is a tetrode and from equation 4(b) calculate grid voltage:

$$-V_g = \frac{300 \times 2}{8} + 12 \times 1 = -87\,\text{V}.$$

From equation (5) calculate $v_{g(pk)} = 87 + 12 = 99\,\text{V}.$

Calculate: $\dfrac{V_g}{v_{g(pk)}} = \dfrac{87}{99} = 0.88$

and from Fig 8 read values of F_5 and F_6. These are 11·7 and 1·975, respectively.

From the grid current (I_g), anode voltage (V_a) curves of the TT21 (7623) a peak grid current of 32 mA occurs at $V_a = 150\,\text{V}$ and $V_{g1} = +12\,\text{V}$.

From equation (6) calculate $I_g = \dfrac{32}{11\cdot7} = 2\cdot75\,\text{mA}.$

From equation (7) calculate $p_{g1} = \dfrac{2\cdot75 \times 1\cdot975 \times 12}{2} = 32\cdot5\,\text{mW}.$

From equation (8) calculate $P_{dr} = 32\cdot5 + (2\cdot75 \times 87) = 273\,\text{mW}.$

The driver stage should produce considerably more than this minimum power in order to allow for losses in the coupling system.

From the screen grid current (I_{g2}) anode voltage (V_a) curves of the TT21 (7623), a peak screen current of 80 mA occurs at $V_a = 150\,\text{V}$ and $V_{g1} = +12\,\text{V}$.

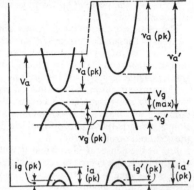

Fig 9. Phase relationship at the carrier and modulation crest for an anode modulated Class C amplifier

From equation (9) calculate $I_{g2} = \dfrac{80}{5\cdot8} = 13\cdot8\,\text{mA}$.

From equation (10) calculate $p_{g2} = 300 \times 13\cdot8 = 4\cdot15\,\text{W}$.
This dissipation is within the maximum rating of 6 W and is acceptable.

From equation (11) calculate $R_a = \dfrac{850}{150 \times 1\cdot8} = 3\cdot16\,\text{k}\Omega$

It is now possible to design a pi coupler to match $3\cdot16\,\text{k}\Omega$ to the impedance of the load. A suitable value of loaded Q would be 10–12 (see p 58 for pi and l-pi coupler data).

(The symbol R_a has been used for output impedance in preference to the more usual symbol Z_a, because it is less confusing in the pi and l-pi coupler design on p 58.)

Anode-modulated amplifiers

Anode-modulated amplifiers are designed in a similar manner to that given for Class C telegraphy, but checks must be made to ensure that the required conditions at the modulation crest are met.

At the modulation crest, the anode and screen voltages will be increased but the bias will be unchanged; hence the angle of anode current flow will increase. Typical values are between 150° and 180°. In making a design, it is best to assume an angle and later check the accuracy of the assumption.

In the following equations, values at the crest of modulation are indicated by ($'$), thus θ' may be between 75° and 90°.

Since the amplifier is assumed to be linear, then:

$$P'_{\text{out}} = 4\,P_{\text{out}} \tag{12}$$
$$v'_{a(pk)} = 2v_{a(pk)} \tag{13}$$
Hence $\qquad v'_{a(min)} = 2v_{a(min)} \tag{14}$

By using equation (3) rearranged, the anode current at modulation crest can be calculated from

$$I'_a = \frac{P'_{\text{out}} \times 2}{F'_2 \times v_{a(pk)}} \tag{15}$$

and from equation (1)

$$i'_{a(pk)} = F'_1 \times I'_a$$

Normally, the positive grid voltage may be assumed to have the same value as calculated at the carrier.

The peak working point corresponding to $i'_{a(pk)}$, $v'_{a(min)}$ and $v_{g1-k(pk)}$ must be located on the anode current (I_a) anode voltage (V_a) curves.

In the case of a tetrode, a value of the screen voltage must be found which satisfies these conditions. In triodes, it may be found that a different (usually greater) value of $v_{g-k(pk)}$ is required to satisfy $i'_{a(pk)}$ and $v'_{a(min)}$.

The grid current at the modulation crest is usually significantly less than at the carrier. By using some grid leak bias, the angle of flow can be increased to 180°, requiring less bias, and hence making available an increased positive grid excursion. An alternative is to supply sufficient modulation to the driver stage to provide the required positive excursion.

For convenience of illustration it will be assumed that the foregoing Class C telegraphy design is now to be modulated, but it should be noted that this will not necessarily give a practical result since the anode dissipation rating may be exceeded during modulation.

It is usual practice to quote anode dissipation ratings at carrier (unmodulated) conditions of two-thirds of the maximum valve rating. This is based on the assumption that the average power dissipation will be increased by 1·5 times when modulation is applied. In the valve used for the example, the anode dissipation under modulation must be reduced to

$$\frac{37\cdot5}{1\cdot5} = 25\,\text{W}.$$

In practice, however, with speech waveforms of relatively high peak-to-mean ratio, it is satisfactory to use a rather higher dissipation rating. When speech compression is used, or continuous 100 per cent tone modulation is applied, it is important to ensure that the actual anode dissipation under modulation conditions is within the maximum rating.

Returning to the previous design

From equation (12) calculate $P'_{out} = 4 \times 115 = 460\,\text{W}$

From equation (13) calculate $v'_{a(pk)} = 2 \times 850 = 1,700\,\text{V}$

From equation (14) calculate $v'_{a(min)} = 2 \times 150 = 300\,\text{V}$

Assuming an angle of anode current flow ($2\theta'$) = 150°, then:

$$F'_1 = 3\cdot75$$
$$F'_2 = 1\cdot69$$
$$F'_3 = 1\cdot35$$

From equation (15) calculate $I'_a = \dfrac{460 \times 2}{1\cdot69 \times 1,700} = 320\,\text{mA}$

From equation (1) calculate $I'_{a(pk)} = 3\cdot75 \times 320 = 1,200\,\text{mA}$.

In order to obtain a peak working point where $i'_a = 1,200\,\text{mA}$ at $v'_{a(min)} = 300\,\text{V}$, it is necessary to find the correct value of screen voltage, it being assumed that the grid voltage for the carrier conditions is still available (+12 V).

From the I_a/V_a curves for the valve at various screen voltages when $V_{g1} = 0$, it is now necessary to predict the screen voltage required to produce $I_{a(pk)} = 1,200\,\text{mA}$ at $v'_{a(min)} = 300\,\text{V}$ and $v'_{g1} = +12\,\text{V}$.

From the TT21 data, the mutual conductance (g_m) at $I_a = 140\,\text{mA}$ is $11\,\text{mA/V}$, therefore, at $I_a = 1,200\,\text{mA}$, the mutual conductance will increase to:

$$\left(\frac{(I'_{a(pk)})}{I_a}\right)^{1/3} \text{ or } \left(\frac{1,200}{140}\right)^{1/3}$$

which gives $22\,\text{mA/V}$.

From this it follows that the anode current at $V_{g1} = +12\,$V will be $12 \times 22 = 264\,$mA greater than the value at $V_{g1} = 0\,$V.

The point on the characteristic curve that now has to be found is for $V_{a'} = 300\,$V, I_a $1,200 - 264 = 936\,$mA. This corresponds to a screen voltage of 465 V.

The screen voltage should therefore be increased by slightly more than 1·5 times when the anode voltage is doubled by modulation. The modulation transformer should be designed to provide this screen modulation point either by a tap on the main winding or by additional winding.

The assumed angle of flow can be checked to see if it is realistic, by calculation of the bias from equation (4b).

$$-V'_{g1} = \frac{465 \times 1\cdot35}{8} + 12 \times 0\cdot35 = -82\cdot5\,\text{V}$$

This is close enough to the original value of $-87\,$V for a practical design.

In practice, the regulation of the driver source, the change of grid current when the screen voltage is raised and the method of obtaining the bias will modify the available positive grid voltage at the crest, but the calculation gives sufficient guide as a practical starting point.

Class AB and Class B linear amplifiers

In Class AB and Class B linear service, the amplifier is required to handle modulated waveforms without distortion. The amplification of ssb signals is the most usual example.

In a Class B amplifier, the angle of flow of anode current is close to 180°. An acceptable design can be made using the procedure given for Class C telegraphy but with $\theta = 90°$.

In practice, however, such amplifiers are operated with some standing anode current ($I_{a(o)}$) in the absence of a signal, as a means of improving the linearity.

Class AB amplifiers invariably operate at significant standing anode current. Design curves based on angle of flow are therefore inconvenient; curves based on the ratio of mean anode current under driven conditions to standing anode current are more useful.

The curves given in Fig 10 are suitable. In these, F_7 corresponds to F_1 and F_8 to F_2; from which, under these new conditions:

$$\text{Peak anode current } I_{a(pk)} = F_7 \times I_a \tag{16}$$

$$\text{Power output } P_{out} = \frac{F_8}{2} \times I_a \times v_{a(pk)} \tag{17}$$

In a typical Class AB amplifier driven to maximum peak envelope power the valve will have an anode efficiency of about 70 per cent. The anode dissipation is a maximum at some value of drive less than the maximum. The anode dissipation at maximum drive must therefore be less than the maximum rating, say 80 per cent.

Taking the same example as used for the Class C calculations, the TT21 (7623), an anode dissipation of 30 W is a suitable starting point. In a final design the values must be chosen so that taking into account the peak-to-mean ratio of the modulation waveform does not cause excessive anode dissipation.

Taking anode dissipation as 30 W and anode efficiency of 70 per cent, then:

$$\text{Anode input } P_{in} = \frac{30}{1 - 0\cdot7} = 100\,\text{W}.$$

Decide on the anode voltage; in this case, take $V_a = 1,000\,$V; then the anode current $I_a = 100\,$mA.

Next, it is necessary to decide the zero signal (standing) anode current $I_{a(o)}$; this

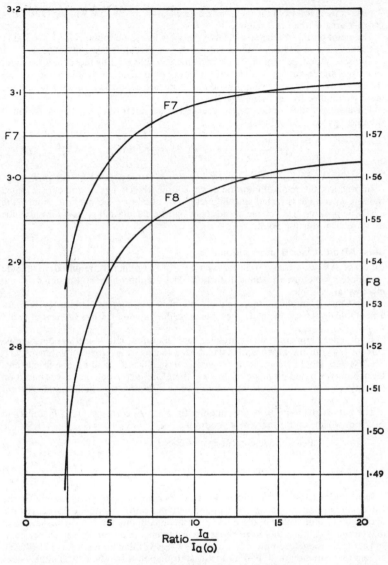

Fig 10

depends on a compromise between efficiency and intermodulation distortion. Generally a current corresponding to about 66 per cent of the rated anode dissipation is typical from which

$$I_{a(o)} = \frac{2}{3} \times 37 \cdot 5 = 25 \, \text{mA}$$

108 PART 4

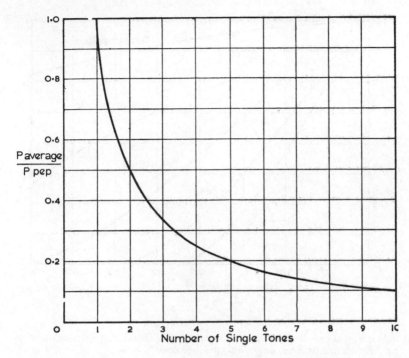

Fig 11

Then
$$\frac{I_a}{I_{a(o)}} = 4$$

from Fig 8 $F_5 = 2 \cdot 99$ and $F_6 = 1 \cdot 53$

and from equation (16) $I_{a(pk)} = 2 \cdot 99 \times 100 = 299$ mA.

Locate this current on the I_a / V_a characteristic curve to find the value of $v_{a(min)}$. To preserve linearity it is important that this point is not in the curved part of the knee characteristic.

From the curve a value of 100 V is suitable.

Hence:

$$v_{a(pk)} = 1,000 - 100 = 900 \text{ V}$$

and from equation (7) $P_{out} = \dfrac{1 \cdot 53}{2} \times 0 \cdot 10 \times 900 = 69$ W

Anode dissipation $p_a = 100 - 69 = 31$ W.

The calculation of driving power (if any) and anode load impedance follow the same procedure as for Class C telegraphy. The bias will, however, be decided by the chosen value of $I_{a(o)}$. The approximate value can be taken from the characteristic curve, but in practice should be set to give the required value of $I_{a(o)}$.

The intermodulation of linear amplifiers is frequently assessed by using a test signal consisting of two or more signals (tones) of equal amplitude. The average power output will decrease as the number of tones is increased in the test signal as shown in Fig 11.

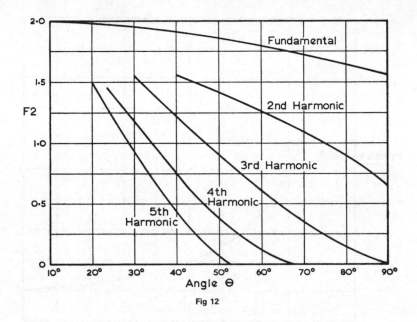

Fig 12

In the usual case of a two-tone test signal, and assuming ideal linear characteristics, the relation between single and two-tone conditions is:

$$I_{a \text{ (two tone)}} = \frac{2}{\pi} I_{a \text{ (single tone)}}$$

Average input power:

$$P_{\text{in (two tone)}} = V_a \times I_{a \text{ (two tone)}}$$

Average output power:

$$P_{\text{out (two tone)}} = \frac{1}{2} P_{\text{out (single tone)}}$$

Grounded grid operation

All the preceding designs are based on the assumption that the signal is applied to the grid and the cathode earthed (grid drive or common cathode connection). Sometimes the signal is applied to the cathode and the grid earthed (grounded grid or cathode drive connection).

This arrangement has the advantage of improved stability usually without neutralizing. It has the disadvantage that much greater driving power is required than that needed for grid drive connection, but some of the driving power is recovered in the output circuit.

The driving power $P_{dr} = (V_g \times I_g) + p_{g1} + \left(\dfrac{v_{g1(pk)} \times F_2 \times I_a}{2} \right)$

The drive power which appears in the output $= \left(\dfrac{v_{g1(pk)} \times F_2 \times I_a}{2} \right)$

In the case of a tetrode there is a small additional driving power which is not

110   PART 4

recovered in the output; this occurs due to the product of peak drive voltage and the fundamental component of the screen current. It is usually sufficiently small to be ignored.

Frequency multipliers

Frequency multipliers are Class C amplifiers in which the anode circuit is tuned to a harmonic of the drive frequency, and may be designed in the same way as a Class C amplifier. In general, smaller angles of flow are used, as this tends to increase the harmonic output.

The factor F_2, which in the amplifier design gives the ratio of peak fundamental to dc anode current, is replaced by a factor giving the ratio for peak harmonic to dc anode current. These factors for harmonics up to the fifth are shown in Fig 12.

Factors

F_1 and F_7 $\quad \dfrac{\text{Peak anode current}}{\text{DC anode current}}$ (assuming sine waveform)

F_2 and F_8 $\quad \dfrac{\text{Peak fundamental component of anode current}}{\text{DC anode current}}$ (assuming sine waveform)

F_3 $\quad \dfrac{1}{1 - \cos \theta}$

F_4 $\quad \dfrac{\text{Peak screen current}}{\text{DC screen current}}$ (assuming squared sine waveform)

F_5 $\quad \dfrac{\text{Peak grid current}}{\text{DC grid current}}$ (assuming squared sine waveform)

F_6 $\quad \dfrac{\text{Peak fundamental component of grid current}}{\text{DC grid current}}$ (assuming squared sine waveform)

GRID CIRCUIT CHART

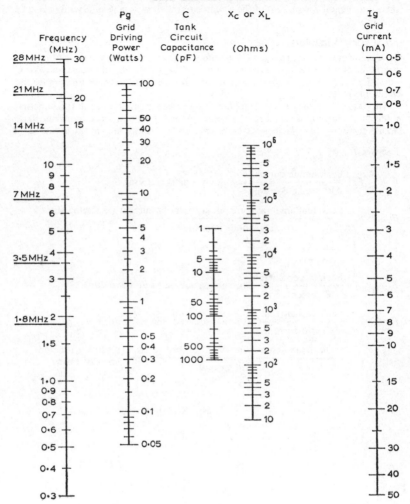

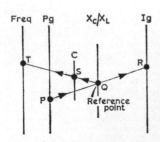

Abac for determining grid tank circuit capacitance for a Q value of 12. Use of the abac is illustrated at right. Join the selected values of *Pg* and *Ig* by a line *PQR*. Note the point *Q* on the X_C/X_L scale. Join the point *Q* to the appropriate frequency *T* on the extreme left-hand scale. The required value of *C* is given at the point *S*. The corresponding value of *L* is given by the reactance value X_L at the point *Q* divided by 6·28 × frequency (MHz). Alternatively, *L* can be obtained from the reactance chart (p 31). For push-pull and parallel connections, the appropriate values of grid current and power are those for the two valves together

ANODE CIRCUIT CHART

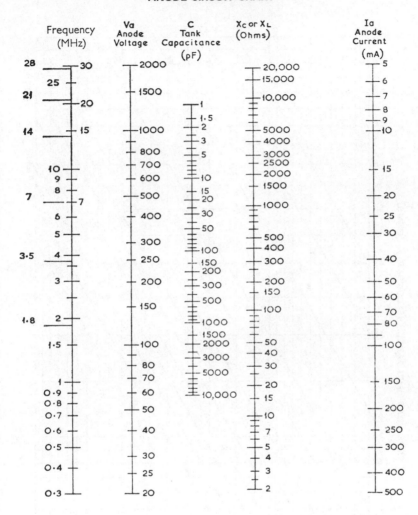

Frequency (MHz)	Va Anode Voltage	C Tank Capacitance (pF)	Xc or XL (Ohms)	Ia Anode Current (mA)

(Chart scales:)

Frequency (MHz): 28 — 30, 25, 21 — 20, 14 — 15, 10, 9, 8, 7 — 7, 6, 5, 3·5 — 4, 3, 1·8 — 2, 1·5, 1, 0·9, 0·8, 0·7, 0·6, 0·5, 0·4, 0·3

Va Anode Voltage: 2000, 1500, 1000, 800, 700, 600, 500, 400, 300, 250, 200, 150, 100, 80, 70, 60, 50, 40, 30, 25, 20

C Tank Capacitance (pF): 1, 1·5, 2, 3, 5, 10, 15, 20, 30, 50, 100, 150, 200, 300, 500, 1000, 1500, 2000, 3000, 5000, 10,000

Xc or XL (Ohms): 20,000, 15,000, 10,000, 5000, 4000, 3000, 2500, 2000, 1500, 1000, 500, 400, 300, 200, 150, 100, 50, 40, 30, 20, 15, 10, 7, 5, 4, 3, 2

Ia Anode Current (mA): 5, 6, 7, 8, 9, 10, 15, 20, 25, 30, 40, 50, 60, 70, 80, 100, 150, 200, 250, 300, 400, 500

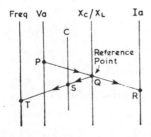

Abac for determining anode tank-circuit capacitance for a loaded Q of 12. For push-pull and parallel connections, the appropriate value of anode current is that for the two valves taken together. Use of the abac is illustrated at left. Join the selected values of V_a and I_a by a line PQR. Note the point Q on the X_C/X_L scale. Join the point Q to the appropriate frequency T on the extreme left-hand scale. The required value of C is given at the point S. The corresponding value of L is given by the reactance value X_L at the point Q divided by $6·28 \times$ frequency (MHz). Alternatively, L can be obtained from the reactance chart on p 31

CIRCUIT DESIGN   113

MODULATION TRANSFORMER RATIOS

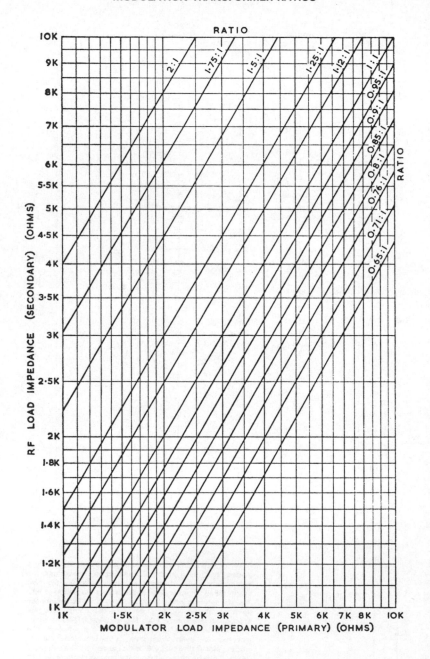

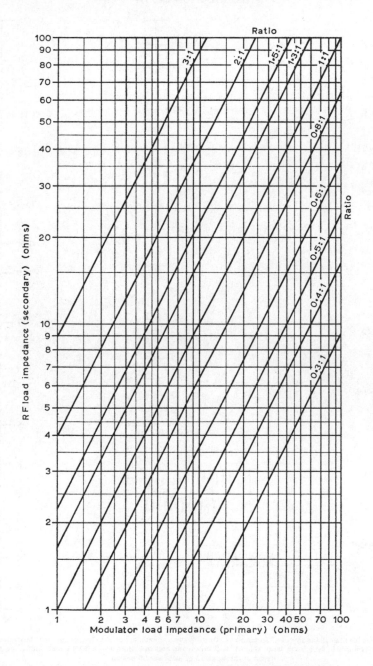

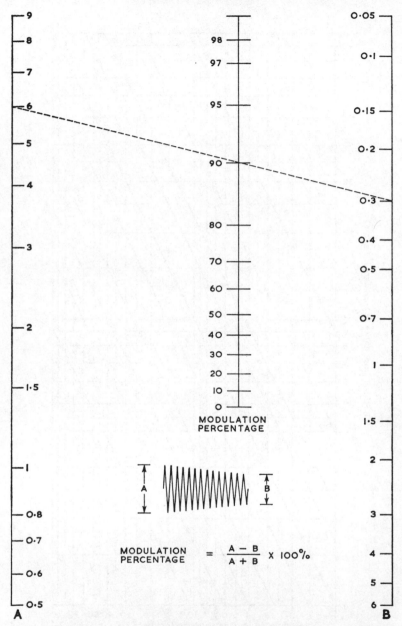

MODULATION
PERCENTAGE

$$\text{MODULATION PERCENTAGE} = \frac{A - B}{A + B} \times 100\%$$

Abac for the calculation of modulation depth from the trapezoidal pattern. The dotted line illustrates an example in which the large side (A) is 6 units long and the shorter one (B) 0·3 unit, indicating a depth of modulation of just over 90 per cent

POWER SUPPLIES

POWER RECTIFICATION

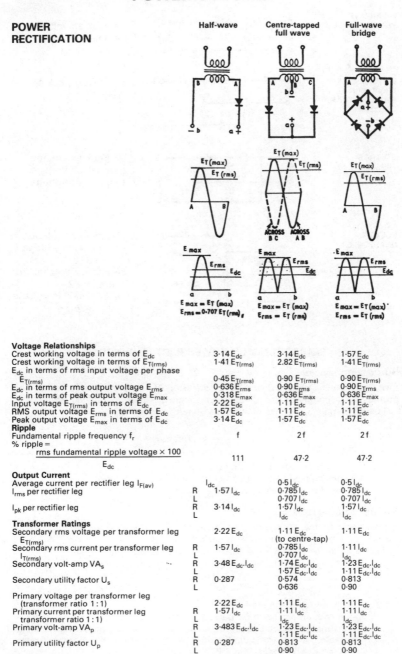

		Half-wave	Centre-tapped full wave	Full-wave bridge
Voltage Relationships				
Crest working voltage in terms of E_{dc}		$3.14\,E_{dc}$	$3.14\,E_{dc}$	$1.57\,E_{dc}$
Crest working voltage in terms of $E_{T(rms)}$		$1.41\,E_{T(rms)}$	$2.82\,E_{T(rms)}$	$1.41\,E_{T(rms)}$
E_{dc} in terms of rms input voltage per phase $E_{T(rms)}$		$0.45\,E_{T(rms)}$	$0.90\,E_{T(rms)}$	$0.90\,E_{T(rms)}$
E_{dc} in terms of rms output voltage E_{rms}		$0.636\,E_{rms}$	$0.90\,E_{rms}$	$0.90\,E_{rms}$
E_{dc} in terms of peak output voltage E_{max}		$0.318\,E_{max}$	$0.636\,E_{max}$	$0.636\,E_{max}$
Input voltage $E_{T(rms)}$ in terms of E_{dc}		$2.22\,E_{dc}$	$1.11\,E_{dc}$	$1.11\,E_{dc}$
RMS output voltage E_{rms} in terms of E_{dc}		$1.57\,E_{dc}$	$1.11\,E_{dc}$	$1.11\,E_{dc}$
Peak output voltage E_{max} in terms of E_{dc}		$3.14\,E_{dc}$	$1.57\,E_{dc}$	$1.57\,E_{dc}$
Ripple				
Fundamental ripple frequency f_r		f	$2f$	$2f$
% ripple = $\dfrac{\text{rms fundamental ripple voltage} \times 100}{E_{dc}}$		111	47.2	47.2
Output Current				
Average current per rectifier leg $I_{F(av)}$		I_{dc}	$0.5\,I_{dc}$	$0.5\,I_{dc}$
I_{rms} per rectifier leg	R	$1.57\,I_{dc}$	$0.785\,I_{dc}$	$0.785\,I_{dc}$
	L		$0.707\,I_{dc}$	$0.707\,I_{dc}$
I_{pk} per rectifier leg	R	$3.14\,I_{dc}$	$1.57\,I_{dc}$	$1.57\,I_{dc}$
	L		I_{dc}	I_{dc}
Transformer Ratings				
Secondary rms voltage per transformer leg $E_{T(rms)}$		$2.22\,E_{dc}$	$1.11\,E_{dc}$ (to centre-tap)	$1.11\,E_{dc}$
Secondary rms current per transformer leg $I_{T(rms)}$	R	$1.57\,I_{dc}$	$0.785\,I_{dc}$	$1.11\,I_{dc}$
	L		$0.707\,I_{dc}$	I_{dc}
Secondary volt-amp VA_s	R	$3.48\,E_{dc}.I_{dc}$	$1.74\,E_{dc}.I_{dc}$	$1.23\,E_{dc}.I_{dc}$
	L		$1.57\,E_{dc}.I_{dc}$	$1.11\,E_{dc}.I_{dc}$
Secondary utility factor U_s	R	0.287	0.574	0.813
	L		0.636	0.90
Primary voltage per transformer leg (transformer ratio 1:1)		$2.22\,E_{dc}$	$1.11\,E_{dc}$	$1.11\,E_{dc}$
Primary current per transformer leg transformer ratio 1:1)	R	$1.57\,I_{dc}$	$1.11\,I_{dc}$	$1.11\,I_{dc}$
	L		I_{dc}	I_{dc}
Primary volt-amp VA_p	R	$3.483\,E_{dc}.I_{dc}$	$1.23\,E_{dc}.I_{dc}$	$1.23\,E_{dc}.I_{dc}$
	L		$1.11\,E_{dc}.I_{dc}$	$1.11\,E_{dc}.I_{dc}$
Primary utility factor U_p	R	0.287	0.813	0.813
	L		0.90	0.90

VOLTAGE MULTIPLIER CIRCUITS

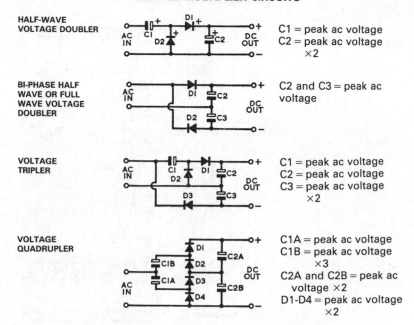

HALF-WAVE VOLTAGE DOUBLER

C1 = peak ac voltage
C2 = peak ac voltage
    ×2

BI-PHASE HALF WAVE OR FULL WAVE VOLTAGE DOUBLER

C2 and C3 = peak ac voltage

VOLTAGE TRIPLER

C1 = peak ac voltage
C2 = peak ac voltage
C3 = peak ac voltage
    ×2

VOLTAGE QUADRUPLER

C1A = peak ac voltage
C1B = peak ac voltage
    ×3
C2A and C2B = peak ac
    voltage ×2
D1-D4 = peak ac voltage
    ×2

SEMICONDUCTOR POWER RECTIFIER DIODES

Surge suppressors

Switching surges can be reduced by the inclusion of a series CR circuit across the primary or secondary of the power transformer or across the dc load circuit.

Typical component values may be calculated from:

$$C = \frac{70\,W}{V^2} \text{ microfarads}$$

where W = power transformer rating in watts
V = rms voltage of the circuit concerned
R = five times the effective load resistance.

Voltage sharing resistors

Equalization of the voltage across series-connected diodes can be effected by connecting a resistor in parallel with each diode.

The value of the required resistors may be calculated from:

$$R = \frac{V}{KI} \text{ ohms}$$

where V = piv rating of the diodes
I = maximum peak reverse current rating of the diodes
K = a constant depending on the number of diodes connected in series: two diodes, $K = 1$; three diodes, $K = 1 \cdot 2$; four diodes, $K = 1 \cdot 5$; five diodes, $K = 1 \cdot 7$; six diodes, $K = 2 \cdot 0$.

118   PART 4

RIPPLE CHART 1

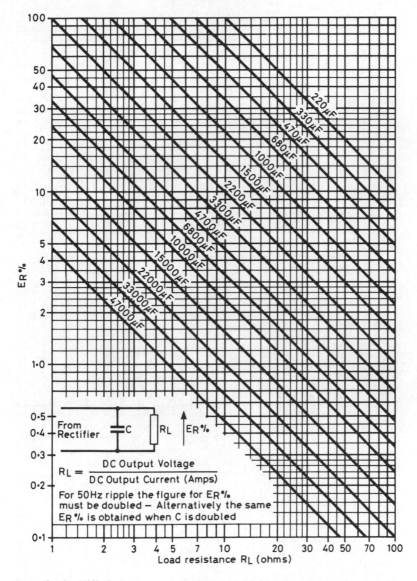

Curves showing 100 Hz ripple component as a percentage of the dc output voltage across a reservoir capacitor

RIPPLE CHART 2

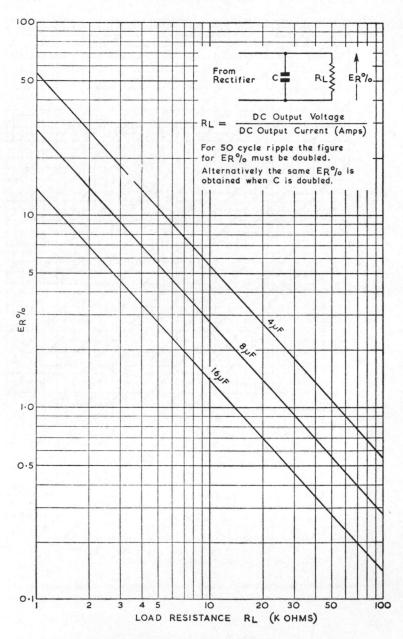

From Rectifier C RL ER%

$$RL = \frac{DC\ Output\ Voltage}{DC\ Output\ Current\ (Amps)}$$

For 50 cycle ripple the figure for $E_R\%$ must be doubled.
Alternatively the same $E_R\%$ is obtained when C is doubled.

4 μF
8 μF
16 μF

LOAD RESISTANCE RL (K OHMS)

Curves showing 100 Hz ripple component as a percentage of the dc output voltage across a reservoir capacitor

RIPPLE CHART 3

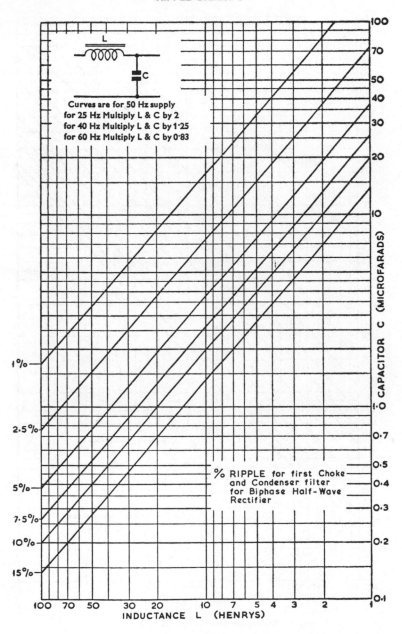

Curves are for 50 Hz supply
for 25 Hz Multiply L & C by 2
for 40 Hz Multiply L & C by 1·25
for 60 Hz Multiply L & C by 0·83

% RIPPLE for first Choke
and Condenser filter
for Biphase Half-Wave
Rectifier

CAPACITOR C (MICROFARADS)

INDUCTANCE L (HENRYS)

RIPPLE CHART 4

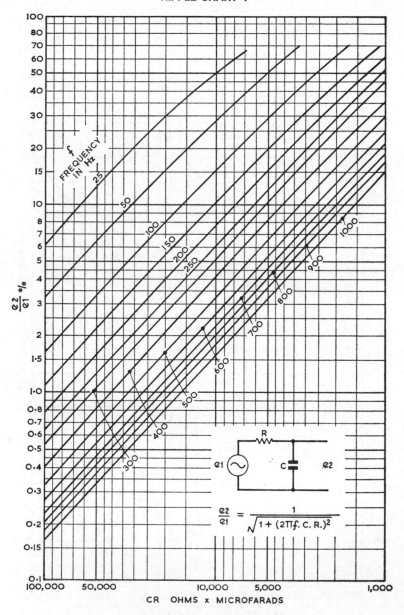

Ripple attenuation of RC filter sections

RIPPLE CHART 5

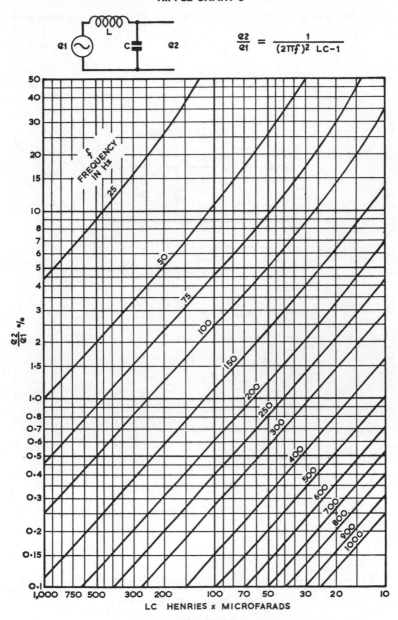

$$\frac{e_2}{e_1} = \frac{1}{(2\pi f)^2 \, LC - 1}$$

Ripple attenuation of LC filter sections

VOLTAGE STABILIZER TUBES

The resistor to be connected in series with a gas-filled voltage stabilizer tube is

$$R = \frac{E_s - E_r}{I} \times 1,000 \ \Omega$$

where E_s = unregulated ht supply voltage (volts)
E_r = regulated ht supply voltage (volts)
I = maximum permissible current in regulator tube (milliamperes)

ZENER DIODES

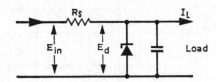

Constant load current/variable input voltage

$$\text{Series resistor } R_s = \frac{E_{in}(\text{min}) - E_d}{1 \cdot 1 \, I_L}$$

$$\text{Diode dissipation } P_d = \left(\frac{E_{in}(\text{max}) - E_d}{R_s} - I_L \right) E_d$$

Variable load current/constant input voltage

$$R_s = \frac{E_{in} - E_d}{1 \cdot 1 \, I_L(\text{max})}$$

$$P_d = \left(\frac{E_{in} - E_d}{R_s} - I_L(\text{min}) \right) E_d$$

Variable load current/variable input voltage

$$R_s = \frac{E_{in}(\text{min}) - E_d}{1 \cdot 1 \, I_L(\text{max})}$$

$$P_d = \left(\frac{E_{in}(\text{max}) - E_d}{R_s} - I_L(\text{min}) \right) E_d$$

PHASE LOCKED LOOPS

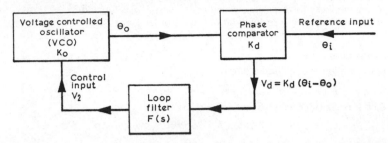

Fig 1. Basic loop

Basic loop

$$\frac{\theta_o(s)}{\theta_i(s)} = H(s) = \frac{K_oK_dF(s)}{s + K_oK_dF(s)}$$

Error response

$$\frac{\theta_i(s) - \theta_o(s)}{\theta_i(s)} = \frac{\theta_e(s)}{\theta_i(s)} = \frac{s}{s + K_oK_dF(s)}$$

Second-order loop

(*a*) *Passive filter*

$$\omega_n = \left(\frac{K_oK_d}{\tau_1 + \tau_2}\right)^{\frac{1}{2}}$$

$$\zeta = \tfrac{1}{2}\left(\frac{K_oK_d}{\tau_1 + \tau_2}\right)^{\frac{1}{2}}\left(\tau + \frac{1}{K_oK_d}\right)$$

(*b*) *Active filter*

$$\omega_n = \left(\frac{K_oK_d}{\tau_1}\right)^{\frac{1}{2}} \qquad \zeta = \frac{\tau_2}{2}\left(\frac{K_oK_d}{\tau_1}\right)^{\frac{1}{2}}$$

where ω_n is the "natural" frequency of the loop in radians per second and ζ is the "damping factor" of the loop (for critical damping $\zeta = 0\cdot707$).

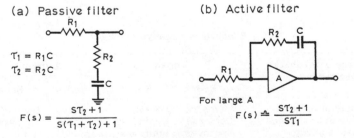

Fig 2. (a) Active and (b) passive filters used in second-order loops

Tracking limits

Hold-in range $\qquad\qquad\Delta\omega_H = \pm K_v \text{ rad/s}$

Maximum locked sweep rate (second-order loop) $\quad \Delta\omega = \omega_n^2 \text{ rad/s}^2$

Maximum frequency step (pull-out of second-order loop)

$$\Delta\omega_{PO} \simeq 1\cdot 8\,\omega_n(\zeta + 1)\,\text{rad/s}$$

Acquisition

Lock-in range (second-order loop)

$$\Delta\omega_L \simeq 2\zeta\omega_n \text{ rads/s}$$

Pull-in range (high-gain, second-order loop)

$$\Delta\omega_P \simeq \sqrt{2}(2\zeta\omega_n K_v - \omega_n^2)^{\frac{1}{2}} \simeq 2\sqrt{\zeta\omega_n K_v}\,\text{rad/s}$$

Pull-in time (high-gain, second-order loop)

$$T_P \simeq \frac{\Delta\omega^2}{2\zeta\omega_n^3}$$

K_v is the dc loop gain $= K_o K_d$, dimensions (second)$^{-1}$.

FEEDBACK

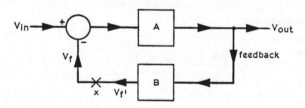

Closed loop

$$\frac{V_{out}}{V_{in}} = \frac{A}{1 + AB}$$

Open loop (break loop at point x)

$$\frac{V_f'}{V_f} = -AB$$

Effective of negative feedback

Type of feedback: Inserted in:	Voltage		Current	
	Series	**Shunt**	**Series**	**Shunt**
Input impedance	Increases	Decreases	Increases	Decreases
Output impedance	Decreases	Decreases	Increases	Increases
Gain stability	Improves	Improves	Improves	Improves
Distortion	Decreases	Decreases	Decreases	Decreases

126

Part 5

Antennas and transmission lines

TYPICAL DIMENSIONS OF YAGI ARRAYS

Element	Element length / Wavelength	Length of elements (in) 70·3 MHz	145 MHz	435 MHz
Reflector	0·495	$83\frac{1}{2}$	40	$13\frac{1}{2}$
Dipole radiator	0·473	$79\frac{1}{2}$	$38\frac{1}{2}$	$12\frac{7}{8}$
Director D1	0·440	74	36	12
Director D2	0·435	$73\frac{1}{4}$	$35\frac{1}{2}$	$11\frac{7}{8}$
Director D3	0·430	$72\frac{1}{2}$	35	$11\frac{3}{4}$
Succeeding directors	0·005 successively	$71\frac{3}{4}$ etc	$34\frac{1}{2}$ etc	$11\frac{1}{2}$ etc
End director	0·007 less than penultimate director	1 in less	$\frac{3}{4}$ in less	$\frac{3}{8}$ in less

Element	Element spacing / Wavelength	Spacing between elements (in) 70·3 MHz	145 MHz	435 MHz
Reflector/Radiator	0·125	21	$10\frac{1}{4}$	$3\frac{3}{8}$
Radiator/Director D1	0·125	21	$10\frac{1}{4}$	$3\frac{3}{8}$
D1—D2	0·25	42	$20\frac{1}{2}$	$6\frac{3}{4}$
D2—D3 etc	0·25	42	$20\frac{1}{2}$	$6\frac{3}{4}$

These dimensions are correct only for elements having diameters in the following ranges:

70·3 MHz	145 MHz	435 MHz
$\frac{1}{2}-\frac{3}{4}$ in	$\frac{1}{4}-\frac{3}{8}$	$\frac{1}{8}-\frac{3}{16}$

GAIN OF YAGI ELEMENTS COMPARED WITH LENGTH

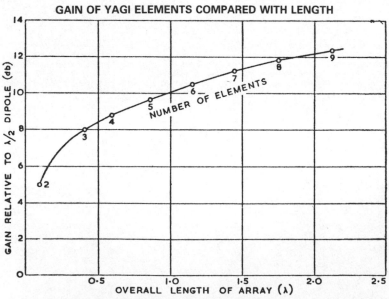

The gain of a Yagi array increases as the number of elements increases. In the graph "2 elements" signifies radiator-plus-reflector: "3 elements" therefore implies one director, and so on. The length of the array is expressed in units of wavelength. The curve shown here is due to S. Kharbanda, G2PU.
(Courtesy Labgear Ltd)

YAGI DESIGN CHART

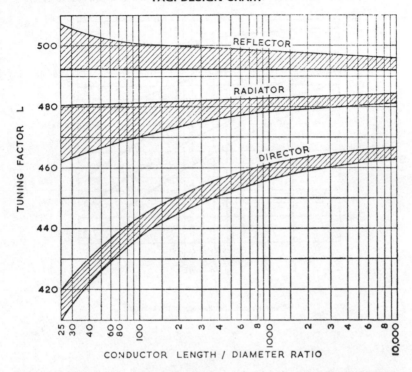

Design chart for Yagi arrays, giving element lengths as a function of conductor length-to-diameter ratio. The tuning factor *L* is divided by the frequency in megahertz to give the lengths in feet. These curves are for arrays of overall length 0·3 λ, with reflector reactance +40 to +60 Ω and director −30 to −40 Ω, and give arrays of input impedance between 15 and 20 Ω. Element lengths which fall within the shaded areas will give an array which can be used without further adjustment, though the front-to-back ratio may be improved by adjusting the reflector

EFFECT OF AMPLITUDE MODULATION ON ANTENNA CURRENT

Depth of modulation (per cent)	Ratio: $\dfrac{\text{af power}}{\text{dc power of pa}}$	Increase in antenna current (per cent)
100	0·5	22·6
90	0·405	18·5
80	0·32	15·1
70	0·245	11·5
60	0·18	8·6
50	0·125	6·0

LENGTH OF YAGI ELEMENTS COMPARED WITH DIAMETER

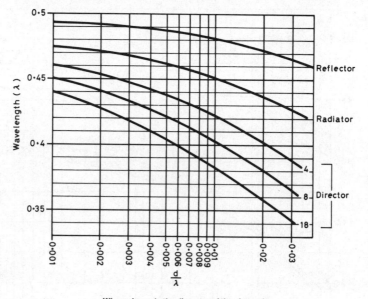

Where d equals the diameter of the element

FOLDED DIPOLE CALCULATIONS

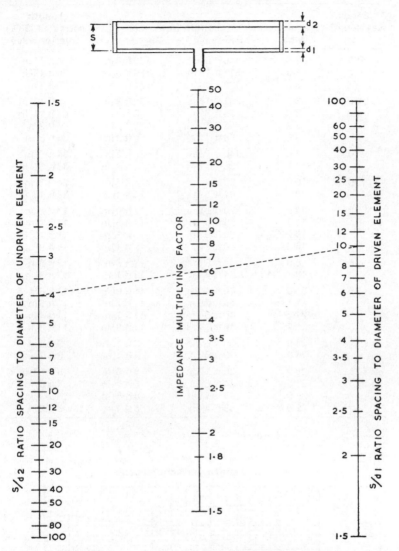

Nomogram for folded dipole calculations. The impedance multiplying factor depends on the two ratios of conductor diameter to spacing between centres, and is always 4:1 when the diameters are equal. A ruler laid across the scales will give pairs of spacing/diameter ratios for any required multiplier. In the example shown the driven element diameter is one-tenth of the spacing and the other element diameter one-quarter of the spacing, resulting in a step up of 6:1. There is an unlimited number of solutions for any given ratio. The chart may also be used to find the step-up ratio of an antenna of given dimensions

HF WIRE ANTENNA LENGTH

Band wavelength (m)	Frequency (MHz)	Length free space Full-wave	Length free space Quarter-wave	Length corrected (98%) Quarter-wave
160	1·8	546 ft 8 in	136 ft 8 in	136 ft 11 in
	1·9	517 ft 11 in	129 ft $5\frac{1}{2}$ in	126 ft $10\frac{1}{2}$ in
	2·0	492 ft	123 ft	123 ft $3\frac{1}{2}$ in
80	3·5	281 ft $1\frac{1}{2}$ in	70 ft 3 in	68 ft $10\frac{1}{2}$ in
	3·6	273 ft $3\frac{1}{2}$ in	68 ft 4 in	66 ft $11\frac{1}{2}$ in
	3·7	265 ft $11\frac{1}{2}$ in	66 ft 6 in	65 ft 2 in
	3·8	258 ft 11 in	64 ft 9 in	63 ft $5\frac{1}{2}$ in
40	7·0	140 ft 7 in	35 ft 2 in	34 ft $5\frac{1}{2}$ in
	7·1	138 ft 7 in	34 ft $7\frac{1}{2}$ in	33 ft $11\frac{1}{2}$ in
30	10·0	98 ft $4\frac{1}{2}$ in	24 ft 7 in	24 ft $1\frac{1}{2}$ in
	10·1	97 ft 5 in	24 ft $4\frac{1}{2}$ in	23 ft $10\frac{1}{2}$ in
20	14·0	70 ft $3\frac{1}{4}$ in	17 ft $6\frac{3}{4}$ in	17 ft $2\frac{1}{2}$ in
	14·1	69 ft $9\frac{1}{2}$ in	17 ft $5\frac{1}{2}$ in	17 ft 1 in
	14·25	69 ft $0\frac{1}{2}$ in	17 ft 3 in	16 ft $10\frac{3}{4}$ in
	14·35	68 ft 7 in	17 ft $1\frac{3}{4}$ in	16 ft $9\frac{3}{4}$ in
16	18·0	54 ft 8 in	13 ft 8 in	13 ft 5 in
	18·1	54 ft $4\frac{1}{4}$ in	13 ft 7 in	13 ft $3\frac{3}{4}$ in
15	21·0	46 ft $10\frac{1}{4}$ in	11 ft $8\frac{1}{2}$ in	11 ft 6 in
	21·1	46 ft $7\frac{1}{2}$ in	11 ft 7 in	11 ft 5 in
	21·25	46 ft $3\frac{1}{2}$ in	11 ft 7 in	11 ft 4 in
	21·35	46 ft 1 in	11 ft $6\frac{1}{4}$ in	11 ft $3\frac{1}{2}$ in
12	24·9	39 ft 6 in	9 ft $10\frac{1}{2}$ in	9 ft 8 in
	25·0	39 ft $4\frac{1}{4}$ in	9 ft 10 in	9 ft $7\frac{1}{2}$ in
10	28·0	35 ft $1\frac{1}{2}$ in	8 ft $9\frac{1}{2}$ in	8 ft $7\frac{1}{4}$ in
	28·5	34 ft $6\frac{1}{4}$ in	8 ft $7\frac{1}{2}$ in	8 ft $5\frac{1}{2}$ in
	29·0	33 ft 11 in	8 ft $5\frac{3}{4}$ in	8 ft $3\frac{3}{4}$ in
	29·5	33 ft $4\frac{1}{4}$ in	8 ft 4 in	8 ft 2 in

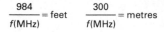

$$\frac{984}{f(\text{MHz})} = \text{feet} \qquad \frac{300}{f(\text{MHz})} = \text{metres}$$

Antenna Length Correction Factor

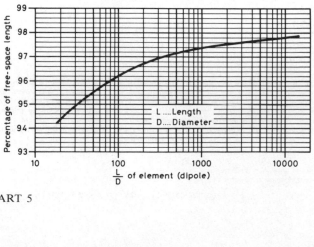

VHF-UHF ANTENNA RADIATOR LENGTH

Band wavelength (m)	Frequency (MHz)	λ (ft)	Free space λ/2 (ft)	λ/4 (ft)	λ/4 (in)	Corrected length Element diam 0·125 (in)	0·25 (in)	0·5 (in)
4	70	14·057	7·028	3·514	42·168	41·02	40·9	40·69
	70·5	13·924	6·962	3·481	41·77	41·64	40·39	40·30
2	144	6·833	3·416	1·708	20·49	19·87	19·72	19·67
	145	6·788	3·394	1·697	20·37	19·76	19·65	19·55
	146	6·779	3·389	1·694	20·23	19·72	19·62	19·52
70 cm	432	2·277	1·138	0·569	6·83	6·57	6·54	6·49
	433	2·272	1·136	0·568	6·82	6·56	6·53	6·47
	434	2·267	1·133	0·567	6·80	6·54	6·51	6·46
Microwaves (cm)		**(cm)**		**(cm)**		**(cm)**	**(cm)**	
23	1,250	23·99	—	5·99	—	5·69	5·63	—
	1,275	23·50	—	5·875	—	5·56	5·52	—
	1,296	23·15	—	5·79	—	5·46	5·43	—
13	2,304	13·015	—	3·25	—	3·09	—	—
9	3,456	8·69	—	2·17	—	2·05	—	—
6	5,750	5·21	—	1·30	—	1·14	—	—
3	10,350	2·88	—	0·72	—	0·66	—	—

V AND RHOMBIC ANTENNAS

Leg length (λ)	Angle A	Gain V antenna (dB)	Gain rhombic (dB)
1	90	3	6
2	72	4·5	7·5
3	60	6	9
4	50	7	10
5	45	8	11
6	40	9	12

Average design figures for V and rhombic antennas. The angle A is the apex angle.

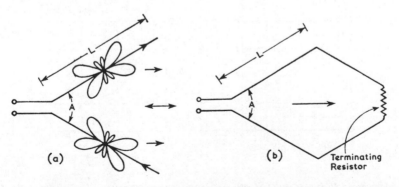

(a)   (b)   Terminating Resistor

V and rhombic antennas. The diagram on the left (a) shows how the main lobes of two long wire radiators are added to form the main beam. The apex angle A is given in the table above

ANTENNAS AND TRANSMISSION LINES   133

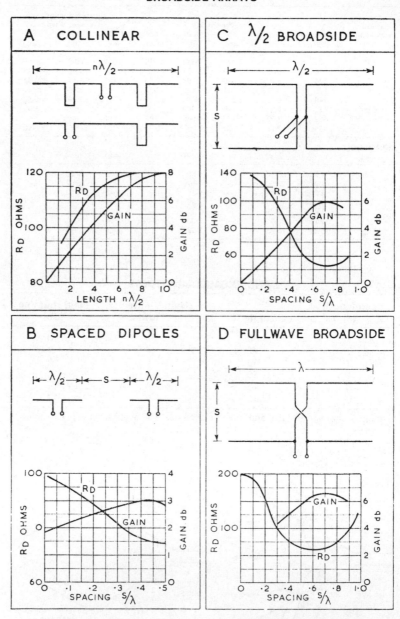

General types of broadside array. (a) Collinear arrays; (b) End-spaced dipoles; (c, d, e) Two-tier, Sterba or Barrage arrays; (f) Pine Tree or Koomans, stacked horizontal $\lambda/2$ or λ dipoles, (g, h) Vertically polarized broadside arrays. Gain figures are with reference to a free-space dipole, in terms of spacing

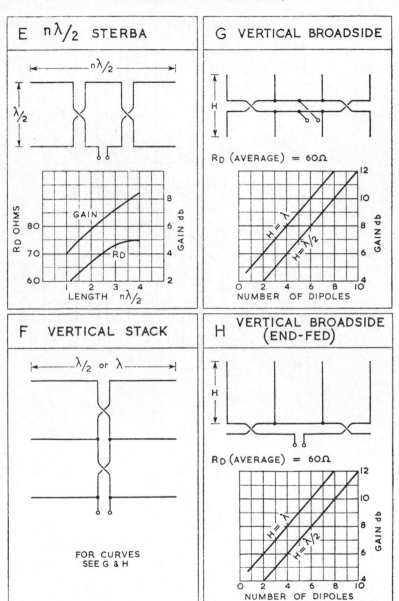

or total length in half-waves. Resistance figures are average over the array, and are added in series or parallel according to the feed arrangements. The antenna in (c) can be arranged to give a broadside beam over a 2:1 frequency range, eg 14, 21 and 28 MHz

ANTENNAS AND TRANSMISSION LINES   **135**

DISH ANTENNA GAIN AND BEAMWIDTH

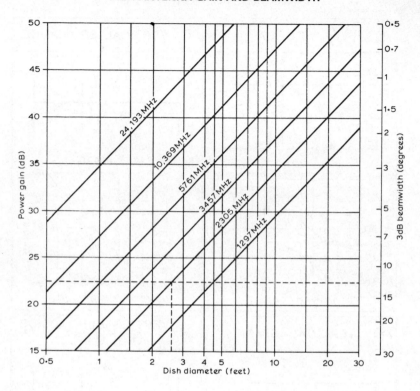

TRANSMISSION LINES

---

1 PARALLEL STRIPS (SLAB LINES)

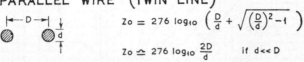

$$Z_0 \cong 377 \frac{a}{b} \qquad \text{if } a << b$$
edge effects neglected

---

2 PARALLEL WIRE (TWIN LINE)

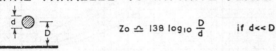

$$Z_0 = 276 \log_{10} \left(\frac{D}{d} + \sqrt{\left(\frac{D}{d}\right)^2 - 1} \right)$$

$$Z_0 \cong 276 \log_{10} \frac{2D}{d} \qquad \text{if } d << D$$

---

3 WIRE PARALLEL TO INFINITE PLATE

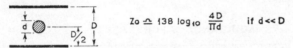

$$Z_0 \cong 138 \log_{10} \frac{D}{d} \qquad \text{if } d << D$$

---

4 WIRE PARALLEL TO TWO INFINITE PLATES

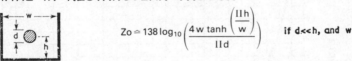

$$Z_0 \cong 138 \log_{10} \frac{4D}{\Pi d} \qquad \text{if } d << D$$

---

5 WIRE IN RECTANGULAR TROUGH

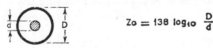

$$Z_0 \cong 138 \log_{10} \left(\frac{4w \tanh\left(\frac{\Pi h}{w}\right)}{\Pi d} \right) \qquad \text{if } d << h, \text{ and } w$$

---

6 CIRCULAR COAXIAL

$$Z_0 = 138 \log_{10} \frac{D}{d}$$

---

7 SQUARE COAXIAL

$$Z_0 \cong 2 + 143 \log_{10} \frac{D}{d}$$

NOTE: In the above, the medium is taken as AIR.
For other medium, the resulting value of Zo
should be multiplied by $\frac{1}{\sqrt{K}}$

where K is the dielectric constant

ANTENNAS AND TRANSMISSION LINES   137

CHARACTERISTIC IMPEDANCE OF PCB TRACKS

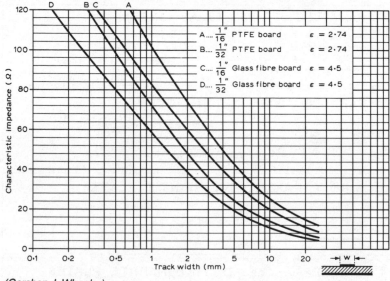

(Gershon J. Wheeler)

INDUCTANCE OF PCB TRACKS

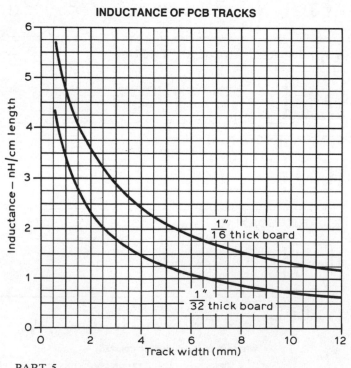

CHARACTERISTIC IMPEDANCE OF PCB TRACKS

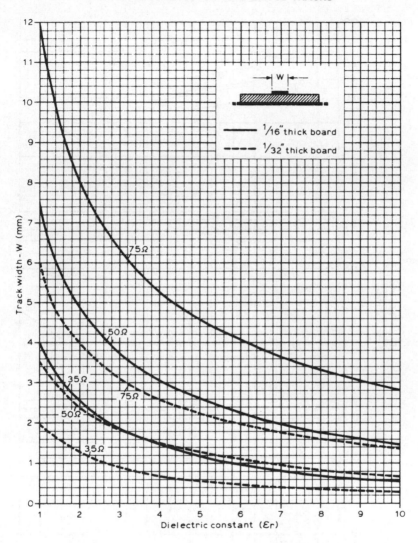

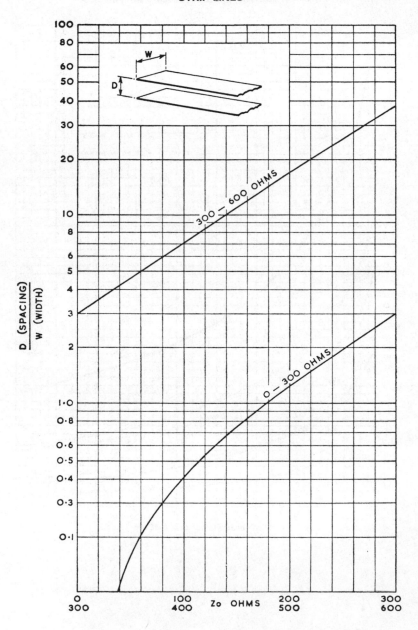

Characteristic impedance of balanced strip transmission line

CHARACTERISTIC IMPEDANCE OF CIRCULAR AND SQUARE COAXIAL LINES

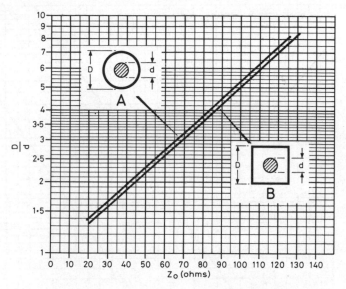

CHARACTERISTIC IMPEDANCE OF TROUGH LINE

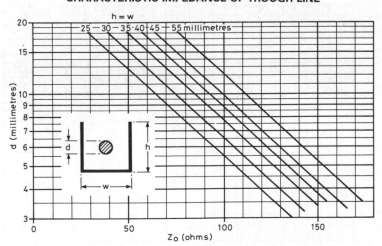

CHARACTERISTIC IMPEDANCE OF TWIN-WIRE COAXIAL LINE

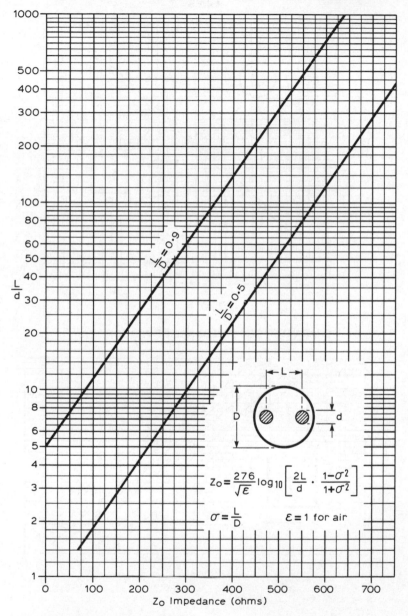

$$Z_0 = \frac{276}{\sqrt{\varepsilon}} \log_{10}\left[\frac{2L}{d} \cdot \frac{1-\sigma^2}{1+\sigma^2}\right]$$

$$\sigma = \frac{L}{D} \qquad \varepsilon = 1 \text{ for air}$$

(Robert Le Blanc)

CAPACITANCE OF COAXIAL LINE

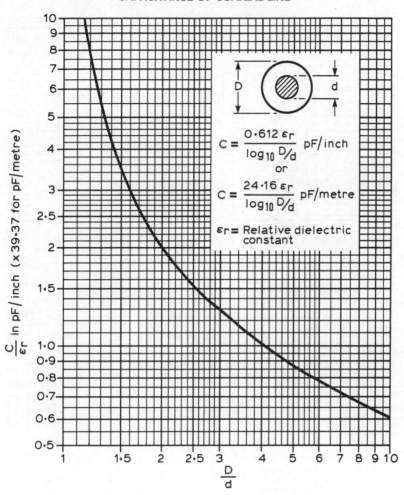

$$C = \frac{0.612\, \varepsilon_r}{\log_{10} D/d} \ \text{pF/inch}$$

or

$$C = \frac{24.16\, \varepsilon_r}{\log_{10} D/d} \ \text{pF/metre}$$

ε_r = Relative dielectric constant

(Robert Le Blanc)

CAPACITANCE OF COAXIAL LINE

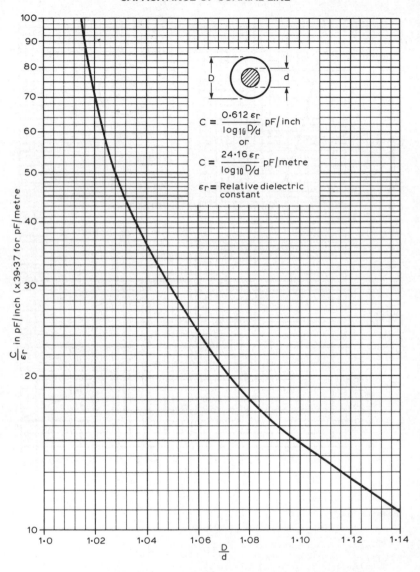

$$C = \frac{0.612\,\varepsilon_r}{\log_{10} D/d} \text{ pF/inch}$$

or

$$C = \frac{24.16\,\varepsilon_r}{\log_{10} D/d} \text{ pF/metre}$$

ε_r = Relative dielectric constant

(Robert Le Blanc)

INDUCTANCE OF COAXIAL LINE

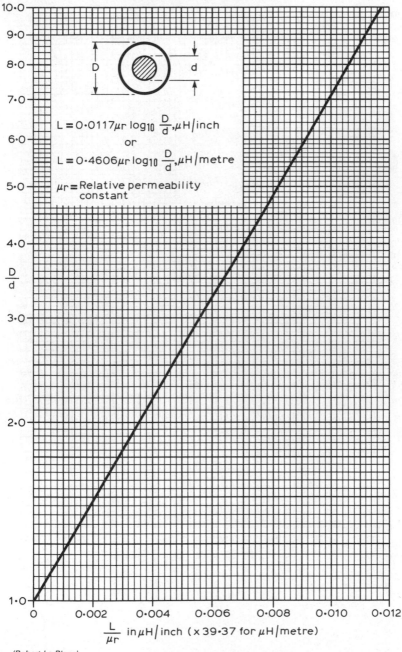

$L = 0.0117\mu_r \log_{10} \dfrac{D}{d}, \mu H/\text{inch}$

or

$L = 0.4606\mu_r \log_{10} \dfrac{D}{d}, \mu H/\text{metre}$

μ_r = Relative permeability constant

$\dfrac{L}{\mu_r}$ in $\mu H/\text{inch}$ (× 39·37 for $\mu H/\text{metre}$)

(Robert Le Blanc)

INDUCTANCE OF COAXIAL LINE

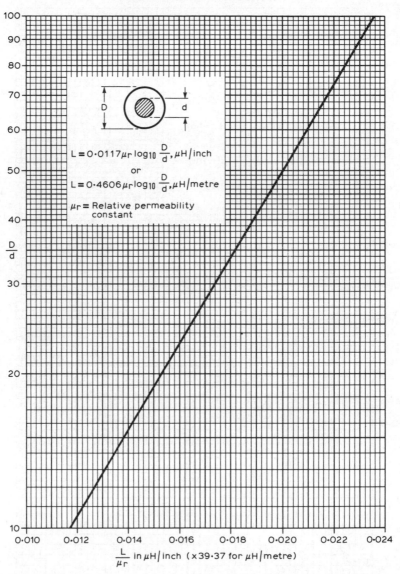

$$L = 0.0117\mu_r \log_{10} \frac{D}{d}, \mu H/\text{inch}$$

or

$$L = 0.4606\mu_r \log_{10} \frac{D}{d}, \mu H/\text{metre}$$

μ_r = Relative permeability constant

(Robert Le Blanc)

STANDING WAVE RATIO CHART

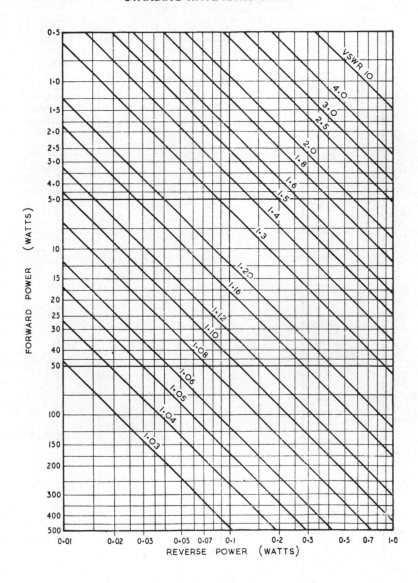

VSWR CHART No 1

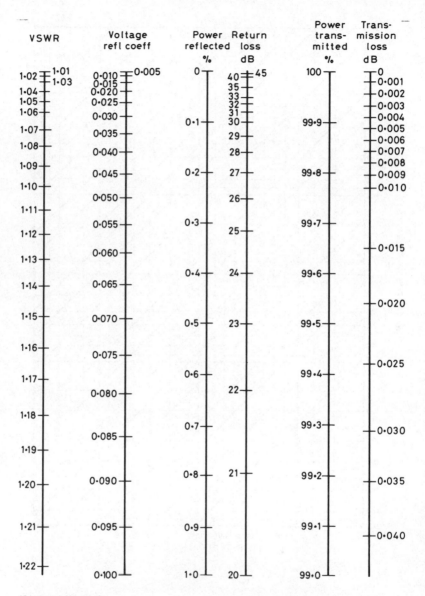

VSWR	Voltage refl coeff	Power reflected %	Return loss dB	Power transmitted %	Transmission loss dB
1·01					
1·02	0·005	0	45	100	0
1·03	0·010		40		0·001
1·04	0·015		35		0·002
1·05	0·020		33		0·003
1·06	0·025		32		0·004
	0·030		31		0·005
1·07		0·1	30	99·9	0·006
1·08	0·035		29		0·007
	0·040		28		0·008
1·09	0·045	0·2	27	99·8	0·009
1·10					0·010
1·11	0·050		26		
	0·055	0·3	25	99·7	
1·12					
1·13	0·060				0·015
1·14	0·065	0·4	24	99·6	
					0·020
1·15	0·070	0·5	23	99·5	
1·16	0·075				
		0·6		99·4	0·025
1·17	0·080		22		
1·18		0·7		99·3	0·030
	0·085				
1·19					
1·20	0·090	0·8	21	99·2	0·035
1·21	0·095	0·9		99·1	0·040
1·22	0·100	1·0	20	99·0	

(Gershon J. Wheeler)

VSWR CHART No 2

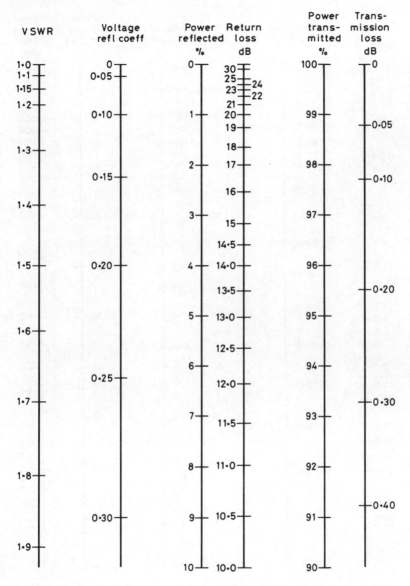

(Gershon J. Wheeler)

VSWR CHART No 3

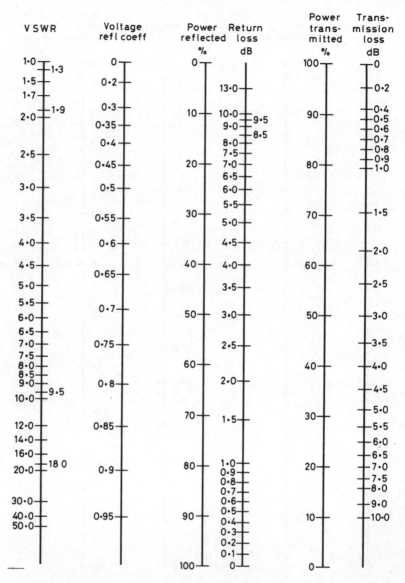

(Gershon J. Wheeler)

ATTENUATORS 50 and 75 Ω

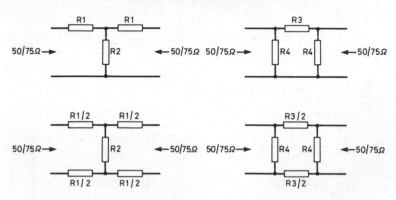

Attenuation (dB)	T pad				π pad			
	50 Ω		75 Ω		50 Ω		75 Ω	
	R1	R2	R1	R2	R3	R4	R3	R4
1	2·9	433	4·3	647	5·8	870	8·6	1,305
2	5·7	215	8·6	323	11·6	436	17·4	654
3	8·5	132	12·8	213	17·6	292	26·4	439
4	11·3	105	17·0	157	23·8	221	35·8	331
5	14·0	82	21·0	123·4	30·4	179	45·6	268
6	16·6	67	25·0	100	37·3	151	56·0	226
7	19·0	54	28·7	83·8	44·8	131	67·2	196
8	21·5	47	32·3	71	52·3	116	79·3	174
9	23·8	41	35·7	61	61·6	105	92·4	158
10	26·0	35	39·0	52·7	70·7	96	107	144
11	28·0	30·6	42·0	45·9	81·6	89	123	134
12	30·0	26·8	45·0	40·2	93·2	84	140	125
13	31·7	23·5	47·6	35·3	106	78·3	159	118
14	33·3	20·8	50·0	31·2	120	74·9	181	112
15	35·0	18·4	52·4	25·0	136	71·6	204	107
20	41·0	10·0	61·4	15·2	248	61	371	91·5
25	44·7	5·6	67·0	8·5	443	56	666	83·9
30	47·0	3·2	70·4	4·8	790	53·2	1,186	79·7
35	48·2	1·8	72·4	2·7	1,406	51·8	2,108	77·7
40	49·0	1·0	73·6	1·5	2,500	51	3,750	76·5

WAVEGUIDE SIZES

| Frequency (GHz) | Wavelength (cm) | WG Internal dimensions (in) | WG Internal dimensions (cm) | RCSC British WG No | British Inter-Service Ref No | | EIA WR ( ) | IEC R ( ) | NATO NWG (1 or 2)* | JAN Type RG ( ) | | | Cut-off Frequency |
					Brass 70/30	Aluminium				Copper or brass	Aluminium	Silver	
0.32–0.49	93.68–61.18	23.0 × 11.5	58.420 × 29.210	00			2,300	3	01				0.265
0.35–0.53	85.65–56.56	21.0 × 10.5	53.34 × 26.670	0			2,100	4	02				0.281
0.41–0.625	73.11–47.96	18.0 × 9.0	45.72 × 22.86	1			1,800	5	03				0.328
0.49–0.75	61.18–39.97	15.0 × 7.5	38.1 × 19.05	2			1,500	6	04				0.393
0.64–0.96	46.84–31.23	11.5 × 5.75	29.210 × 14.605	3			1,150	8	05		201		0.513
0.75–1.12	39.95–26.76	9.75 × 4.875	24.765 × 12.3825	4			975	9	06		202		0.605
0.96–1.45	31.23–20.67	7.7 × 3.85	19.558 × 9.779	5			770	12	07		203		0.766
1.12–1.70	26.76–17.63	6.5 × 3.25	16.510 × 8.255	6		012-0037	650	14	08	69	204		0.908
1.45–2.20	20.67–13.62	5.1 × 2.55	12.954 × 6.477	7			510	18	09		205		1.157
1.70–2.60	17.63–11.53	4.3 × 2.15	10.922 × 5.461	8			430	22	10	104	103		1.372
2.20–3.30	13.63–9.08	3.4 × 1.7	8.636 × 4.318	9A	083-0144	083-0144	340	26	11	112	105		1.763
2.60–3.95	11.53–7.59	2.84 × 1.34	7.2163 × 3.403	10	012-0040	012-0042	284	32	12	48	75		2.078
3.30–4.90	9.08–6.12	2.29 × 1.145	5.8166 × 2.909	11A	083-0068	083-0069	229	40	13		113		2.577
3.95–5.85	7.59–5.12	1.872 × 0.872	4.7549 × 2.2149	12	012-0045	012-0047	187	48	14	49	95		3.152
4.90–7.05	6.12–4.25	1.59 × 0.795	4.0486 × 2.0193	13	083-0077	083-0078	159	58	15				3.711
5.85–8.20	5.12–3.66	1.372 × 0.622	3.4849 × 1.58	14	083-0146	083-0147	137	70	16	50	106		4.301
7.05–10.00	4.25–2.99	1.122 × 0.497	2.880 × 1.2624	15	083-0081	083-0082	112	84	17	51	68		5.259
8.20–12.40	3.66–2.42	0.90 × 0.40	2.286 × 1.016	16	083-0086	083-0087	90	100	18	52	67		6.557
10.00–15.00	2.99–2.00	0.75 × 0.375	1.9050 × 0.9525	17	083-0097	083-0099	75	120	19				7.868
12.40–18.00	2.42–1.66	0.622 × 0.311	1.58 × 0.790	18	083-0101		62	140	20	91		107	9.426
15.00–22.00	2.00–1.36	0.510 × 0.255	1.295 × 0.6477	19			51	180	21				11.574
18.00–26.50	1.66–1.13	0.420 × 0.170	1.0668 × 0.4318	20	Precision		42	220	22	53	121	66	14.047
22.00–33.00	1.36–0.91	0.340 × 0.170	0.8636 × 0.4318	21			34	260	23				17.328
26.50–40.00	1.13–0.75	0.280 × 0.140	0.7112 × 0.3556	22			28	320	24			96	21.081
33.00–50.00	0.91–0.60	0.224 × 0.112	0.5659 × 0.2845	23	083-1500		22	400	25			97	26.342
40.00–60.00	0.75–0.50	0.188 × 0.94	0.4775 × 0.2388	24	083-1501		19	500	26				31.357
50.00–75.00	0.60–0.40	0.148 × 0.074	0.3759 × 0.1880	25	083-1502		15	620	27			98	39.863
60.00–90.00	0.50–0.33	0.122 × 0.061	0.3098 × 0.1550	26	083-1503		12	740	28			99	48.350
75.00–110.0	0.40–0.27	0.100 × 0.050	0.2540 × 0.1270	27	083-1504		10	900	29				59.010
90.00–140.0	0.33–0.22	0.080 × 0.040	0.2032 × 0.1016	28	083-1505		8	1,200	30				73.80
140.00–220.0	0.22–0.14	0.051 × 0.025	0.1295 × 0.0635		083-1506		5	1,800					116.80

* *NB*—(1) Aluminium. (2) Copper based alloy.

The cut-off wavelength of a rectangular waveguide, the wide dimension of which is a cm, is given by $\lambda_{co} = 2a$

For a waveguide $\dfrac{1}{\lambda^2} + \dfrac{1}{\lambda_{co}^2} = \dfrac{1}{\lambda_o^2}$ where λ = waveguide wavelength, λ_{co} = waveguide cut-off wavelength, and λ_o = free space wavelength.

CHARACTERISTICS OF TYPICAL BRITISH RADIO FREQUENCY FEEDER CABLES

Type of cable	Nominal impedance $Z_0(\Omega)$	Dimensions (in)			Velocity factor	Approximate attenuation (dB/100 ft)				Remarks
		Centre conductor	Over outer sheath	Over twin cores		70 MHz	145 MHz	430 MHz	1,250 MHz	
Standard TV feeder	75	7/·0076	0·202	—	0·67	3·5	5·1	9·2	17	—
Low-loss TV feeder (semi-air-spaced)	75	0·048	0·290	—	0·86 approx.	2·0	3·0	5·4	10	Semi-air-spaced or cellular.
Flat twin	150	7/·012	—	0·18×0·09	0·71	2·1	3·1	5·7*	11*	*Theoretical figures, likely to be considerably worsened by radiation
Flat twin	300	7/·012	—	0·405×0·09	0·85	1·2	1·8	3·4*	6·6*	
Tubular twin	300	7/·012	—	0·446	0·85	1·2	1·8	3·4*	6·6*	

This table is compiled from information kindly supplied by Aerialite Ltd and BICC Ltd, and includes data extracted from *Defence Specification*, DEF-14-A (HMSO)

RF CABLES—BRITISH UR SERIES

UR No	Nominal impedance Z_0	Overall diameter (in)	Inner conductor (in)	Capacitance (pF/ft)	Maximum operating voltage rms	Approx attenuation (dB per 100 ft)				Approx RG equivalent
						10 MHz	100 MHz	300 MHz	1,000 MHz	
43	52	0·195	0·032	29	2,750	1·3	4·3	8·7	18·1	58/U
57	75	0·405	0·044	20·6	5,000	0·6	1·9	3·5	7·1	11 A/U
63*	75	0·855	0·175	14	4,400	0·15	0·5	0·9	1·7	—
67	50	0·405	7/0·029	30	4,800	0·6	2·0	3·7	7·5	213/U
74	51	0·870	0·188	30·7	15,000	0·3	1·0	1·9	4·2	218/U
76	51	0·195	19/0·0066	29	1,800	1·6	5·3	9·6	22·0	58C/U
77	75	0·870	0·104	20·5	12,500	0·3	1·0	1·9	4·2	164/U
79*	50	0·855	0·265	21	6,000	0·16	0·5	0·9	1·8	—
83*	50	0·555	0·168	21	2,600	0·25	0·8	1·5	2·8	—
85*	75	0·555	0·109	14	2,600	0·2	0·7	1·3	2·5	—
90	75	0·242	0·022	20	2,500	1·1	3·5	6·3	12·3	59B/U

All the above cables have solid dielectric with a velocity factor of 0·66 with the exception of those marked with an astrisk which are helical membrane and have a velocity factor of 0·96

RF CABLES (USA RG SERIES)

Cable No	Nominal impedance $Z_0(\Omega)$	Cable outside diameter (in)	Velocity factor	Approximate attenuation (dB per 100 ft)					Capacity (pF/ft)	Maximum operating voltage (rms)
				1 MHz	10 MHz	100 MHz	1,000 MHz	3,000 MHz		
RG-5/U	52.5	0.332	0.659	0.21	0.77	2.9	11.5	22.0	28.5	3,000
RG-5B/U	50.0	0.332	0.659	0.16	0.66	2.4	8.8	16.7	29.5	3,000
RG-6A/U	75.0	0.332	0.659	0.21	0.78	2.9	11.2	21.0	20.0	2,700
RG-8A/U	50.0	0.405	0.659	0.16	0.55	2.0	8.0	16.5	30.5	4,000
RG-9/U	51.0	0.420	0.659	0.16	0.57	2.0	7.3	15.5	30.0	4,000
RG-9B/U	50.0	0.425	0.659	0.175	0.61	2.1	9.0	18.0	30.5	4,000
RG-10A/U	50.0	0.475	0.659	0.16	0.55	2.0	8.0	16.5	30.5	4,000
RG-11A/U	75.0	0.405	0.66	0.18	0.7	2.3	7.8	16.5	20.5	5,000
RG-12A/U	75.0	0.475	0.659	0.18	0.66	2.3	8.0	16.5	20.5	4,000
RG-13A/U	75.0	0.425	0.659	0.18	0.66	2.3	8.0	16.5	20.5	4,000
RG-14A/U	50.0	0.545	0.659	0.12	0.41	1.4	5.5	12.0	30.0	5,500
RG-16/U	52.0	0.630	0.670	0.1	0.4	1.2	6.7	16.0	29.5	6,000
RG-17A/U	50.0	0.870	0.659	0.066	0.225	0.80	3.4	8.5	30.0	11,000
RG-18A/U	50.0	0.945	0.659	0.066	0.225	0.80	3.4	8.5	30.5	11,000
RG-19A/U	50.0	1.120	0.659	0.04	0.17	0.68	3.5	7.7	30.5	14,000
RG-20A/U	50.0	1.195	0.659	0.04	0.17	0.68	3.5	7.7	30.5	14,000

Type										
RG-21/AU	50·0	0·332	0·659	1·4	4·4	13·0	43·0	85·0	30·0	2,700
RG-29/U	53·5	0·184	0·659	0·33	1·2	4·4	16·0	30·0	28·5	1,900
RG-34A/U	75·0	0·630	0·659	0·065	0·29	1·3	6·0	12·5	20·5	5,200
RG-34B/U	75	0·630	0·66		0·3	1·4	5·8		21·5	6,500
RG-35A/U	75·0	0·945	0·659	0·07	0·235	0·85	3·5	8·60	20·5	10,000
RG-54A/U	58·0	0·250	0·659	0·18	0·74	3·1	11·5	21·5	26·5	3,000
RG-55/U	53·5	0·206	0·659	0·36	1·3	4·8	17·0	32·0	28·5	1,900
RG-55A/U	50·0	0·216	0·659	0·36	1·3	4·8	17·0	32·0	29·5	1,900
RG-58/U	53·5	0·195	0·659	0·33	1·25	4·65	17·5	37·5	28·5	1,900
RG-58C/U	50·0	0·195	0·659	0·42	1·4	4·9	24·0	45·0	30·0	1,900
RG-59A/U	75·0	0·242	0·659	0·34	1·10	3·40	12·0	26·0	20·5	2,300
RG-59B/U	75	0·242	0·66		1·1	3·4	12		21	2,300
RG-62A/U	93·0	0·242	0·84	0·25	0·85	2·70	8·6	18·5	13·5	750
RG-83/U	35·0	0·405	0·66	0·23	0·80	2·8	9·6	24·0	44·0	2,000
RG-174A/U	50·0	0·615	0·659	0·10	0·38	1·5	6·0	11·5	30·0	5,500
*RG-213/U	50	0·405	0·66	0·16	0·6	1·9	8·0		29·5	5,000
†RG-218/U	50	0·870	0·66	0·066	0·2	1·0	4·4		29·5	11,000
‡RG-220/U	50	1·120	0·66	0·04	0·2	0·7	3·6		29·5	14,000

* Formerly RG8A/U   † Formerly RG17A/U   ‡ Formerly RG19A/U

BALANCE-TO-UNBALANCE TRANSFORMERS

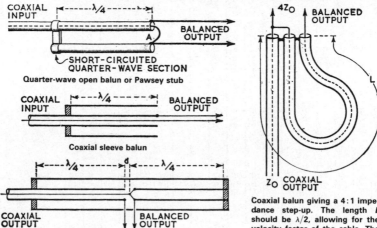

COAXIAL INPUT |←------ λ/4 ------→|

BALANCED OUTPUT

A

SHORT-CIRCUITED QUARTER-WAVE SECTION

Quarter-wave open balun or Pawsey stub

COAXIAL INPUT |←--- λ/4 ---→|

BALANCED OUTPUT

Coaxial sleeve balun

|←---- λ/4 ----→| d |←---- λ/4 ----→|

COAXIAL OUTPUT

BALANCED OUTPUT

Totally enclosed coaxial balun. The right-hand section acts as a "metal insulator"

$4Z_0$ BALANCED OUTPUT

L

Z_0 COAXIAL OUTPUT

Coaxial balun giving a 4:1 impedance step-up. The length L should be $λ/2$, allowing for the velocity factor of the cable. The outer braiding may be joined at the points indicated

IMPEDANCE MATCHING

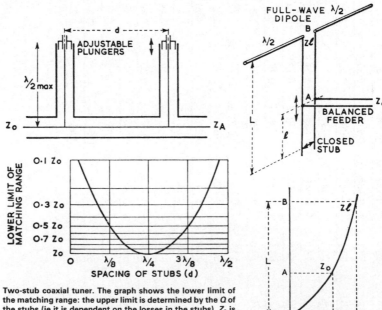

ADJUSTABLE PLUNGERS

|←------ d ------→|

$λ/2$ max

Z_0

Z_A

LOWER LIMIT OF MATCHING RANGE

0·1 Z_0

0·3 Z_0

0·5 Z_0

0·7 Z_0

Z_0

O   λ/8   λ/4   3λ/8   λ/2

SPACING OF STUBS (d)

Two-stub coaxial tuner. The graph shows the lower limit of the matching range: the upper limit is determined by the Q of the stubs (ie it is dependent on the losses in the stubs). Z_0 is the characteristic impedance of the feeder

FULL-WAVE λ/2 DIPOLE

B

λ/2

$Zℓ$

$λ/2$

A

Z_0

BALANCED FEEDER

L

$ℓ$

CLOSED STUB

B

$Zℓ$

L

Z_0

A

O

$Z →$

Stub matching applied to a full-wave dipole

TYPICAL CONNECTIONS FOR TOROIDAL TRANSFORMERS FOR IMPEDANCE TRANSFORMATION (BALUNS)

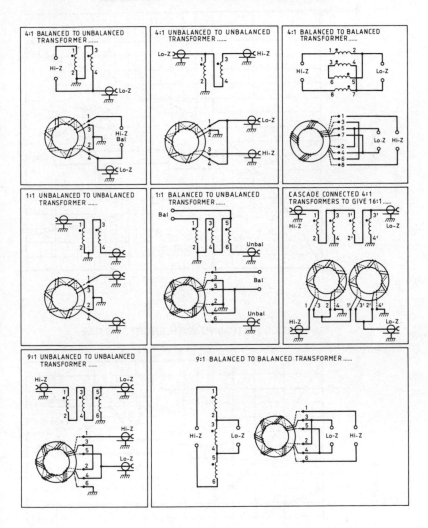

IMPEDANCE MATCHING WITH OPEN STUB

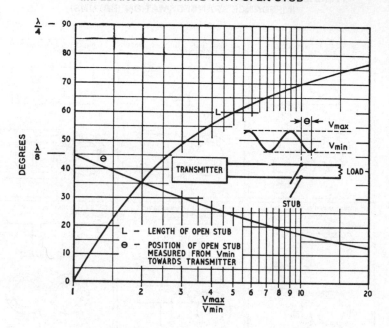

IMPEDANCE MATCHING WITH SHORTED STUB

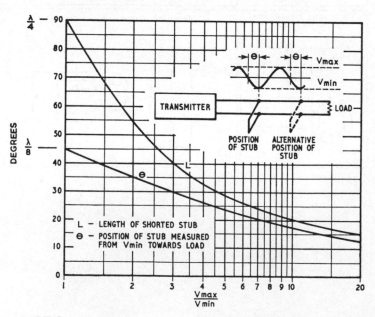

COAXIAL CONNECTORS

Type	Impe-dance (Ω)	Maxi-mum freq. (MHz)	Max. peak voltage (V)	Suitable cable	Notes
BNC	50	10,000	500	URM43	High quality constant impedance bayonet
	75	10,000	500	URM70	fitting connector. Versions with captive pin recommended. Not often used on commercial amateur equipment.
Miniature BNC	50	10,000	500	URM95	
N	50	10,000	1,000	URM67	High quality constant impedance connector 75 Ω type for thinner (URM43) cable available. Recommended for high power circuits above 400 MHz.
PL259/ SO239	50	200	500	URM67 or URM43	Non-constant impe-dance design. Used on most hf/vhf commercial amateur equipment. High vswr makes it unsuitable for use above 144 MHz. Reducers available for different cables.
C	75	—	—	—	Bayonet fitting. Rarely found on amateur equipment.
F	50	—	—	URM43	American cctv connector used on some 144 MHz port-able transceivers. Plugs use inner conductor of cable for centre pin.
Belling Lee	75	—	—	URM70 etc	British tv antenna connector used extensively for home-built equipment and some British commercial equip-ment. Main virtue is low cost but aluminium plugs corrode badly if used outside.

COAXIAL CONNECTORS *(continued)*

Type	Impedance (Ω)	Maximum freq. (MHz)	Max. peak voltage (V)	Suitable cable	Notes
Phono	—	—	—	—	American connector originally designed for audio use. Often found on Japanese hf/vhf transceivers for low power outputs.
GR	50	1,000	—	—	Constant impedance sexless connectors. Most commonly used on measuring equipment.

Part 6

Radio and tv services

THE FREQUENCY SPECTRUM

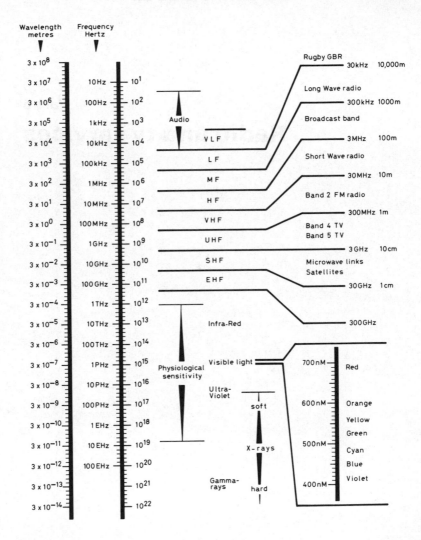

DESIGNATION OF RADIO EMISSIONS

The World Administrative Radio Conference in 1979 (Geneva) agreed a new system of designation for radio transmissions, which became operational on 1 January 1982.

Three symbols are used to describe the class of emission. The first symbol describes the type of modulation of the main carrier, the second symbol indicates the nature of the signal(s) modulating the main carrier and the third symbol indicates the type of information to be transmitted.

The Radio Regulations also require emission characteristics to contain information on bandwidth employed. A new system of bandwidth designation has been introduced; this is a four-symbol code, consisting of three numerals to express the bandwidth and a letter to denote the unit of frequency; the letter is in the position of the decimal point.

Bandwidth

Bandwidths are assigned standard code letters:

H Bandwidths between 0·001 and 999 Hz
K   1·00   and 999 kHz
M   1·00   and 999 MHz
G   1·00   and 999 GHz

Examples:	0·5 Hz	is shown as	H500
	50 Hz		50H0
	250 Hz		250H
	2·4 kHz		2K40
	7 kHz		7K00
	455 kHz		455K
	1·2 MHz		1M20
	22 MHz		22M0

Designation of emission

FIRST SYMBOL—Type of modulation of the main carrier

N   Emission of an unmodulated carrier

Emission in which the main carrier is amplitude-modulated (including cases where sub-carriers are angle-modulated)

A   Double-sideband
H   Single-sideband, full carrier
R   Single-sideband, reduced or variable level carrier
J   Single-sideband, suppressed carrier
B   Independent sideband
C   Vestigial sideband

Emission in which the main carrier is angle-modulated

F   Frequency modulation
G   Phase modulation
D   Emission in which the main carrier is amplitude and angle-modulated, either simultaneously or in pre-established sequence

Emission of pulses

P   Unmodulated sequence of pulses
K   A sequence of pulses modulated in amplitude
L   A sequence of pulses modulated in width/duration
M   A sequence of pulses modulated in position/phase
Q   A sequence of pulses in which the carrier is angle-modulated during the period of the pulse

V   A sequence of pulses which is a combination of the foregoing or is produced by other means
W   Cases not covered above in which an emission consists of the main carrier modulated either simultaneously or in a pre-established sequence of a combination of two or more of the following modes: amplitude, angle, pulse
X   Cases not otherwise covered

SECOND SYMBOL—Nature of signal(s) modulating the main carrier

0   No modulating signal
1   A single channel containing quantized or digital information without the use of a modulating sub-carrier
2   A single channel containing quantized or digital information with the use of a modulating sub-carrier (excluding time-division multiplex)
3   A single channel containing analogue information
7   Two or more channels containing quantized or digital information
8   Two or more channels containing analogue information
9   Composite system with one or more channels containing quantized or digital information, together with one or more channels containing analogue information
X   Cases not otherwise covered

THIRD SYMBOL—Type of information to be transmitted

N   No information transmitted
A   Telegraphy, for aural reception
B   Telegraphy, for automatic reception
C   Facsimile
D   Data transmission, telemetry, telecommand
E   Telephony (including sound broadcasting)
F   Television (video)
W   Combination of any of the above
X   Cases not otherwise covered

Note Modulation used for short periods and for incidental purposes (such as, in many cases, for identification or calling) may be ignored provided that the necessary bandwidth is not thereby increased

Common symbols

N0N	CW no modulation
A1A	CW keyed carrier
A2A	MCW double-sideband keyed tone
R2A	MCW single-sideband reduced carrier
H2A	MCW single-sideband full-carrier keyed tone
J2A	MCW single-sideband suppressed-carrier keyed tone
A3E	AM double-sideband telephony
R3E	Single-sideband reduced-carrier telephony
B8E	Two independent sidebands telephony
H3E	Compatible a.m. single sideband plus full carrier telephony
J3E	Single-sideband suppressed-carrier telephony
F1B	FSK without use of modulating audio frequency
F2B	FSK with use of modulating audio frequency
F3E	FM telephony

FREQUENCY BAND DESIGNATIONS

	New		Old
A	0–250 MHz	P	80–390 MHz
B	250–500 MHz	L	390–2,500 MHz
C	500–1,000 MHz	S	2·5–4·1 GHz
D	1–2 GHz	C	4·1–7 GHz
E	2–3 GHz	X	7–11·5 GHz
F	3–4 GHz	J	11·5–18 GHz
G	4–6 GHz	K	18–33 GHz
H	6–8 GHz	Q	33–40 GHz
I	8–10 GHz	O	40–60 GHz
J	10–20 GHz	V	60–90 GHz
K	20–40 GHz		
L	40–60 GHz		
M	60–100 GHz		

Notes
(i) Each band is subdivided into 10 equal channels numbered 1–10. To indicate a narrower band of frequencies, use the letter followed by the appropriate channel figure.

Examples:
B1	250–275 MHz
B2	275–300 MHz
B9	450–475 MHz
B10	475–500 MHz
J1	10–11 GHz
K2	22–24 GHz
M3	68–72 GHz

(ii) To specify a precise frequency, identify designator letter and channel figure then add the megahertz necessary counted from the lowest channel frequency.

Examples: 260 MHz B1 plus 10
10,500 MHz J1 plus 500

(iii) To ensure that the upper and lower limit frequencies relevant to each letter designator are not included in two adjacent bands, the upper limit is taken to mean "up to but not including".

Example: Band A covers 0–249·999 MHz

ISO 7-BIT DATA INTERCHANGE CODE (CCITT ALPHABET NO 5)

Hexa-decimal	Abbrevia-tion	Meaning	Hexa-decimal	Abbrevia-tion	Meaning
00	NUL	Null	40	@	—
01	SOH	Start heading	41	A	—
02	STX	Start of text	42	B	—
03	ETX	End of text	43	C	—
04	EOT	End of transmission	44	D	—
05	ENQ	Enquiry	45	E	—
06	ACK	Acknowledge	46	F	—
07	BEL	Bell	47	G	—
08	BS	Backspace	48	H	—
09	HT	Horizontal tabulation	49	I	—
0A	LF	Line feed	4A	J	—
0B	VT	Vertical tabulation	4B	K	—
0C	FF	Form feed	4C	L	—
0D	CR	Carriage return	4D	M	—
0E	SO	Shift-out	4E	N	—
0F	SI	Shift-in	4F	O	—
10	DLE	Data link escape	50	P	—
11	(DC1)	(Device control)	51	Q	—
12	(DC2)	(Device control)	52	R	—
13	(DC3)	(Device control)	53	S	—
14	(DC4)	(Device control)	54	T	—
15	NAK	Negative acknowledge	55	U	—
16	SYN	Synchronous idle	56	V	—
17	ETB	End of transmission block	57	W	—
			58	X	—
18	CAN	Cancel	59	Y	—
19	EM	End of medium	5A	Z	—
1A	SUB	Substitute character	5B	[	—
1B	ESC	Escape	5C	\	—
1C	FS	File separator	5D	]	—
1D	GS	Group separator	5E	^	—
1E	RS	Record separator	5F	⎵	—
1F	US	Unit separator	60	`	—
20	(space)	—	61	a	—
21	!	—	62	b	—
22	"	—	63	c	—
23	# or £	—	64	d	—
24	$	—	65	e	—
25	%	—	66	f	—
26	&	—	67	g	—
27	'	—	68	h	—
28	(	—	69	i	—
29	)	—	6A	j	—
2A	*	—	6B	k	—
2B	+	—	6C	l	—
2C	,	—	6D	m	—
2D	−	—	6E	n	—
2E	.	—	6F	o	—
2F	/	—	70	p	—
30	0	—	71	q	—
31	1	—	72	r	—
32	2	—	73	s	—
33	3	—	74	t	—
34	4	—	75	u	—
35	5	—	76	v	—
36	6	—	77	w	—
37	7	—	78	x	—
38	8	—	79	y	—
39	9	—	7A	z	—
3A	:	—	7B	{	—
3B	;	—	7C			—
3C	<	—	7D	}	—
3D	=	—	7E	~	—
3E	>	—	7F	DEL	Delete
3F	?	—			

AMATEUR RTTY STANDARDS

(*a*) RTTY signalling speeds to be 45·45, 50, 75 and 100 bauds.

(*b*) RTTY transmission mode to be fsk (fm) on all bands with a preferred shift of 170 Hz on hf bands (ie 30 MHz and below), and 170/850 Hz on vhf. Mark signal to be the higher radiated radio frequency.

(*c*) Reception of rtty by means of a two-tone system is encouraged for optimum communication effectiveness.

(*d*) In the interests of bandwidth efficiency and communication effectiveness afsk operation on am transmitters is *not* encouraged. Where afsk operation is used on vhf/uhf for local and autostart communication the use of fm transmitters is strongly encouraged. In the interests of bandwidth efficiency the use of a standard afsk shift of 170 Hz is recommended. In this case the standard afsk tones should be 1,275 Hz (space) and 1,445 Hz (mark). If 850 Hz shift is used the mark tone should be 2,125 Hz.

SSTV STANDARDS

Parameter	50 Hz Mains	60 Hz Mains
Line speed	50 Hz ÷ 3 = 16·6 Hz (60 ms)	60 Hz ÷ 4 = 15 Hz (66 ms)
Line performance	120	120
Frame speed	7·2 s	8 s
Picture aspect ratio	1 to 1	1 to 1
Scanning direction		
Horizontal	left to right	left to right
Vertical	top to bottom	top to bottom
Sync pulse duration		
Horizontal	5 ms	5 ms
Vertical	30 ms	30 ms
Subcarrier frequency		
Sync	1,200 Hz	1,200 Hz
Black	1,500 Hz	1,500 Hz
White	2,300 Hz	2,300 Hz
Required transmission bandwidth	1·0 to 2·5 kHz	1·0 to 2·5 kHz

PHONETIC ALPHABET

A	Alfa	J	Juliett	S	Sierra
B	Bravo	K	Kilo	T	Tango
C	Charlie	L	Lima	U	Uniform
D	Delta	M	Mike	V	Victor
E	Echo	N	November	W	Whiskey
F	Foxtrot	O	Oscar	X	X-ray
G	Golf	P	Papa	Y	Yankee
H	Hotel	Q	Quebec	Z	Zulu
I	India	R	Romeo		

Amateurs are not restricted to any particular phonetic code. They should, however, be conversant with the above which is now regularized for world-wide use. (ITU Regulations, Geneva, 1968.)

WATTS/dBW CONVERSION

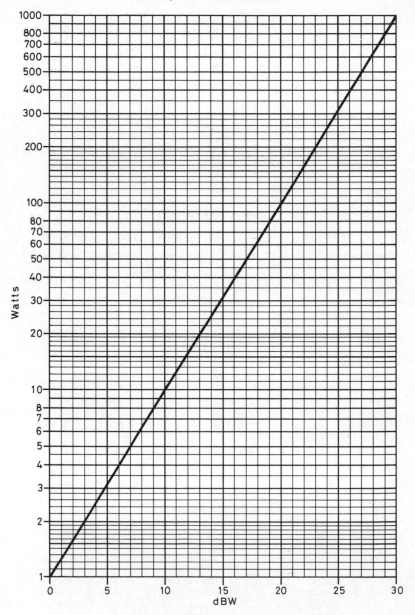

STANDARD FREQUENCY STATIONS

The standard frequencies are maintained to an accuracy of typically one part in 10^{-11}. However, if the sky-wave is used there could be a larger error in reception due to Doppler shift and there will be fading of the signal. These problems can be avoided by using a low-frequency transmission such as those from MSF or WWVB.

Times are announced in gmt or utc (coordinated universal time), the latter being the official standard time as maintained by atomic clocks. Any difference or error is likely to be of the order of 0·1 ms. Since the earth's rotation is somewhat irregular, astronomical time (ut1) can vary slightly from utc and some stations broadcast the difference (dut1).

For further information on the facilities provided by these stations see the *List of Radiodetermination and Special Service Stations* published by the ITU.

ARGENTINA

Callsign: LOL2.
Standard frequencies: 5,000, 10,000, 15,000 kHz simultaneous (1100–1200, 1400–1500, 1700–1800, 2000–2100, 2300–2400).
Time interval signals: 3 min of 1 kHz and 440 Hz modulation (A2A) alternately, commencing all the minutes which are multiples of 5, except the 55th minute, this being reserved for a precision time signal which consists of a 5 ms pulse every second for 3 min (except the 59th second) at 1 kHz.
Announcements: In between the 3 min tone periods. For the first minute a dut1 code is sent. For the second minute the station callsign in morse code is sent followed by the origin of the transmission, ie "Observatorio Naval Buenos Aires".
Location: Buenos Aires.

AUSTRALIA

Callsign: VNG.
Standard frequencies: 4,500 kHz (0945–2130), 7,500 kHz (2245–2230), 12,000 kHz (2145–0930).
Time interval signals: Seconds pulses are normally 50 cycles of 1 kHz modulation (A2A); shortened pulses precede the minute which is marked by 500 cycles of 1 kHz.
Announcements: Voice identification (A3E) precedes the hour and quarter hours.
Location: Lyndhurst, Victoria.

CANADA

Callsign: CHU.
Standard frequencies: 3,330, 7,335, 14,670 kHz simultaneous (24 h).
Time interval signals: Seconds pulses are 300 cycles of 1 kHz tone (A2H): the beginning of each pulse marks the exact second. The zero pulse of each minute is 0·5 s long, and the zero pulse of each hour is 1 s long. The sequence and form of the pulses are also modified as follows:
1. The 29th pulse of each minute is omitted.
2. The 1st to 9th pulses are omitted from the first minute of each hour.
3. The 1st to 15th pulses of each minute may be split so as to indicate the difference dut1 between ut1 and utc in magnitude to the nearest 0·1 s and in sign.
4. The 31st to 39th pulses of each minute are shortened to 10 cycles of 1 kHz

and each is followed by a frequency shift code which can be employed to synchronize remote clocks to utc (NRC).
Announcements: The 51st to 59th pulses of each minute are omitted. During this time station indentification and time are announced in both French and English.
Location: Ottawa.

FRANCE

Callsign: FFH.
Standard frequencies: 2,500 kHz (0800–1625 except Sundays).
Time interval signals: Seconds pulses are five cycles of 1 kHz modulation (A2A), except at the zero second of each minute when the total duration is 0·5 s.
Announcements: The callsign is transmitted on morse code (A2A) after the 30th second of 0, 10, 20, 30, 40 and 50 minutes of the hour.
Location: S Assise.

ITALY

Callsign: IBF.
Standard frequency: 5,000 kHz (from minute 45 to 60 of 0700, 0900, 1000, 1100, 1200, 1300, 1400, 1500, 1600, 1700, 1800). The schedule is advanced by 1 h in summer.
Time interval signals: Seconds pulses are five cycles of 1 kHz modulation (A2A). These pulses are repeated seven times on the minute.
Announcements: Voice announcement (A3A) at the beginning and end of each 15 min transmission. Time announcement by morse code every 10 min beginning at 0000.
Location: Turin.

JAPAN

Callsign: JJY.
Standard frequencies: 2,500, 5,000, 10,000, 15,000 kHz simultaneous (24 h).
Time interval signals: These are active for the 5 min following each multiple of 10 min and are followed by the standard frequency only radiated for 4 min. (The transmitter does not radiate between the 35th and 39th minute). Seconds pulses are 5 ms of 1·6 kHz modulation. The beginning of each pulse marks the exact second. (There are 1 kHz pulses in between the second markers). The minute is a 5 ms pulse of 1·6 kHz preceded by a 655 ms pulse of 600 Hz.
Announcements: At the minute preceding multiples of 10 min, the callsign is sent twice by morse code at 1 kHz modulation followed by Japanese Standard Time (four figures) once. This information is then transmitted by voice in Japanese. A warning of radio propagation is then sent by morse code at 1 kHz modulation ("N" denotes normal, "U" unstable, "W" warning).
Location: Tokyo.

UNITED KINGDOM

Callsign: MSF.
Standard frequencies: 2,500, 5,000, 10,000 kHz simultaneous (24 h).
Time interval signals: Seconds pulses are five cycles of 1 kHz modulation (A2A) which is lengthened to 100 ms at each minute. These signals are radiated for the 5 min following each multiple of 10 min.

Announcements: The callsign is given twice in morse code (A2A) during the 5 s immediately preceding each transmission period.
Location: Rugby.

Callsign: MSF.
Standard frequency: 60 kHz (24 h).
Time interval signals: Carrier interruptions (A1A) lasting 100 ms at each second and lengthened to 500 ms at each minute. The start of the interruption denotes the precise time.
Announcements: Each minute is also indicated by a bcd signal inserted in the 500 ms carrier interruption. This consists of 13 bits at 100 bit/s giving hour and minute information, together with a final parity bit. The signal can be decoded by suitable circuitry to give a continuous clock display. No transmissions are made for 5 s preceding each hour when the callsign is given in morse code (A1A).
Location: Rugby.

USA

Callsigns: WWV and WWVH.
Standard frequencies: 2,500, 5,000, 10,000, 15,000, 20,000 kHz (plus 25,000 kHz from WWV only), simultaneous (24 h).
Time interval signals: Seconds pulses are five cycles of 1 kHz on WWV (or six cycles of 1,200 Hz on WWVH) and occur each second except the 29th and 59th seconds. A long pulse (0·8 s) marks the beginning of each minute. A modified IRIG-H time code is broadcast continuously on a 100 Hz subcarrier. The format is 1 pulse per second with a 1 min time frame. It gives a day of the year, hours and minutes in bcd form.
Announcements: The time in gmt is announced once a minute with a male voice at WWV and a female voice at WWVH. The WWVH announcement occurs at 15 s before the minute, while that of WWV occurs at 7·5 s before the minute. Propagation forecasts are sent by voice during the 15th minute of each hour from WWV. They are short-term forecasts in the following format: "The radio propagation quality forecast at . . . (0100, 0700, 1300, or 1900) is . . . (excellent, very good, good etc). Current geomagnetic activity is . . . (quiet, unsettled or disturbed)". Geophysical alerts are sent by voice during the 19th minute from WWV and the 46th minute from WWVH. These describe events in progress followed by a summary of events over the last 24 h.
Locations: Fort Collins, Colorado (WWV) and Kekaha-Kauai, Hawaii (WWVH).

Callsign: WWVB.
Standard frequency: 60 kHz (24 h).
Time interval signals: One pulse per second special binary code giving minutes, hours, days, and dut1.
Location: Fort Collins, Colorado.

USSR

Callsign: RWM.
Standard frequencies: 4,996, 9,996, 14,996 kHz simultaneous (24 h).
Time interval signals: Second pulses from 10 min 00 s to 19 min 55 s and 40 min 00 s to 49 min 55 s. Signals at the beginning of each minute are prolonged to 0·5 s. From 20 min 00 s to 29 min 55 s and 50 min 00 s to 59 min 55 s there are signals with a 10 Hz repetition rate. Signals at the beginning of each minute are prolonged.
Announcement: The callsign is sent at 9 min and 39 min past each hour.
Location: Moscow.

WWV SCHEDULE

WWV BROADCAST FORMAT

VIA TELEPHONE (303) 499-7111
(NOT A TOLL-FREE NUMBER)

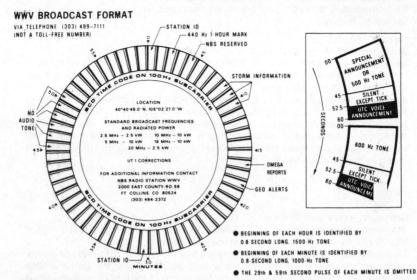

● BEGINNING OF EACH HOUR IS IDENTIFIED BY
0.8-SECOND LONG, 1500-Hz TONE.

● BEGINNING OF EACH MINUTE IS IDENTIFIED BY
0.8-SECOND LONG, 1000-Hz TONE.

● THE 29th & 59th SECOND PULSE OF EACH MINUTE IS OMITTED.

WWVH BROADCAST FORMAT

VIA TELEPHONE (808) 335-4363
(NOT A TOLL-FREE NUMBER)

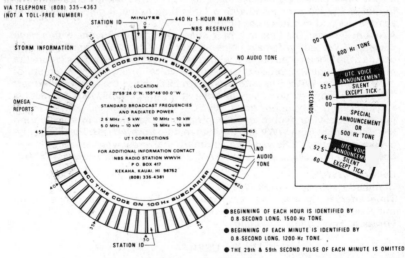

● BEGINNING OF EACH HOUR IS IDENTIFIED BY
0.8-SECOND LONG, 1500-Hz TONE.

● BEGINNING OF EACH MINUTE IS IDENTIFIED BY
0.8-SECOND LONG, 1200-Hz TONE.

● THE 29th & 59th SECOND PULSE OF EACH MINUTE IS OMITTED.

TIME-OF-DAY INFORMATION ON RUGBY MSF

Fast code

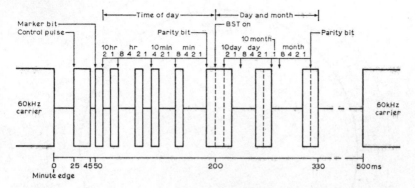

Fig 1. Fast-code information inserted in Rugby MSF standard frequency 60 kHz transmission. The time indicated in bit form is 1248 bst, 22 May.

The 60 kHz carrier is interrupted for 100 ms at each second and for 500 ms at each minute. The time of day in bcd code is inserted into this 500 ms "minute window." As can be seen from Fig 1 the code consists of 13 bits of bcd information giving hours and minutes in the Universal Time Coordinated (utc) scale with the addition of a final parity bit, each bit being 10 ms wide. This time code is preceded by two pulses; a control pulse 20 ms wide delayed 25 ms from the start of the minute edge shown in the figure and a marker pulse 10 ms wide which starts 5 ms after the control pulse.

Slow code

The slow-code time-and-date information is transmitted over the period between the 17th and 59th seconds, as shown in Fig 2. The carrier drop-out pulses, occurring each second, are coded for this transmission by extending their width from the normal 100 ms (binary "0") to 200 ms (binary "1"). Normal bcd coding is used for the transmitted information, consisting of the year, month, day-of-month, day-of-week, hour and minute. A group of "minute identifier" pulses are then transmitted, including the parity bits for the slow-code time-and-date information.

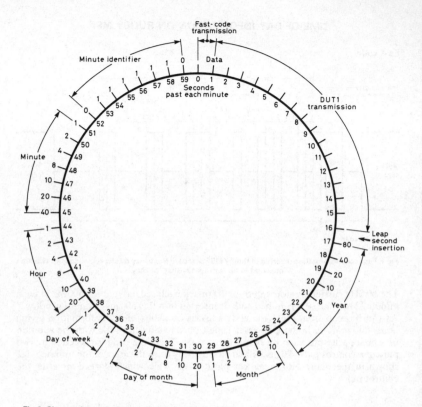

Fig 2. Slow-code transmissions inserted in Rugby MSF standard frequency 60 kHz transmission

UK CITIZENS BANDS

27 MHz (Specification MPT 1320)

Chan	MHz	Chan	MHz	Chan	MHz	Chan	MHz
1	27·60125	11	27·70125	21	27·80125	31	27·90125
2	27·61125	12	27·71125	22	27·81125	32	27·91125
3	27·62125	13	27·72125	23	27·82125	33	27·92125
4	27·63125	14	27·73125	24	27·83125	34	27·93125
5	27·64125	15	27·74125	25	27·84125	35	27·94125
6	27·65125	16	27·75125	26	27·85125	36	27·95125
7	27·66125	17	27·76125	27	27·86125	37	27·96125
8	27·67125	18	27·77125	28	27·87125	38	27·97125
9	27·68125	19	27·78125	29	27·88125	39	27·98125
10	27·69125	20	27·79125	30	27·89125	40	27·99125

P_{erp} = 4 W. Mod = frequency modulation (F3E). f = 27·6–27·99 MHz (10 kHz spacing)

934 MHz (Specification MPT 1321)

Chan	MHz	Chan	MHz	Chan	MHz	Chan	MHz
1	934·025	6	934·275	11	934·525	16	934·775
2	934·075	7	934·325	12	934·575	17	934·825
3	934·125	8	934·375	13	934·625	18	934·875
4	934·175	9	934·425	14	934·675	19	934·925
5	934·225	10	934·475	15	934·725	20	934·975

P_{erp} = 25 W (3 W hand held). Mod = frequency modulation (F3E). f = 934·025–934·975 MHz (50 kHz spacing)

COASTAL RADIO STATIONS

Station	Callsign	Frequencies (MHz)	VHF chans
Anglesey	GLV	1·925	16, 26
Wick	GKR	1·927, 3·610	16, 26
Niton	GNI	1·834	4, 16, 25, 28
Lands End	GLD	1·841	16, 27
North Foreland	GNF	1·848	5, 16, 26, 28
Stonehaven	GND	1·856, 1·946	16, 26
*Hebrides		1·866	
Humber	GKZ	1·869, 3·738, 3·778	16, 26
Port Patrick	GPK	1·883, 3·610	16, 27
Ilfracombe	GIL	1·885	16, 25
Cullercoats	GCC	1·838	16, 26
Malin Head	EJM	1·827	
Valentia	EJK	1·927	
Ostend	OST	1·817, 1·820, 1·908, 3·629, 3·632, 3·684	
Boulogne	FFB	3·795	
Brest le Conquet	FFU	1·806, 3·722	
Scheveningen	PCH	1·862, 1·890, 1·939, 3·673	

* Controlled by Stonehaven with same callsign.

Distress frequencies: 2·182 MHz telephony, 500 kHz cw.
Silent periods for distress listening on 2·182 MHz and vhf channel 16: 3 min at the hour and half hour. On 500 kHz: 3 min at 15 and 45 min past the hour.
Coastguard and lifeboat use vhf channel 0 (156·000 MHz).

COASTAL RADIO SERVICES

Channel	Transmit (MHz)	Receive (MHz)	Channel	Transmit (MHz)	Receive (MHz)
4	160·8	156·2	25	161·85	157·25
5	160·85	156·25	26	161·9	157·3
7	160·95	156·35	27	161·95	157·35
16	156·8	156·8	28	162·0	157·4

Navigational warnings
0403, 0803, 1603 and 2003 gmt broadcast by Wick, North Foreland, Lands End and Malin.
0433, 0833, 1633 and 2033 gmt broadcast by Humber, Niton, Port Patrick and Valentia.

Gale warnings
0303, 0903, 1503 and 2103 gmt.

Weather bulletins
0803 and 2003 gmt by Cullercoats, Lands End, North Foreland, Oban and Wick.
0833 and 2033 gmt by Humber, Ilfracombe, Niton, Port Patrick, Stonehaven and Valentia.

MARITIME VHF SERVICES

Channel numbers, related frequency in megahertz, and use in order of priority are as follows. It will be seen that any one channel may be put to different uses.

Calling and safety: Chan 16 (Coastguard Chan 67)
Intership: Chan 6, 8, 10, 13, 9, 67, 77, 15, 17 (Marinas use 157·85 MHz)
Port operations (simplex): Chan 12, 14, 11, 13, 9, 68, 71, 74, 10, 67, 69, 73, 17, 15
Port operations (duplex): Chan 20, 22, 18, 19, 21, 5, 7, 2, 3, 1, 4, 78, 82, 79, 81, 80, 60, 63, 66, 62, 65, 64, 61, 84
Public correspondence: Chan 26, 27, 25, 24, 23, 28, 4, 1, 3, 2, 7, 5, 84, 87, 86, 83, 85, 88, 61, 64, 65, 62, 66, 63, 60, 82

Chan		Transmitter frequency (MHz)		Chan		Transmitter frequency (MHz)		Chan		Transmitter frequency (MHz)	
		Ship	Shore			Ship	Shore			Ship	Shore
	60	156·025	160·625		70	156·525			80	157·025	161·625
1		156·050	160·650	11		156·550					156·050
	61	156·075	160·675		71	156·575		21		157·050	OR
											161·650
2		156·100	160·700	12		156·600			81	157·075	161·675
	62	156·125	160·725		72	156·625		22		157·100	161·700
3		156·150	160·750	13		156·650			82	157·125	161·725
	63	156·175	160·775		73	156·675					156·150
4		156·200	160·800	14		156·700		23		157·150	OR
											161·750
	64	156·225	160·825		74	156·725					156·175
5		156·250	160·850	15		156·750		83		157·175	OR
											161·775
	65	156·275	160·875		75	156·7625	156·7875	24		157·200	161·800
6		156·300		16		156·800	156·800		84	157·225	161·825
	66	156·325	160·925		76	156·8125	156·8375	25		157·250	161·850
7		156·350	160·950	17		156·850			85	157·275	161·875
	67	156·375			77	156·875		26		157·300	161·900
8		156·400		18		156·900	161·500		86	157·325	161·925
	68	156·425			78	156·925	161·525	27		157·350	161·950
9		156·450		19		156·950	161·550		87	157·375	161·975
	69	156·475			79	156·975	161·575	28		157·400	162·000
10		156·500		20		157·000	161·600		88	157·425	162·025

75 and 76 guard channels for 16. Simplex channels are shown by the single frequency given.

BROADCAST RADIO SERVICES

UK LONG AND MEDIUM WAVE BROADCAST FREQUENCIES

Programme	Frequencies (kHz)
BBC Radio 1	1,053, 1,089, 1,107, 1,485
BBC Radio 2	693, 909, 1,026, 1,116 (CI)
BBC Radio 3	1,215
BBC Radio 4	200, 603, 720, 756, 774, 1,449, 1,485
BBC Radio 4 Scotland	585, 657, 810, 990
BBC Radio 4 Wales	882
BBC Overseas Service	648
Manx Radio (commercial)	1,295, 1,594
Radio Ulster	1,341

UK MEDIUM WAVE LOCAL RADIO STATIONS

BBC	Frequency (kHz)	Power (kW)	BBC	Frequency (kHz)	Power (kW)
Brighton	1,485	1	Leeds	774	0·5
Bristol	1,548	2	Leicester	837	7
Cambridgeshire	1,026	0·5	Lincolnshire	1,368	2·0
Cleveland	1,548	1	London	1,458	50
Cornwall	657	0·5	Manchester	1,458	0·5
	630	2	Merseyside	1,485	2
Cumbria	756	1	Newcastle	1,458	2
Whitehaven relay	1,458	0·5	Norfolk	855	1
Derby	1,116	0·5	Northampton	1,107	0·5
Devon	801	2	Nottingham	1,584	0·25
Furness	837	1	Oxford	1,485	0·5
Guernsey	1,116	0·5	Sheffield	1,035	1
Humberside	1,485	1·5	Solent	1,359	0·25
Jersey	1,035	0·5	Stoke-on-Trent	1,503	1
Kent	1,035	0·5	Sussex	1,485	1
Lancashire	1,557	0·25	West Midlands	1,458	7

ILR	Fre-quency (kHz)	Power (kW)	ILR	Fre-quency (kHz)	Power (kW)
Aberdeen (North Sound)	1,035	0·5	Londonderry (Northside		
Ayr (West Sound)	1,035	0·32	Sound)	990	0·25
Belfast (Downtown Radio)	1,026	1·0	Luton (Chilton Radio)	828	0·27
Birmingham (BRMB Radio)	1,152	0·8	Maidstone (Northdown		
Bradford (Pennine Radio)	1,278	0·1	Radio)	954	0·25
Brighton (Southern Sound)	1,332	0·5	Manchester (Piccadilly Radio)	1,151	0·35
Bristol (Radio West)	1,260	1·6	Newport (Gwent		
Bournemouth (Two Counties			Broadcasting)	1,305	0·2
Radio)	823	0·5	Norwich (Radio		
Bury St Edmunds			Broadland)	1,152	0·25
(Saxon Radio)	1,251	0·76	Nottingham (Radio Trent)	999	0·2
Cardiff (Cardiff Broadcasting)	1,359	0·25	Peterborough (Hereward		
Cheltenham (Severn Sound)	774	0·2	Radio)	1,332	0·5
Coventry (Mercia Sound)	1,359	0·1	Plymouth (Plymouth Sound)	1,152	0·5
Dundee/Perth (Radio Tay)	1,161	0·5	Portsmouth (Radio Victory)	1,170	0·2
Edinburgh (Radio Forth)	1,548	2	Preston (Red Rose		
Exeter/Torbay (Devon Air			Radio)	999	0·8
Radio)	666	0·5	Reading (Radio 210)	1,435	0·1
Glasgow (Radio Clyde)	1,152	2	Reigate (Radio Mercury)	1,521	0·2
Guildford (County			Sheffield & Rotherham (Radio		
Sound)	1,476	0·5	Hallam)	1,548	0·3
Hereford (Radio Wyvern)	1,530	0·44	Southend (Essex Radio)	1,431	0·35
Humberside (Viking Radio)	1,161	0·25	Stoke (Signal Radio)	1,170	0·2
Ipswich (Radio Orwell)	1,170	0·3	Swansea (Swansea Sound)	1,169	0·8
Inverness (Moray Firth Radio)	1,107	1·0	Teesside (Radio Tees)	1,170	0·5
Leeds (Centre Radio)	828		Tyne/Wear (Metro Radio)	1,152	1
Leicester (Centre Radio)	1,260	0·29	Wolverhampton (Beacon		
Liverpool (Radio City)	1,546	1·2	Radio)	990	0·1
London (Capital Radio)	1,548	27·5	Wrexham (Marcher		
(LBC)	1,151	5·5	Sound)	1,260	0·64

Many stations use directional antennas.

UK VHF FM STATIONS
BAND II

Station	Frequencies (MHz) R1/2	R3	R4*	Polar- ization	Max erp (kW)
ENGLAND AND ISLE OF MAN					
Belmont	88·8s	90·9s	93·1s	H	8
Holme Moss	89·3s	91·5s	93·7s	M	240
Douglas (IOM)	84·4	90·6	92·8	M	12
Kendal	88·7s	90·9s	93·1s	H	0·025
Morecambe Bay	90·0s	92·2s	94·4s	M	11
Sheffield	89·9s	92·1s	94·3s	M	0·32
Wensleydale	88·3s	90·5s	92·7s	H	0·025
Windermere	88·6s	90·8s	93·0s	H	0·02
Oxford	89·5s	91·7s	93·9s	H	22
Peterborough	90·1s	92·3s	94·5s	M	44
Cambridge	88·9s	91·1s	93·3s	M	0·26
Northampton	88·9s	91·1s	93·3s	M	0·123
Pontop Pike	88·5s	90·7s	92·9s	H	60
Chatton	90·1s	92·3s	94·5s	M	5·6
Weardale	89·7s	91·9s	94·1s	H	0·1
Whitby	89·6s	91·8s	94·0s	H	0·04
Rowridge	88·5s	90·7s	92·9s	H	60
Ventnor	89·4s	91·7s	93·8s	H	0·02
Sandale	88·1s	90·3s	94·7s	H	120
Sutton Coldfield	88·3s	90·5s	92·7s	M	240
Churchdown Hill	89·0s	91·2s	93·4s	M	0·072
Hereford	89·7s	91·9s	94·1s	H	0·026
Swingate (Dover)	90·0s	92·4s	94·4s	M	10
Talconeston	89·7s	91·9s	94·1s	H	120
Wenvoe	89·9s	92·1s	94·3s	M	240
Bath	88·8s	91·0s	93·2s	M	0·07
Brighton	90·1s	92·3s	94·5s	M	0·5
Bristol (Ilchester Crescent)	89·3s	91·5s	93·7s	M	1·3
Guildford	88·1s	90·3s	92·5s	M	3
Olivers Mount	89·9s	92·1s	94·3s	M	0·25
St Thomas (Exeter)	89·0s	91·2s	93·4s	M	0·055
Wharfedale	88·4s	90·6s	92·8s	M	0·04
Wrotham	89·1s	91·3s	93·5s	M	240
Les Platons (CI)	91·1	94·75	97·1	M	16
North Hessary Tor	88·1s	90·3s	92·5	H	80
Barnstaple	88·5s	90·7s	92·7s	H	1
Okehampton	88·7s	90·9s	93·1	M	0·07
Redruth	89·7s	91·9s	94·1	H	9
Isles of Scilly	88·8s	91·0s	93·2	M	0·06
NORTHERN IRELAND					
Ballycastle	89·0s	91·2s	93·5s	H	0·04
Brougher Mountain	88·9s	91·1s	93·3s	M	5
Divis	90·1s	92·3s	94·5s	H	60
Kilkeel	88·8s	91·05	93·2s	H	0·025
Larne	89·1s	91·3s	93·5s	H	0·015
Londonderry	88·3s	90·55s	92·7sf	H	13

Station	Frequencies (MHz) R1/2	R3	R4*	Polar- ization	Max erp (kW)
Maddybenny More	88·7s	90·9s	93·1s	H	0·03
Newry South	89·5	91·7	93·9	M	0·044
Rostrevor Forest	88·6	90·8	93·0	M	0·064
SCOTLAND					
Ashkirk	89·1s	91·3s	93·5st	H	18
Ayr	88·7s	90·9s	93·1s	H	0·055
Bowmore	88·1	90·3	92·5	V	0·08
Campbeltown	88·6s	90·8s	93·0	H	0·035
Durris	89·4s	91·6s	93·8sa	M	2
Forfar	88·3s	90·5s	92·7s	H	10
Girvan	88·9s	91·5s	93·3s	V	0·1
Innerleithan	89·5s	91·7s	93·9st	M	0·02
Keeleylang Hill	89·3s	91·5s	93·7sao	M	40
Kirk O'Shotts	89·9s	92·1s	94·3s	H	120
Knock More	88·2s	90·4s	92·6sh	M	0·5
Lethanhill	88·3s	90·5s	92·7s	M	0·2
Lochgilphead	88·3s	90·5s	97·9 (92·7s)	H	0·01
Milburn Muir	88·8s	91·0s	93·2s	H	0·025
Peebles	88·4s	90·6s	92·8st	M	0·01
Perth	89·0	91·2	93·4	H	0·012
Pitlochry	89·2	91·4	93·6	H	0·2
Port Ellen	89·4	91·6	93·8	V	0·01
Rosneath	89·2s	91·4s	93·6s	H	0·025
Rothesay	88·5s	90·7s	92·9s	M	0·72
South Knapdale	89·3s	91·5s	98·9 (93·7s)	H	1·1
Strachur	86·6s	90·8s	98·2 (93·0s)	M	0·02
Tullich	90·1s	92·3s	94·5sa	M	0·042
Meldrum	88·7s	90·9s	93·1sa	H	60
Bressay	88·3	90·5	92·7aoz	H	10
Rosemarkie	89·6s	91·8s	94·0sh	H	12
Ballachulish	88·1	90·3	97·7 (92·0h)	H	0·015
Fort William	89·3	91·5	98·9 (93·7h)	H	1·5
Glengorm	89·5	91·7	99·1 (93·9h)	H	1·1
Grantown	89·8s	92·0s	94·6sh	H	0·35
Kingussie	89·1s	91·3s	93·5sh	H	0·035
Kinlockleeven	89·7	91·9	99·3 (94·1h)	H	0·002
Mallaig	88·1	88·1	97·7 (90·3hn)	H	0·02
Melvaig	89·1	91·3	98·7 (93·5hn)	H	22
Oban	88·9	91·1	98·5 (93·3h)	M	5
Penfiler	89·5s	91·7	98·1 (93·9hn)	H	0·006
Skriaig	88·5	90·7	98·1 (92·9hn)	H	10
Sandale	88·1s	90·3s	92·5sd	H	120
Cambret Hill	88·7s	90·9s	93·1sd	H	0·064
Stranraer	89·5s	91·7s	93·9sd	V	0·031
WALES					
Blaenplwyf	88·7s	90·9s	93·1s	H	60
Dolgellau	90·1	92·3	94·5	H	0·015
Ffestiniog	88·1s	90·3s	92·5s	H	0·05
Llandifriog	90·1s	92·3s	94·5s	M	0·087
Machynlleth	89·4s	91·3s	93·8s	H	0·06
Haverfordwest	89·3s	91·5s	93·7s	H	10

Station	Frequencies (MHz)			Polar- ization	Max erp (kW)
	R1/2	R3	R4*		
Llandonna	89·6s	91·8s	94·0s	M	24
Betws-y-Coed	88·2	90·4	92·6	H	0·01
Llandinam	90·1s	92·3s	94·5	H	0·02
Llangollen	88·85s	91·05s	93·25s	M	22
Long Mountain	89·6s	91·8s	94·0	H	0·024
Wenvoe	89·9s	92·1s	96·8s	M	240
Abergavenny	88·6s	90·8s	93·0s	H	0·017
Blaenavon	88·5s	90·7s	92·9s	V	0·01
Brecon	88·9s	91·1s	93·3	H	0·01
Carmarthen	88·9s	91·1s	93·3s	M	0·02
Carmel	88·4s	90·6s	92·8s	M	3·2
Ebbw Vale	88·4s	90·6s	92·8s	H	0·01
Kilvey Hill	89·5s	91·7s	93·9s	M	1
Llandrindod Wells	89·1s	91·3s	93·5s	H	1·5
Llanidloes	88·1s	90·3s	92·5s	H	0·005
Pontypool	89·2s	91·4s	93·6s	H	0·026
Varteg Hill	88·9s	91·1s	93·3s	M	0·05
Blaenavon	—	—	103·0sm	M	0·5
Christchurch	—	—	95·1sm	V	0·01
Mynydd Pencarrey	89·7s	91·9s	94·1s	M	0·4
Llanddona	89·6s	91·8s	94·0s	M	24
Llanfyllin	89·1s	91·3s	93·5	M	0·014
Llanrhaeadr-ym- Mochnant	89·8s	92·0s	94·2	M	0·05

* Radio Ulster in Northern Ireland, Radio Scotland in Scotland and Radio Cymru in Wales.
s—transmits stereophonic programmes
a—carries Radio Aberdeen
c—carries Radio Clwyd
d—carries Radio Solway
f—carries Radio Fogle
g—carries Radio Guernsey
h—carries Radio Highland
j—carries Radio Jersey
m—carries Radio Gwent
n—carries Radio nan Eilean
o—carries Radio Orkney
t—carries Radio Tweed
z—carries Radio Shetland
Further information from BBC Engineering Information Department, Broadcasting House, London W1A 1AA.

VHF LOCAL RADIO STATIONS

BBC	Fre-quency (MHz)	ERP (kW)	BBC	Fre-quency (MHz)	ERP (kW)
Radio London	94·9s	16·5	Radio Bristol	95·5	5·0
Medway	96·7	5·5	Humberside	96·9	4·5
Oxford	95·2	4·5	Leeds	92·4	5·2
Birmingham	95·6	5·5	Sheffield main	97·4	5·2
Derby	96·5	5·5	relay	88·6	0·05
relay	94·2	0·01	Blackburn	96·4	1·5
Leicester	95·1	0·3	Manchester	95·1	4·2
Nottingham	95·4s	0·3	Merseyside	95·8	5·0
Stoke-on-Trent	96·1	2·5	Carlisle	95·6	5·0
Brighton	95·3	0·5	Newcastle	95·4	3·5
Solent	96·1	5·0	Cleveland	96·6	5·0

s = stereo programmes.

ILR	Frequency (MHz)	ERP (kW)
Belfast (Downtown Radio)	96·0	1
Birmingham (BRMB Radio)	94·8	2
Bradford (Pennine Radio)	96·0	0·5
Edinburgh (Radio Forth)	96·8	0·5
Glasgow (Radio Clyde)	95·1	3·4
Ipswich (Radio Orwell)	97·1	1
Liverpool (Radio City)	96·7	5
London (Capital Radio)	95·8	2
(LBC)	97·3	2
Manchester (Piccadilly Radio)	97·0	2
Nottingham (Radio Trent)	96·2	0·3
Plymouth (Plymouth Sound)	96·0	1
Portsmouth (Radio Victory)	95·0	0·2
Reading (Thames Valley Broadcasting)	97·0	0·5
Sheffield (Radio Hallam)	95·2	0·1
Rotherham (Radio Hallam)	95·9	0·05
Swansea (Swansea Sound)	95·1	1
Teesside (Radio Tees)	95·0	2
Tyne/Wear (Metro Radio)	97·0	5
Wolverhampton (Beacon Radio)	97·2	1
Aberdeen (North Sound)	96·9	0·25
Ayr (West Sound)	96·2	0·5
Bournemouth (Two Counties Radio)	97·2	0·6
Cardiff (Cardiff Broadcasting)	96·0	0·5
Coventry (Mercia Sound)	95·9	0·25
Dundee/Perth (Radio Tay)	95·8	0·3
	96·4	0·25
Exeter/Torbay (Devon Air Radio)	95·2	0·5
	95·1	0·25
Gloucester/Cheltenham (Severn Sound)	95·0	0·3

ILR	Frequency (MHz)	ERP (kW)
Inverness (Moray Firth Radio)	95·9	1·4
Leeds (Radio Aire)	94·6	
Leicester (Centre Radio)	97·1	0·5
Peterborough (Hereward Radio)	95·7	0·5
Southend/Chelmsford (Essex Radio)	95·3	0·5
Wrexham/Deeside (Marcher Sound)	95·4	0·5

All stations carry stereo programmes.

TELEVISION SERVICES

TELEVISION SYSTEMS

Parameter	A	M	(N)	B	C	G	(H)	I	D K	(K1)	L	E
						System code						
Lines per picture	405	525	(625)	625	625	625		625	625		625	819
Field frequency (Hz)	50	60	(50)	50	50	50		50	50		50	50
Line frequency (Hz)	10,125	15,734	(15,625)	15,625	15,625	15,625		15,625	15,625		15,625	20,475
Video bandwidth (MHz)	3	4·2		5	5	5		5·5	6		6	10
Channel bandwidth (MHz)	5	6		7	7	8		8	8		8	14
Nearest edge of channel relative to vision carrier (MHz)	+1·25	−1·25		−1·25	−1·25	−1·25		−1·25	−1·25		−1·25	±2·83
Sound carrier frequency relative to vision carrier (MHz)	−3·5	+4·5		+5·5	+5·5	+5·5		+6	+6·5		+6·5	±11·15
Width of vestigial sideband (MHz)	0·75	0·75		0·75	0·75	0·75	(1·25)	1·25	0·75	(1·25)	1·25	2
Vision modulation polarity	positive	negative		negative	positive	negative		negative	negative		positive	positive
Sound modulation	a.m.	fm ± 25 kHz		fm ± 50 kHz	a.m.	fm ± 50 kHz	fm ± 50 kHz	fm ± 50 kHz	fm ± 50 kHz		a.m.	a.m.
pre-emphasis (μs)		75		50	50	50	50	50	50			

Notes
1. Figures quoted are nominal.
2. Data in brackets refers to system code shown in brackets at top of column.
3. For further information reference should be made to Report 624 (Rev 76) of the Interim Meeting of CCIR Study Group II, Geneva 1976.

NATIONAL STANDARDS (END OF 1978)

Country	System used in bands I–III	System used in bands IV–V
Afghanistan	B	
Albania	B	
Algeria	B/PAL	
American Forces Radio (Germany)	M/NTSC	M/NTSC
Angola	I	
Antigua	M/NTSC	
Argentina	N/PAL	N
Australia	B/PAL	
Austria	B/PAL	G/PAL
Azores	B	
Bahamas	M	
Bahrain	B/PAL	
Bangladesh	B/PAL	
Barbados	N/NTSC	
Belgium	B/PAL	H/PAL
Bermuda	M/NTSC	
Bolivia	N	
Brazil	M/PAL	M/PAL
British Forces Broadcasting Service (Germany)		I/PAL
Brunei	B/PAL	
Bulgaria	D/SECAM	
Cambodia	M	
Cameroon	K1	K1
Canada	M/NTSC	M/NTSC
Canary Islands	B/PAL	
Cape Verde	I	
Central African Republic	B	
Chile	M/PAL	
China (PR)	D/PAL	
Colombia	M/SECAM	
Congo (Peoples Republic and Democratic Republic)	D/SECAM	
Costa Rica	M/NTSC	
Cuba	D/SECAM	
Cyprus	B	H
Czechoslovakia	D/SECAM	K/SECAM
Denmark	B/PAL	
Diego Garcia	M	
Dominican Republic	M/NTSC	
Ecuador	M/NTSC	
Egypt (Arab Republic)	B/SECAM	
El Salvador	M/NTSC	
Ethiopia	B	
Finland	B/PAL	G/PAL
France	E	L/SECAM
Gabon	K/SECAM	
Gambia	I	
Germany (Democratic Republic)	B/SECAM	G/SECAM
Germany (Federal Republic)	B/PAL	G/PAL

Country	System used in bands I–III	IV–V
Ghana	B/PAL	
Gibraltar	B/PAL	
Great Britain	A	I/PAL
Greece	B	G
Greenland (US air base)	M/NTSC	
Guadeloupe	K	
Guam	M/NTSC	
Guatemala	M/NTSC	
Guinea	I	
Guyana (French)	K/SECAM	
Haiti	M/SECAM	
Holland	B/PAL	G/PAL
Honduras (Republic of)	M	
Hong Kong		I/PAL
Hungary	D/SECAM	K/SECAM
India	B	
Indonesia	B/PAL	
Iran	B/SECAM	
Iraq	B/SECAM	
Ireland (Rep)	AI/PAL	I/PAL
Israel	B	G
Italy	B/PAL	G/PAL
Ivory Coast	K1/SECAM	
Jamaica	M	
Japan	M/NTSC	M/NTSC
Jibuti (Republic of)	K1	
Johnston Island (US Terr.)	M/NTSC	
Jordan	B/PAL	
Kenya	B/PAL	
Korea (Republic of)	M/NTSC	M/NTSC
Kuwait	B/PAL	
Leeward Island	M	
Lebanon	B/SECAM	
Lesotho	I	
Liberia	B/PAL	
Libya (Arab Republic of)	B/SECAM	
Luxembourg	C/PAL	L/SECAM
Maco Island	I	
Madagascar	K	
Madeira	B	
Malaysia	B/PAL	
Malta	B	G
Martinique	K1/SECAM	
Mauritius	B/SECAM	
Mexico	M/NTSC	M/NTSC
Midway Island (US Terr.)	M/NTSC	
Monaco	C/SECAM	L/G/SECAM
Mongolia	D	
Morocco	B/SECAM	
Mozambique	I	
Netherlands Antilles	M/NTSC	
New Caledonia	K1	

Country	System used in bands I–III	IV–V
New Zealand	B/PAL	
Nicaragua	M/NTSC	
Nigeria (Federal Republic of)	B/PAL	
Norway	B/PAL	G/PAL
Okinawa	M/NTSC	
Oman	B/PAL	G/PAL
Pakistan	B/PAL	
Panama	M/NTSC	
Paraguay	N	
Peru	M/NTSC	
Philippines	M/NTSC	
Poland	D/SECAM	K/SECAM
Portugal	B/PAL	G/PAL
Puerto Rico	M/NTSC	M/NTSC
Qatar	B/PAL	
Reunion (French)	K1/SECAM	
Romania	D	
Samoa (American)	M/NTSC	
Saudi Arabia	B/SECAM	
	M/PAL	
Senegal	K1	
Seychelles Islands	I	
Sierra Leone	B/PAL	
Singapore	B/PAL	
Somalia	B	
Society Islands	K1	
South Africa	I/PAL	I/PAL
Spain	B/PAL	G/PAL
Sri Lanka	B	
St Helena Island	I	
St Kitts	M/NTSC	
St Pierre & Miquelon	K1	
Sudan	B/PAL	
Surinam	M/NTSC	
Swaziland	I	
Sweden	B/PAL	G/PAL
Switzerland	B/PAL	G/PAL
Syrian Arab Rep.	B	
Tahiti	K1/SECAM	
Taiwan	M/NTSC	
Tanzania	B/PAL	
Thailand	M/B/PAL	
Togo	K1	
Trinidad & Tobago	M/NTSC	
Trust Terr. of Pacific	M	
Tunisia	B/SECAM	
Turkey	B/PAL	
Uganda	B/PAL	
United Arab Emirates	B/PAL	
Upper Volta (Burkino Fasa)	K1	
Uruguay	M	

Country	System used in bands I–III	IV–V
USA	M/NTSC	M/NTSC
USSR	D/SECAM	K/SECAM
Venezuela	M/NTSC	
Virgin Islands (American)	M/NTSC	
Virgin Islands (British)	M/NTSC	
Yemen (PDR)	B	
Yugoslavia	B/PAL	H/PAL
Zaire (Republic of)	K/SECAM	
Zambia	B	
Zimbabwe	B	

SATELLITE TELEVISION AND BROADCASTING BAND

CHANNEL NUMBERS AND ASSIGNED FREQUENCIES FOR THE 12 GHz SATELLITE BROADCASTING BAND

Channel No	Assigned frequency (MHz)	Channel No	Assigned frequency (MHz)
1	11,727·48	21	12,111·08
2	11,746·66	22	12,130·26
3	11,765·84	23	12,149·44
4	11,785·02	24	12,168·62
5	11,804·20	25	12,187·80
6	11,823·38	26	12,206·98
7,	11,842·56	27	12,226·16
8	11,861·74	28	12,245·34
9	11,880·92	29	12,264·52
10	11,900·10	30	12,283·70
11	11,919·28	31	12,302·88
12	11,938·46	32	12,322·06
13	11,957·64	33	12,341·24
14	11,976·82	34	12,360·42
15	11,996·00	35	12,379·60
16	12,015·18	36	12,398·78
17	12,034·36	37	12,417·96
18	12,053·54	38	12,437·14
19	12,072·72	39	12,456·32
20	12,091·90	40	12,475·50

UK channels are 4, 8, 12, 16 and 20, orbit position 31°W polarization left-hand circular.

PROPOSED BROADCAST SATELLITE PARAMETERS FOR THE FREQUENCY BAND 11·7–12·5 GHz

Type of modulation	fm	
Number of lines	625	
Sound sub-carrier frequency	6 MHz	
Peak-peak deviation	13·3 MHz	
Peak deviation of sound sub-carrier	50 kHz	
Receiver equivalent rectangular noise bandwidth	27 MHz	
Angle of elevation	15°	40°
Luminance signal—unweighted noise for 99% of worst month	34 dB	33 dB
Sound signal to weighted noise ratio for 99% of worst month	51 dB	50 dB

UNITED KINGDOM CHANNEL FREQUENCIES

BAND IV

Channel	Frequency (MHz) Vision	Sound	Channel	Frequency (MHz) Vision	Sound
21	471·25	477·25	28	527·25	533·25
22	479·25	485·25	29	535·25	541·25
23	487·25	493·25	30	543·25	549·25
24	495·25	501·25	31	551·25	557·25
25	503·25	509·25	32	559·25	565·25
26	511·25	517·25	33	567·25	573·25
27	519·25	525·25	34	575·25	581·25

All transmissions on 625 line system (System I).

BAND V

Channel	Frequency (MHz) Vision	Sound	Channel	Frequency (MHz) Vision	Sound
39	615·25	621·25	54	735·25	741·25
40	623·25	629·25	55	743·25	749·25
41	631·25	637·25	56	751·25	757·25
42	639·25	645·25	57	759·25	765·25
43	647·25	653·25	58	767·25	773·25
44	655·25	661·25	59	775·25	781·25
45	663·25	669·25	60	783·25	789·25
46	671·25	677·25	61	791·25	797·25
47	679·25	685·25	62	799·25	805·25
48	687·25	693·25	63	807·25	813·25
49	695·25	701·25	64	815·25	821·25
50	703·25	709·25	65	823·25	829·25
51	711·25	717·25	66	831·25	837·25
52	719·25	725·25	67	839·25	845·25
53	727·25	733·25	68	847·25	853·25

All transmissions on 625 line system (System I).

AUSTRALIAN TELEVISION CHANNEL FREQUENCIES

Channel	Frequencies (MHz)	Channel	Frequencies (MHz)
0	46·25– 51·75	6	175·25–180·75
1	57·25– 62·75	7	182·25–187·75
2	64·25– 69·75	8	189·25–194·75
3	86·25– 91·75	9	196·25–201·75
4	95·25–100·75	10	209·25–214·75
5	102·25–107·75	11	216·25–221·75
5A	138·25–143·75		

All transmissions on 625 line system (System B).

NEW ZEALAND TELEVISION CHANNEL FREQUENCIES

Channel	Frequencies (MHz)	Channel	Frequencies (MHz)
1	45·25– 50·75	6	189·25–194·75
2	55·25– 60·75	7	196·25–201·75
3	62·25– 67·75	8	203·25–208·75
4	175·25–180·75	9	210·25–215·75
5	182·25–187·75		

All transmissions on 625 line system (System B).

REPUBLIC OF IRELAND TELEVISION CHANNEL FREQUENCIES

Channel	Frequencies (MHz)	Channel	Frequencies (MHz)
7*	181·25–184·75	IE	183·25–189·25
11*	201·25–204·75	IF†	191·25–197·25
IA†	45·75– 51·75	IG†	199·25–205·25
IB†	53·75– 59·75	IH†	207·25–213·25
IC†	61·75– 67·75	IJ†	215·25–221·25
ID†	175·25–181·25		

* 425 line system (System A).   † 625 line system (System I).

SOUTH AFRICA TELEVISION CHANNEL FREQUENCIES

Channel	Frequencies (MHz)	Channel	Frequencies (MHz)
4	175·25–181·25	9	215·25–221·25
5	183·25–189·25	10	223·25–229·25
6	191·25–197·25	11	231·25–237·25
7	199·25–205·25	13	247·43–253·43
8	207·25–213·25		

All transmissions on 625 line system (System I).

USA TELEVISION CHANNEL FREQUENCIES

VHF

Channel	Frequencies (MHz)	Channel	Frequencies (MHz)
2	55·25– 59·75	8	181·25–185·75
3	61·25– 65·75	9	187·25–191·75
4	67·25– 71·75	10	193·25–197·75
5	77·25– 81·75	11	199·25–203·75
6	83·25– 87·75	12	205·25–209·75
7	175·25–179·75	13	211·25–215·75

UHF

Channel	Frequencies (MHz)	Channel	Frequencies (MHz)
14	471·25–475·75	49	681·25–685·75
15	477·25–481·75	50	687·25–691·75
16	483·25–487·75	51	693·25–697·75
17	489·25–493·75	52	699·25–703·75
18	495·25–499·75	53	705·25–709·75
19	501·25–505·75	54	711·25–715·75
20	507·25–511·75	55	717·25–721·75
21	513·25–517·75	56	723·25–727·75
22	519·25–523·75	57	729·25–733·75
23	525·25–529·75	58	735·25–739·75
24	531·25–535·75	59	741·25–745·75
25	537·25–541·75	60	747·25–751·75
26	543·25–547·75	61	753·25–757·75
27	549·25–553·75	62	759·25–763·75
28	555·25–559·75	63	765·25–769·75
29	561·25–565·75	64	771·25–775·75
30	567·25–571·75	65	777·25–781·75
31	573·25–577·75	66	783·25–787·75
32	579·25–583·75	67	789·25–793·75
33	585·25–589·75	68	795·25–799·75
34	591·25–595·75	69	801·25–805·75
35	597·25–601·75	70	807·25–811·75
36	603·25–607·75	71	813·25–817·75
37	609·25–613·75	72	819·25–823·75
38	615·25–619·75	73	825·25–829·75
39	621·25–625·75	74	831·25–835·75
40	627·25–631·75	75	837·25–841·75
41	633·25–637·75	76	843·25–847·75
42	639·25–643·75	77	849·25–853·75
43	645·25–649·75	78	855·25–859·75
44	651·25–655·75	79	861·25–865·75
45	657·25–661·75	80	867·25–871·75
46	663·25–667·75	81	873·25–877·75
47	669·25–673·75	82	879·25–883·75
48	675·25–679·75	83	885·25–889·75

All transmissions on 525 line system (System M).

UK BANDS IV AND V STATIONS

UHF station name	BBC1	Channels BBC2	ITV	Four	Polar- ization	ERP (kW)
LONDON AND SOUTH-EAST ENGLAND						
Bluebell Hill	40	46	43	65	H	30
Crystal Palace	26	33	23	30	H	1,000
Guildford	40	46	43	50	V	10
Hemel Hempstead	51	44	41	47	V	10
Hertford	58	64	61	54	V	2
High Wycombe	55	62	59	65	V	0·5
Reigate	57	63	60	53	V	10
Tunbridge Wells	51	44	41	47	V	10
Woolwich	57	63	60	67	V	0·63
Dover	50	56	66	53	H	100
Heathfield	49	52	64	67	H	100
Hastings	22	25	28	32	V	1
Newhaven	39	45	43	41	V	2
Oxford	57	63	60	53	H	500
MIDLANDS						
Ridge Hill	22	28	25	32	H	100
Sutton Coldfield	46	40	43	50	H	1,000
Brierly Hill	57	63	60	53	V	10
Bromsgrove	31	27	24	21	V	2
Fenton	31	27	24	21	V	10
Kidderminster	58	64	61	54	V	2
Larkstoke	33	26	23	29	V	6·3
Leek	22	28	25	32	V	1
Malvern	56	62	66	68	V	2
Nottingham	21	27	24	31	V	2
Stanton Moor	55	62	59	65	V	2
The Wrekin	26	33	23	29	H	100
Waltham	58	64	61	54	H	250
SOUTH ENGLAND						
Brighton	57	63	60	63	V	10
Hannington	39	45	42	66	H	250
Midhurst	61	55	58	68	H	100
Rowridge	31	24	27	21	H	500
Salisbury	57	63	60	53	V	10
Ventnor	39	45	49	42	V	2
Winterbourne Stickland	40	46	43	50	V	1
SOUTH-WEST ENGLAND						
Beacon Hill	57	63	60	53	H	100
Carodon Hill	22	28	25	32	H	500
Ivybridge	39	45	42	49	V	0·5
Plympton	58	64	61	54	V	2
Huntshaw Cross	55	62	59	65	H	100
Redruth	51	44	41	47	H	100
Isles of Scilly	21	27	24	31	V	0·5
Stockland Hill	33	26	23	29	H	250
Weymouth	40	46	43	50	V	2

UHF station name	Channels				Polar-ization	ERP (kW)
	BBC1	BBC2	ITV	Four		
Channel Islands						
Fremont Point	51	44	41	47	H	20
Les Toillets	56	48	54	52	H	2
WEST ENGLAND						
Mendip	58	64	61	54	H	500
Bristol Ilchester Crescent	40	46	43	50	V	0·5
Bristol Kings Weston Hill	45	48	42	52	V	1
Stroud	48	45	42	52	V	0·5
BORDERS						
Billsdale West Moor	33	26	29	23	H	500
Caldbeck	30	34	28	32	H	500
Haltwhistle	55	62	59	65	V	2
Whitehaven	40	46	43	50	V	2
Chatton	39	45	49	42	H	100
Pontop Pike	58	64	61	54	H	500
Fenham	21	27	24	31	V	2
Newton	33	26	23	29	V	2
Weardale	44	51	41	47	V	1
EAST ENGLAND						
Sandy Heath	31	27	24	21	H	1,000
Sudbury	51	44	41	47	H	250
Talconeston	62	55	59	65	H	250
Aldeburgh	33	26	23	30	V	10
West Runton	33	26	23	29	V	2
NORTH-WEST ENGLAND						
Winter Hill	55	62	59	65	H	500
Buxton	21	27	24	31	V	1
Darwen	39	45	49	42	V	0·5
Haslingden	33	26	23	29	V	10
Kendal	58	64	61	54	V	2
Ladder Hill	33	26	23	29	V	1
Lancaster	31	27	24	21	V	10
Littleborough	21	27	24	31	V	0·5
Pendle Forest	22	28	25	32	V	0·5
Saddleworth	52	45	49	42	V	2
Sedburgh	40	46	43	50	V	0·5
Storeton	22	28	25	32	V	2·8
Todmorden	39	45	49	42	V	0·5
Windermere	51	44	41	47	V	0·5
Douglas (IOM)	68	66	48	56	V	2
NORTH-EAST ENGLAND						
Belmont	22	28	25	32	H	500
Emley Moor	44	51	47	41	H	870
Beecroft Hill	55	62	59	65	V	1
Chesterfield	33	26	23	29	V	2
Cop Hill	22	28	25	32	V	1
Halifax	21	27	24	31	V	0·5
Heyshaw	57	63	60	53	V	0·5
Keighley	58	64	61	54	V	10
Oliver's Mount	57	63	60	53	V	1

UHF station name	Channels				Polar-ization	ERP (kW)
	BBC1	BBC2	ITV	Four		
Shalton Edge	52	58	48	54	V	1
Sheffield	31	27	24	21	V	5
Skipton	39	45	49	42	V	10
Wharfedale	22	28	25	32	V	2
WALES						
Blaenplwyf	31	27	24	21	H	100
Longmountain	58	64	61	54	V	1
Carmel	57	63	60	53	H	100
Llandrindod Wells	39	45	49	42	V	2·25
Llanddona	57	63	60	53	H	100
Arfon	51	44	41	47	V	3
Betws-y-Coed	21	27	24	31	V	0·5
Conway	40	46	43	50	V	2
Ffestiniog	22	28	25	32	V	1·2
Moel-y-Parc	52	45	49	42	H	100
Preseley	46	40	43	50	H	100
Wenvoe	44	51	41	47	H	500
Aberdare	21	27	24	31	V	0·5
Abergavenny	39	45	49	42	V	1
Brecon	58	64	61	54	V	1
Ebbw Vale	55	62	59	65	V	0·5
Kilvey Hill	33	26	23	29	V	10
Mynydd Machen	33	26	23	29	V	2
Pontypridd	22	28	25	32	V	0·5
Rhondda	33	26	23	29	V	4
SCOTLAND						
Angus	57	63	60	53	H	100
Taybridge	51	44	41	47	V	0·5
Black Hill	40	46	43	50	H	500
Biggar	22	28	25	32	V	0·5
Glengorm	56	52	48	54	V	1·1
Killearn	65	62	59	55	V	0·5
South Knapdale	57	63	60	53	V	1·45
Torosay	22	28	25	32	V	20
Sandale	22	—	—	⎤	H	500
Caldbeck	—	34	28	32 ⎦		
Barskeoch Hill	55	62	59	65	V	2
Cambret Hill	44	51	41	47	H	16
Thornhill	57	63	60	53	V	0·5
Craigkelly	31	27	24	21	H	100
Penicuik	58	64	61	64	V	2
Perth	39	45	49	42	V	1
Darvel	33	26	23	29	H	100
Rosneath	58	64	61	54	V	10
Rothesay	22	28	25	32	V	2
Durris	22	28	25	32	H	500
Gartly Moor	58	64	61	54	V	2·2
Rosehearty	51	44	41	47	V	2
Eitshal	33	26	23	29	H	100
Clettraval	51	44	41	47	V	2
Keelylang Hill	40	46	43	50	H	100

UHF station name	Channels BBC1	BBC2	ITV	Four	Polar-ization	ERP (kW)
Bressay	22	28	25	32	V	10
Knock More	33	26	23	29	H	100
Rosemarkie	39	45	49	42	H	100
Rumster Forest	31	27	24	21	H	100
Selkirk	55	62	59	65	H	50
Eyemouth	33	26	23	29	V	2
NORTHERN IRELAND						
Brougher Mountain	22	28	25	32	H	100
Divis	31	27	24	21	H	500
Kilkeel	39	45	49	42	V	0·5
Larne	39	45	49	42	V	0·5
Newcastle	55	62	59	65	V	1
Limavady	55	62	59	65	H	100
Londonderry	51	44	41	47	V	3·2
Strabane	39	45	49	42	V	2

Only stations with an erp of 0·5 kW and above listed. Many other low-power relays are in operation. Further information from: BBC Engineering Information Department, Broadcasting House, London W1A 1AA, and IBA Engineering Information Service, Crawley Court, Winchester, Hampshire SO21 2QA.

Part 7

Geographical and meteorological data

HORIZON DISTANCE

Horizon distance can be calculated from the formula

$$S = 1{\cdot}42\sqrt{H}$$

where S = distance in miles and H = height of the observer's eyes in feet above sea level, assuming normal air refractivity and a sea-level horizon.

Height of antenna above ground (ft)	Limit of optical range (miles)	Height of antenna above sea level (ft)	Limit of optical range (miles)
5	3·2	1,000	45·0
20	6·4	2,000	63·5
50	10·0	3,000	78·0
100	14·2	4,000	90·0
500	32·0	5,000	100·0

GREAT CIRCLE CALCULATIONS

The shortest distance between two points on the surface of the earth lies along the great-circle which passes through them. On a globe this great-circle path can be represented by a tightly-stretched thread joining the two locations.

It is sometimes useful to be able to calculate the great-circle bearing, and the distance of one point from another, and the expressions which follow enable this to be done.

First label the two points A and B.

Then let L_a = latitude of point A

L_b = latitude of point B

L_o = the difference in longitude between A and B

C = the direction of B from A, in degrees east or west from north in the northern hemisphere, or from south in the southern hemisphere.

D = the angle of arc between A and B.

It follows that $\cos D = \sin L_a \cdot \sin L_b + \cos L_a \cdot \cos L_b \cdot \cos L_o$

D can be converted to distance, knowing that

1 degree of arc = 111·1 km or 69·06 miles
1 minute of arc = 1·853 km or 1·151 miles

Once D is known (in angle of arc), then,

$$\cos C = \frac{\sin L_b - \sin L_a \cdot \cos D}{\cos L_a \cdot \sin D}$$

Note:
1. For stations in the northern hemisphere call latitudes positive.
2. For stations in the southern hemisphere call latitudes negative.
3. $\cos L_a$ and $\cos L_b$ are always positive.
4. $\cos L_o$ is positive between 0 and 90°, negative between 90° and 180°.
5. $\sin L_a$ and $\sin L_b$ are negative in the southern hemisphere.
6. The bearing for the reverse path can be found by transposing the letters on the two locations.

It is advisable to make estimates of the bearings on a globe, wherever possible, to ensure that they have been placed in the correct quadrant.

METEOROLOGICAL DATA

THE BEAUFORT SCALE

Beaufort force	Description	Specification on land	Speed (mph)	(km/h)
0	Calm	Smoke rises vertically	Less than 1	
1	Light air	Direction of wind shown by smoke drift	1–3	1–5
2	Light breeze	Wind felt on face, leaves rustle	4–7	6–11
3	Gentle breeze	Leaves and small twigs in constant motion	8–12	12–19
4	Moderate breeze	Wind raises dust and small branches move	13–18	20–29
5	Fresh breeze	Small trees in leaf start to sway, crested wavelets on inland waters	19–24	30–39
6	Strong breeze	Large branches in motion, whistling in telegraph wires	25–31	40–50
7	Near gale	Whole trees in motion, inconvenient to walk against wind	32–38	51–61
8	Gale	Twigs break from trees, difficult to walk	39–46	62–74
9	Strong gale	Slight structural damage occurs, chimney pots and slates removed	47–54	75–87
10	Storm	Trees uprooted, considerable structural damage occurs	55–63	88–101
11	Violent storm	Widespread damage	64–73	102–117
12	Hurricane	Widespread damage	≥74	≥119

RELATIVE HUMIDITY (%)

Dry bulb temperature (°C)	Wet bulb temperature depression												
	1	2	3	4	5	6	8	10	12	14	16	18	20
0	82	65	48	31	—	—	—	—	—	—	—	—	—
2	84	68	52	37	22	—	—	—	—	—	—	—	—
4	85	70	56	42	29	—	—	—	—	—	—	—	—
6	86	73	60	47	35	23	—	—	—	—	—	—	—
8	87	75	63	51	40	29	—	—	—	—	—	—	—
10	88	76	65	54	44	34	—	—	—	—	—	—	—
15	90	80	71	61	52	44	27	12	—	—	—	—	—
20	91	83	74	66	59	51	37	24	12	—	—	—	—
25	92	84	77	70	63	57	44	33	22	12	—	—	—
30	—	86	—	73	—	61	50	39	30	21	13	5	—
35	—	87	—	75	—	64	53	44	35	27	20	13	7
40	—	87	—	76	—	66	56	47	39	32	26	20	14

ATMOSPHERIC PRESSURE CONVERSION TABLE

Millibars	Inches	mm	Millibars	Inches	mm	Millibars	Inches	mm
960	28·35	720	990	29·23	742	1,020	30·12	765
965	28·50	724	995	29·38	746	1,025	30·27	769
970	28·64	727	1,000	29·53	750	1,030	30·42	773
975	28·79	731	1,005	29·68	754	1,035	30·56	776
980	28·94	735	1,010	29·83	758	1,040	30·71	780
985	29·09	739	1,015	29·97	761	1,045	30·86	784

Typical average pressure at sea level = 1,014 millibars.

CLOUD CLASSIFICATION

Genus (with abbreviation	Height of base (ft)	(m)	Notes
Cirrus (Ci)	16,500–45,000	5,000–13,700	Detached clouds in the form of white, delicate filaments, often called "Mares tails".
Cirrocumulus (Cc)	16,500–45,000	5,000–13,700	Thin, white patch, sheet or layer of cloud without shading.
Cirrostratus (Cs)	16,500–45,000	5,000–13,700	Transparent, whitish cloud veil of fibrous or smooth appearance.
Altocumulus (Ac)	6,500–23,000	2,000–7,000	White or grey, sheet or layer of cloud, generally with shading.
Altostratus (As)	6,500–23,000	2,000–7,000	Greyish or bluish cloud sheet or layer of striated, fibrous or uniform appearance.
Nimbostratus (Ns)	3,000–10,000	900–3,000	Grey cloud layer, often dark.
Stratocumulus (Sc)	1,500–6,500	460–2,000	Grey or whitish patch, sheet or layer of cloud which almost always has dark parts.
Stratus (St)	surface–1,500	surface–460	Generally grey cloud layer with a fairly uniform base, which may give drizzle, ice prisms or snow grains.
Cumulus (Cu)	1,500–6,500	460–2,000	Detached clouds, generally dense and with sharp outlines, developing vertically in the form of rising mounds, often resembling a cauliflower.
Cumulonimbus (Cb)	15–6,500	460–2,000	Heavy and dense cloud, with a considerable vertical extent, in the form of a mountain, often with an anvil-shaped plume.

VISIBILITY

Dense fog	Less than 50 yards
Fog	50–200 yards
Slight fog	200–1,000 yards
Mist	1,100–2,200 yards
Haze	1,100–2,200 yards
Poor visibility	$1\frac{1}{4}$–$2\frac{1}{2}$ miles
Moderate visibility	$2\frac{1}{2}$–$6\frac{1}{4}$ miles
Good visibility	$6\frac{1}{4}$–25 miles

WIND VELOCITIES AND PRESSURES

Indicated velocities (mph) V_i	Actual velocities (mph) V_a	Cylindrical surfaces pressure (lb/sq ft) projected areas $P = 0.0025\,V_a^2$	Flat surfaces pressure (lb/sq ft) $P = 0.0042\,V_a^2$
10	9·6	0·23	0·4
20	17·8	0·8	1·3
30	25·7	1·7	2·8
40	33·3	2·8	4·7
50	40·8	4·2	7·0
60	48·0	5·8	9·7
70	55·2	7·6	12·8
80	62·2	9·7	16·2
90	69·2	12·0	20·1
100	76·2	14·5	24·3
110	83·2	17·3	29·1
120	90·2	20·3	34·2
125	93·7	21·9	36·9
130	97·2	23·6	39·7
140	104·2	27·2	45·6
150	111·2	30·9	51·9
160	118·2	34·9	58·6
170	125·2	39·2	65·7
175	128·7	41·4	69·5
180	132·2	43·7	73·5
190	139·2	48·5	81·5
200	146·2	53·5	89·8

* As measured with a cup anemometer, these being the average maximum for a period of 5 min.

COMPARISON OF CELSIUS AND FAHRENHEIT THERMOMETER SCALES

Celsius	Fahrenheit	Celsius	Fahrenheit	Celsius	Fahrenheit
−50	−58	+ 35	+ 95	+120	+248
−45	−49	+ 40	+104	+125	+257
−40	−40	+ 45	+113	+130	+266
−35	−31	+ 50	+122	+135	+275
−30	−22	+ 55	+131	+140	+284
−25	−13	+ 60	+140	+145	+293
−20	− 4	+ 65	+149	+150	+302
−15	+ 5	+ 70	+158	+155	+311
−10	+14	+ 75	+167	+160	+320
− 5	+23	+ 80	+176	+165	+329
0	+32	+ 85	+185	+170	+338
+ 5	+41	+ 90	+194	+175	+347
+10	+50	+ 95	+203	+180	+356
+15	+59	+100	+212	+185	+365
+20	+68	+105	+221	+190	+374
+25	+77	+110	+230	+195	+383
+30	+86	+115	+239	+200	+392

BOUNDARIES OF SEA AREAS, AS USED IN BBC
AND BT WEATHER FORECASTS

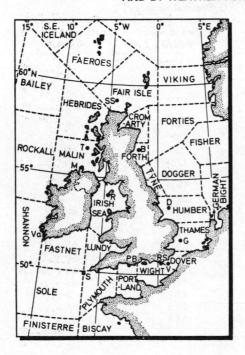

Stations whose latest reports are broadcast in the 5 min forecasts on Radio 2 (200kHz) at 0033, 0633 and 1755 (daily), 1155 (Sundays) and 1355 (weekdays).

T   Tiree
SS Sule Skerry Lighthouse
B   Bell Rock Lighthouse
D   Dowsing light-vessel
G   Galloper light-vessel
V   Varne light-vessel
RS Royal Sovereign Light-tower
PB Portland Bill
S   Scilly (St Mary's)
Va Valentia
R   Ronaldsway
M   Malin Head Lighthouse

Part 8

Materials and engineering data

PROPERTIES OF METALS

Material	Relative resistance	Temp coeff of resistivity at 20°C ($\times 10^{-6}$)	Specific gravity	Thermal conductivity at 20°C	Coeff of linear expansion ($\times 10^{-6}$)	Melting point (°C)
Aluminium	1·64	40	2·7	0·48	25·5	660
Brass	3·9	20	8·47	0·26	18·9	920
Cadmium	4·4	38	8·64	0·222	28·8	321
Cobalt	5·6	33	8·71		12·3	1,480
Constantan	28·45	0·1	8·9	0·054	17·0	1,210
Copper	1·00	39·3	8·89	0·918	16·7	1,083
Carbon (gas)	29·00	−5	1·88	0·0004	5·4	3,500
Eureka	28·45	0·1	8·9	—	—	—
Gold	1·446	34	19·32	0·705	13·9	1,063
Iron (cast)	5·6	60	7·87	0·18	10·2	1,535
Lead	12·78	42	11·37	0·083	29·1	327
Magnesium	2·67	40	1·74	0·376	25·4	651
Manganin	26·0	0·2	8·5	0·053	18·0	910
Mercury	55·6	9·8	13·55	0·0148	—	−38·87
Molybdenum	3·3	45	10·2	0·346	5·0	2,622
Monel	27·8	20	8·8	0·06	14	1,350
Nichrome	65	1·7	8·25	0·035	12·5	1,350
Nickel	5·05	47	8·85	0·142	12·8	1,452
Nickel silver	16	2·6	8·72	0·07	18·36	1,110
Palladium	6·39	33	12·2	0·168	—	—
Phosphor bronze	5·45	—	8·9	0·15	19·0	1,050
Platinum	6·16	38	21·4	0·166	8·9	1,773
Silver	0·95	40	10·5	1·006	19·5	960·5
Steel (stainless)	52·8	—	7·9	0·069	10–11	1,410
Tantalum	9·0	33	16·6	0·130	6·5	2,850
Tin	6·7	42	7·3	0·155	21·4	231·9
Tungsten	3·25	45	19·2	0·476	4·44	3,370
Zinc	3·4	37	7·14	0·265	26·3	419·5
Zirconium	2·38	44	6·4	—	—	1,860

MELTING AND FREEZING POINTS OF "SOFT SOLDER"

Tin (wt %)	Lead (wt %)	Melting point (°C)	Freezing point (°C)
0	100	327	327
10	90	300	275
20	80	277	183
30	70	256	183
40	60	237	183
50	50	215	183
60	40	190	183
70	30	192	183
80	20	203	183
90	10	215	183
100	0	232	232

CORROSION TABLE

Metal or alloy ↓ \ Contact metal →	Gold, silver	Copper brasses, nickel silver	Nickel	Lead tin, soft solders	Steel, cast iron	Cadmium	Zinc	"Stainless" steels Austenitic 18/8	18/2 Cr/Ni	13%Cr	Chromium	Aluminium, aluminium alloys
Gold, silver	—	A	A	A	A	A	A	A	A	A	A	A
Copper, brasses and nickel silver	C(1)	—	B or C	B or C	A	A	A	B or C	B or C	A	B or C	A
Nickel	C	A	—	A	A	A	A	B or C	B or C	A	B or C	A
Lead, tin, soft solders	C	B or C	B	—	A or C	A	A or C	B or C	B or C	B or C	B or C	A
Steel, cast iron	C	C	C(1)	C(1)	—	—	A	C	C	C	C(1)	B
Cadmium	C	C	C	B	C	—	A	C	C	C	C	B
Zinc	C	C	C	B	C	B	—	C	C	C	C	C
"Stainless" steel Austenitic 18/8	A	A	A	A	A	A	A	(2)	A	A	A	A
"Stainless" steel 18/2 Cr/Ni	C	A or C(3)	A	A	A	A	A	A	(2)	A	A	A
"Stainless" steel 13% Cr	C	C	B or C	A	A	A	A	C	C	(2)	C	A
Chromium	A	A	A	A	A	A	A	A	A	A	—	A
Aluminium, aluminium alloys	D	D	C(1)	B or C	B or C	A	A	B or C	B or C	B or C	B or C	(2)

Key to table

A—The corrosion of metal or alloy is not increased by contact with "contact metal".

B—The corrosion of metal or alloy may be slightly increased by contact with "contact metal".

C—The corrosion of metal or alloy may be markedly increased by contact with "contact metal".

D—When moisture may be present, combination inadvisable without adequate protection measures.

(1)—May be satisfactory as plating if of high quality.
(2)—Crevices should be filled with jointing compound.
(3)—Corrosion may be severe in crevices.

SYNTHETIC INSULATING MATERIALS

	Electrical					Mechanical				General		
	Power factor at 1 MHz	Permittivity at 1 MHz	Surface resistivity (MΩ)	Volume resistivity (MΩ)	Electric strength at 90°C (V/mil)	Tensile strength (UTS) (lb/in²)	Cross breaking strength (lb/in²)	Impact strength	Water absorption (mg)	Plastic yield (m/max°C)	Max operating temp (°)	Filler
Thermo-setting												
Polyester-fastcure												
High impact	0·018	4·5	10^5	10^7	200	6,000	20,000	4	100	2 at 160	100	glass fibre
General purpose	0·014	5·0	10^6	10^8	250	3,000	7,000	0·12	130	3 at 160	100	mineral
General purpose (imp)	0·016	4·5	10^6	10^7	260	4,200	10,000	0·25	160	3 at 160	100	mineral
Diallyl phthalate -												
High impact	—	—	10^8	10^7	250	5,000	12,000	3·0	150	—	110	glass fibre
General purpose	0·05	5·5	10^5	10^8	200	3,000	6,000	0·12	80	—	110	mineral
General purpose (imp)	0·04	5·0	5×10^6	10^9	250	4,500	6,500	0·14	55	—	110	mineral
Polyester dough												
General purpose	0·02	6·0	10^6	10^7	200	7,000	—	7·0	35	—	—	glass fibre
General purpose	0·02	6·0	10^7	10^7	240	7,000	—	7·0	25	—	—	glass fibre
Melamine formaldehyde	0·06	7·0	10^5	3×10^4	130	3,000	5,000	0·1	30	6 at 180	110	—
Phenolic												
Electrical Type L4	0·015	5·5	10^7	10^7	200	4,000	8,300	0·09	15	6 at 100	90	mica
Type L	0·025	5·8	10^6	10^6	150	4,000	8,300	0·10	20	6 at 140	100	mica
Type L1	0·025	4·8	3×10^5	3×10^5	75	6,000	10,000	0·14	27	6 at 100	90	nylon
Type L2	0·035	5·0	10^5	10^5	100	6,500	10,000	0·12	27	6 at 140	100	nylon & cellulose
Type L3	0·040	5·5	3×10^5	3×10^5	130	4,000	7,500	0·12	20	6 at 140	100	nylon & mica
Type HD	0·050	6·0	$1·6 \times 10^3$	2×10^5	90	6,500	9,500	0·11	75	6 at 140	100	wood flour
Mechanical Type MS	—	—	8×10^2	10^3	30	6,000	9,500	0·25	80	6 at 140	100	ground cotton
Type MHS	—	—	2×10^2	10^3	30	5,400	9,200	0·55	85	6 at 140	100	cotton
Type HS	—	—	25	10^3	30	5,500	9,200	0·75	110	6 at 180	100	fabric
Heat resistant HR	0·058	7·3	5×10^3	5×10^3	120	3,500	7,000	0·07	37	—	140	asbestos
Silicone moulding (dry)	0·004	3·5	28×10^8	80×10^6	100–200	4,400	14,000	15	0·10	—	230	—
(wet)	0·020	3·6	28×10^8	$0·09 \times 10^6$	100–200	1,300	5,000	11	0·13	—	230	—
Thermoplastic												
Polyamides (nylon) (dry)												
General purpose 66GP	0·05	4·0	10^6	10^6	220	11,000	—	—	—	—	80	—

General purpose 6GP	—	—	10^6	10°	220	10,000	—	—	—	—	80	—
General purpose 11GP	—	—	10^6	10^6	220	8,000	—	—	—	—	80	—
General purpose 610GP	—	—	10^6	10^6	220	8,000	—	—	—	—	80	—
Weather resistant 66 W	—	—	10^6	10^6	220	11,500	—	—	—	80	—	—
Weather resistant 6 W	—	—	10^6	10^6	220	10,500	—	—	—	—	80	—
Weather resistant 11 W	—	—	10^6	10^6	220	8,500	—	—	—	—	80	—
Hot air 66 HL	—	—	10^6	10^6	220	11,000	—	—	—	—	105	—
Hot air 6 HL	—	—	10^6	10^6	220	9,000	—	—	—	—	105	—
Hot air 11 HL	—	—	10^6	10^6	220	8,000	—	—	—	—	105	—
Polyethylene												
Low density	0·00015/ 0·0003	2·35	10^8	3×10^9	1,000 at 20°C	1,000/ 1,500	—	3	3	—	70	—
High density	0·00015/ 0·003	2·35	10^8	3×10^9	1,000 at 20°C	3,700	—	1–10	3	—	95	—
Polypropylene	0·0005	2·2	10^8	10^8	600	4,500	—	1	0·03	—	90	—
Polystyrene										softening		
Normal Type A	0·0005	2·7	10^8	10^8	400	4,000	5,400	0·12	5	100	70	—
Type B	0·0005	2·7	10^8	10^8	400	4,000	5,400	0·12	5	90	60	—
Type C	0·0005	2·7	10^8	10^8	400	4,000	5,400	0·12	5	85	55	—
Type D	0·0007	2·7	10^8	10^8	400	—	—	—	—	75	50	—
Toughened Type 1	0·001	2	10^8	10^8	400	3,000	—	—	20	80	—	—
Type 2	0·001	2	10^8	10^8	400	3,500	—	—	15	85	—	—
Type 3	0·001	2	10^8	10^8	400	4,000	—	—	20	90	—	—
PTFE	0·00025	2·12	10^8	10^{11}	500	2,000	—	4	1	7,150	250	—
Laminates					edgewise							
Phenolic board												
Paper base for rf Type H	0·038	5	5×10^4	—	25 kV	8,000	10,000	0·08	13	—	100	—
Paper base for rf Type L	0·045	5·8	5×10^2	—	25 kV	8,000	12,000	0·15	32	—	100	—
Paper base non-rf Type P3	—	—	10^3	—	20 kV	8,000	12,000	0·15	32	—	100	—
Paper base non-rf Type P4	—	—	10^4	—	20 kV	8,000	10,000	0·08	13	—	100	—
Fabric base for rf Type 1A	0·04	5·8	10^6	—	50 kV	—	10,000	0·3	65	—	100	—
Fabric base for rf Type 1B	0·045	5·8	10^5	—	25 kV	8,000	13,000	0·45	65	—	100	—
Fabric base for non-rf Type 2A	—	—	5×10^2	—	20 kV	—	15,000	0·45	65	—	100	—
Asbestos paper non-rf	—	—	20	—	3 kV	12,000	—	0·45	55	—	130	—

SYNTHETIC INSULATING MATERIALS (continued)

	Electrical					Mechanical			General			
	Power factor at 1 MHz	Permittivity at 1 MHz	Surface resistivity (MΩ)	Volume resistivity (MΩ)	Electric strength at 90°C (V/mil)	Tensile strength (UTS) (lb/in²)	Cross breaking strength (lb/in²)	Impact strength	Water absorption (mg)	Plastic yield (m/max°C)	Max operating temp (°)	Filler
Epoxide resin glass fabric	0·035	5·5	10^3	—	15 kV	26,000	35,000	3	12	—	140	—
Melamine resin glass fabric	—	—	50	—	6 kV	15,000	12,000	3	118	—	130	—
Silicone resin glass fabric (S1)	0·005	4	10^4	—	13 kV	12,000	15,000	13	10	—	200	—
Silicone resin glass fabric (S2)	0·01	4·5	100	—	8 kV	14,000	16,000	4	20	—	200	—

CERAMIC INSULATING MATERIALS

Material	Dielectric				Thermal				Strength		
	Strength at 50 Hz (V/0·001")	Constant at 1 MHz	Power factor at 1 MHz	Volume resistivity at 20°C (ohms/cm³)	Conductivity at 20°C (CGS units)	Expansion at 0–200°C (ppm/°C)	Working temperature (°C)	Water absorption (%)	Specific gravity	Tensile (lb/sq in)	Compressive (lb/sq in)
Alumina (95%)	500	9·6	0·006	10^{16}	0·054	6·3	1,400	0	3·72	18,300	240,000
Alumina (99·5%)	200	9·0	0·0005	10^{16}	0·06	7·6	1,600	0	3·9	35,000	300,000
Aluminium silicate	80	5·3	0·01	10^{14}	0·003	3·3	1,100	2–3	2·3	2,500	40,000
Boron nitrite	900	4·15	0·0002	10^{14}	0·064	10·0	1,700	0·17	2·1	5,500	45,000
Beryllium oxide	400	7·0	0·0004	10^{13}	0·02	7·0	1,800	0	3·01	17,500	200,000
Corderite	100	5·0	0·004	10^{14}	0·003	2·2	1,250	10–15	2·1	3,500	30,000
Fosterite	250	6·2	0·0004	10^{14}	0·0024	10·0	1,000	0	2·8	10,000	85,000
Lithium-aluminium silicate	300	6·0	0·005	10^{14}	0·005	1·2	1,000	0–2	2·0	350	4,000
Magnesium silicate	100	5·8	0·0003	10^{14}	0·005	10·7	1,250	2–3	2·8	2,500	90,000
Porcelain	300	5·6	0·0055	10^{13}–10^{14}	0·0024	4–6	1,000	0–0·5	2·4	4,250	110,000
Steatite	230	6·0	0·0021	10^{14}–10^{16}	0·0035	8	1,000	0	2·6	8,000	120,000
Zircon	220	8·8	0·001	10^{14}	0·015	4·5	1,200	0	3·7	12,000	100,000

OTHER INSULATING MATERIALS

Material	Dielectric constant at 50 Hz	Power factor 50 Hz	Power factor 1 MHz	Power factor 100 MHz	Dielectric strength V/0·001"	Resistance (Ω/cm)	Softening temp (°C)	Coeff of expansion— 10^6 per °C
Air (NP)	1	—	—	—	19·8–22·8	—	—	—
Cellulose acetate	6–8	6	10	—	250–1,000	$4·5 \times 10^{10}$	70	160
Cellulose nitrate	4–7	5–15	7–10	—	300–780	$2–30 \times 10^{10}$	85	90–160
Fibre	2·5–5	6–9	5	5	150–180	5×10^9	130	25
Glass, crown	6·2	—	1	—	500	—	1,100	8·9
Glass, photographic	7·5	—	0·8–1	—	—	—	—	—
Glass, Pyrex	4–5	—	0·2–0·7	0·54	335	10^{14}	600	3·2
Mica	2·5–8	0·2	0·2–6	—	—	2×10^{17}	—	—
Mica, clear Indian	7–7·3	0·03–0·05	0·02–0·03	0·03	600–1,500	5×10^{12}	1,200	3–7
Micalex	6–8	0·64	0·21	0·22	350	—	348	8–9
Paper	2–2·6	—	—	—	1,250	—	—	—
Paraffin wax	2·25	0·02	0·02	0·02	203–305	10^{16}	MP56	—
Pyrophillite	5·2	—	0·2–0·7	0·36	500	$1·3 \times 10^{15}$	—	—
Quartz	3·5–4·2	0·09	0·02	0·02	200	$10^{14}–10^{18}$	1,430	0·45
Rubber, hard	2–3·5	1	0·5–1	—	450	$10^{12}–10^{15}$	70	70–80
Shellac	2·5–4	0·6–2·5	0·9–31	3	900	10^{16}	85	—
Urea formaldehyde	5–7	3–5	2·8	5	300–550	$10^{12}–10^{13}$	200	70
Vinyl resins	4	—	1·7	—	400–500	10^{14}	—	70
Wood, dry oak	2·5–6·8	—	4·2	—	—	—	—	—

WEIGHTS OF MATERIALS

| | | | Weight in lb per | |
| | | | in² | ft² |
Material	Specific gravity	in³	(0·001 in thick)	(0·001 in thick)
Aluminium 99·4%	2·706	0·0977	0·0000977	0·0140688
Aluminium alloy DTD 249	2·7	0·0975	0·0000975	0·0140400
Aluminium alloy DTD 290	2·8	0·1011	0·0001011	0·0145584
Aluminium magnesium alloy	2·68	0·0967	0·0000967	0·0139248
Aluminium manganese alloy	2·7	0·0975	0·0000975	0·0140400
Antimony	6·71	0·2422	0·0002422	0·0348768
Asbestos	2·8	0·1011	0·0001011	0·0145584
Bronze phosphor 92/8	8·8	0·3177	0·0003177	0·0457488
Bismuth	9·8	0·3538	0·0003538	0·0509472
Brass 65/35	8·47	0·3058	0·0003058	0·0440352
Bronze 2/10/88	8·78	0·3170	0·0003170	0·045648
Bronze phosphor sheet	8·8	0·3180	0·0003180	0·0457920
Celluloid	1·35	0·0487	0·0000487	0·0070128
Chromium	6·5	0·2347	0·0002347	0·0337968
Copper	8·93	0·3224	0·0003224	0·0464256
Cork	0·24	0·0087	0·0000087	0·0012528
Dow metal magnesium	1·78	0·0643	0·0000643	0·0092592
Duralumin	2·85	0·1029	0·0001029	0·0148176
Ebony wood, dry	1·25	0·045	0·000045	0·00648
Elektron	1·83	0·0661	0·0000661	0·0095184
Fibre, vulcanized	1·41	0·0510	0·000051	0·007344
Gold cast, hammered	19·32	0·6975	0·0006975	0·10044
Iridium	22·42	0·8094	0·0008094	0·1165536
Iron, cast	7·2	0·2599	0·0002599	0·0374256
Iron, ferrosilicon	7·01	0·2530	0·0002530	0·036432
Iron, pure	7·87	0·2841	0·0002841	0·0409104
Iron, sheet	7·7	0·2780	0·0002780	0·040032
Iron, wrought	7·78	0·2807	0·0002807	0·0404208
Lead	11·37	0·4105	0·0004105	0·059112
Leather	0·94	0·0341	0·0000341	0·0049104
Magnesium	1·74	0·0628	0·0000628	0·0090432
Magnesium aluminium alloy 7%	2·63	0·0949	0·0000949	0·0136656
Manganese	7·42	0·2679	0·0002679	0·0385776
Mercury	13·6	0·4910		
Mica	2·8	0·1011	0·0001011	0·0145584
Micarta	1·24	0·0446	0·0000446	0·0064224
Molybdenum	10·2	0·3682	0·0003682	0·0530208
Monel metal, cast	8·8	0·3177	0·0003177	0·0457488
Monel metal, rolled	8·9	0·3212	0·0003212	0·0462528
Nickel	8·8	0·3177	0·0003177	0·0457488
Nickel alloy 45%	8·0	0·2888	0·0002888	0·0415872
Paper	0·93	0·0336	0·0000336	0·0048384
Pewter	7·49	0·2703	0·0002703	0·0389232
Platinum sheet	21·54	0·7776	0·0007776	0·1119744
Platinum wire	21·04	0·7595	0·0007595	0·109368

WEIGHTS OF MATERIALS *(continued)*

Material	Specific gravity	Weight in lb per		
		in³	in² (0·001 in thick)	ft² (0·001 in thick)
Rubber, soft	0·95	0·0341	0·0000341	0·0049104
Rubber, hard ebonite	1·15	0·0416	0·0000416	0·0059904
Silicon	2·42	0·0874	0·0000874	0·0125856
Silver	10·78	0·3890	0·000389	0·056016
Silver, German or nickel	8·75	0·3160	0·000316	0·045504
Steel, crucible sheet	7·9	0·2853	0·0002853	0·0410832
Steel, machinery	7·81	0·2818	0·0002818	0·0405792
Steel, rolled sheet	7·85	0·2833	0·0002833	0·0407952
Steel, stainless	8·4	0·3033	0·0003033	0·0436752
Steel, tool	7·9	0·2853	0·0002853	0·0410832
Steel, 2½% silicon transformer grade	7·42	0·268	0·000268	0·038592
Tin	7·30	0·2635	0·0002635	0·037944
Tungsten	18·77	0·6776	0·0006776	0·0975744
Vanadium	5·5	0·1986	0·0001986	0·0285984
Zinc, cast	7·11	0·2567	0·0002567	0·0369648
Zinc, rolled	7·2	0·26	0·000260	0·03744

METRIC THREADS

No	Outside diameter (mm)	Pitch (mm)	Tapping (mm)	Clearance (mm)
M1	1·0	0·25	0·75	1·1
	1·6	0·35	1·25	1·7
M2	2·0	0·4	1·6	2·2
	2·5	0·45	2·05	2·7
	2·6	0·45	2·2	2·8
M3	3·0	0·5	2·5	3·2
M4	4·0	0·7	3·3	4·3
M5	5·0	0·8	4·2	5·3
M6	6·0	1·0	5·0	6·4
M8	8·0	1·25	6·7	8·4
M10	10·0	1·25	8·5	10·5
M12	12·0	1·75	10·3	13·0
M14	14·0	2·0	12·0	15·0
M16	16·0	2·0	14·0	17·0
M18	18·0	2·5	15·5	19·0
M20	20·0	2·5	17·5	21·0

STANDARD WIRE GAUGE AND STANDARD DRILL SIZES

Standard wire gauge	Standard drill size in mm	Decimal inch equivalent	Nearest obsolete number drill	Standard wire gauge	Standard drill size in mm	Decimal inch equivalent	Nearest obsolete number drill
50		0·0010		23		0·0240	
49		0·0012			0·62	0·0244	
48		0·0016			0·65	0·0256	72, 71
47		0·0020			0·68	0·0268	
46		0·0024			0·70	0·0276	70
45		0·0028		22		0·0280	
44		0·0032			0·72	0·0283	
43		0·0036			0·75	0·0295	69
42		0·0040			0·78	0·0307	
41		0·0044		$\frac{1}{32}$		0·0312	68
40		0·0048			0·80	0·0315	
39		0·0052		21		0·0320	
38		0·0060			0·82	0·0323	67
37		0·0068			0·85	0·0335	66
36		0·0076			0·88	0·0346	
35		0·0084			0·90	0·0354	65
34		0·0092		20		0·0360	
33		0·0100			0·92	0·0362	64
32		0·0108			0·95	0·0374	63
31		0·0116			0·98	0·0386	62
30		0·0124			1·00	0·0394	61, 60
	0·32	0·0126		19		0·0400	
29		0·0136			1·05	0·0413	59, 58
	0·35	0·0138	80		1·10	0·0433	57
28		0·0148			1·15	0·0453	
	0·38	0·0150	79	$\frac{3}{64}$		0·0469	56
$\frac{1}{64}$		0·0156			1·20	0·0472	
	0·40	0·0157	78	18		0·0480	
27		0·0164			1·25	0·0492	
	0·42	0·0165			1·30	0·0512	55
	0·45	0·0177	77		1·35	0·0532	
26		0·0180			1·40	0·0551	54
	0·48	0·0189	76	17		0·0560	
	0·50	0·0197			1·45	0·0571	
25		0·0200			1·50	0·0591	53
	0·52	0·0205	75		1·55	0·0610	
	0·55	0·0217		$\frac{1}{16}$		0·0625	
24		0·0220			1·60	0·0630	52
	0·58	0·0228	74	16		0·0640	
	0·60	0·0236	73		1·65	0·0650	

STANDARD WIRE GAUGE AND STANDARD DRILL SIZES *(continued)*

Standard wire gauge	Standard drill size in mm	Decimal inch equivalent	Nearest obsolete number drill	Standard wire gauge	Standard drill size in mm	Decimal inch equivalent	Nearest obsolete number drill
	1·70	0·0669	51		3·40	0·1339	
	1·75	0·0689			3·50	0·1378	29
	1·80	0·0709	50	$\frac{9}{64}$		0·1406	28
15		0·0720			3·60	0·1417	
	1·85	0·0728	49	9		0·1440	
	1·90	0·0748			3·70	0·1457	27, 26
	1·95	0·0768	48		3·80	0·1496	25
$\frac{5}{64}$		0·0781			3·90	0·1535	24, 23
	2·00	0·0787	47	$\frac{5}{32}$		0·1562	
14		0·0800			4·00	0·1575	22, 21
	2·05	0·0807	46	8		0·1600	
	2·10	0·0827	45		4·10	0·1614	20
	2·15	0·0846			4·20	0·1654	19
	2·20	0·0866	44		4·30	0·1693	18
	2·25	0·0886	43	$\frac{11}{64}$		0·1719	
	2·30	0·0906			4·40	0·1732	17
13		0·0920		7		0·1760	
	2·35	0·0925			4·50	0·1772	16
$\frac{3}{32}$		0·0938	42		4·60	0·1811	15, 14
	2·40	0·0945			4·70	0·1850	13
	2·45	0·0965	41	$\frac{3}{16}$		0·1875	
	2·50	0·0984	40		4·80	0·1890	12
	2·55	0·1004	39	6		0·1920	
	2·60	0·1024	38		4·90	0·1929	11, 10
12		0·1040			5·00	0·1968	9
	2·65	0·1043	37		5·10	0·2008	8, 7
	2·70	0·1063	36	$\frac{13}{64}$		0·2031	
	2·75	0·1083			5·20	0·2047	6, 5
$\frac{7}{64}$		0·1094			5·30	0·2087	4
	2·80	0·1102	35, 34	5		0·2120	
	2·85	0·1122	33		5·40	0·2126	3
	2·90	0·1142			5·50	0·2165	
11		0·1160		$\frac{7}{32}$		0·2188	
	2·95	0·1161	32		5·60	0·2205	2
	3·00	0·1181	31		5·70	0·2244	
	3·10	0·1220			5·80	0·2283	1
$\frac{1}{8}$		0·1250		4		0·2320	
	3·20	0·1260			5·90	0·2323	
10		0·1280		$\frac{15}{64}$		0·2344	A
	3·30	0·1299	30		6·00	0·2362	B

Standard wire gauge	Standard drill size in mm	Decimal inch equivalent	Nearest obsolete number drill	Standard wire gauge	Standard drill size in mm	Decimal inch equivalent	Nearest obsolete number drill
	6·10	0·2402	C		9·00	0·3543	
	6·20	0·2441	D		9·10	0·3583	T
	6·30	0·2480		$\frac{23}{64}$		0·3594	
$\frac{1}{4}$		0·2500	E		9·20	0·3622	
3	6·40	0·2520			9·30	0·3661	U
	6·50	0·2559	F		9·40	0·3701	
	6·60	0·2598	G	3/0		0·3720	
	6·70	0·2638			9·50	0·3740	
$\frac{17}{64}$		0·2656	H	$\frac{3}{8}$		0·3750	V
	6·80	0·2677			9·60	0·3780	
	6·90	0·2717	I		9·70	0·3819	
	7·00	0·2756	J		9·80	0·3858	W
2		0·2760			9·90	0·3898	
	7·10	0·2795		$\frac{25}{64}$		0·3906	
$\frac{9}{32}$		0·2812	K		10·00	0·3937	
	7·20	0·2835			10·10	0·3976	X
	7·30	0·2874		4/0		0·4000	
	7·40	0·2913	L		10·20	0·4016	
	7·50	0·2953	M		10·30	0·4055	Y
$\frac{19}{64}$		0·2969		$\frac{13}{32}$		0·4062	
	7·60	0·2992			10·40	0·4094	
1		0·3000			10·50	0·4134	Z
	7·70	0·3032	N		10·60	0·4173	
	7·80	0·3071			10·70	0·4213	
	7·90	0·3110		$\frac{27}{64}$		0·4219	
$\frac{5}{16}$		0·3125			10·80	0·4252	
	8·00	0·3150	O		10·90	0·4291	
	8·10	0·3189		5/0		0·4320	
	8·20	0·3228	P		11·00	0·4331	
0		0·3240			11·10	0·4370	
	8·30	0·3268		$\frac{7}{16}$		0·4375	
$\frac{21}{64}$		0·3281			11·20	0·4409	
	8·40	0·3307	Q				
	8·50	0·3346					
	8·60	0·3386	R				
	8·70	0·3425					
$\frac{11}{32}$		0·3438					
	8·80	0·3465	S				
00		0·3480					
	8·90	0·3504					

Drill sizes proceed thus:
$\frac{1}{2}$ in to 2 in in $\frac{1}{64}$ in steps; 12·7 mm to 14 mm in 0·1 mm steps; 14 mm to 25 mm in 0·25 mm steps; 25 mm to 50·5 mm in 0·5 mm steps.

TAPPING AND CLEARANCE DRILL SIZES FOR BSF AND BSW THREADS

Tapping sizes for BSF	BSW	Clearance for BSW–BSF	Standard drill size (in)	(mm)	Decimal inch equivalent
	$\frac{3}{16}$			3·80	0·1496
		$\frac{3}{16}$		4·90	0·1929
	$\frac{1}{4}$		$\frac{13}{64}$		0·2031
$\frac{1}{4}$				5·40	0·2126
		$\frac{1}{4}$		6·50	0·2559
	$\frac{5}{16}$			6·60	0·2598
$\frac{5}{16}$				6·80	0·2677
	$\frac{3}{8}$		$\frac{5}{16}$		0·3125
		$\frac{5}{16}$		8·20	0·3228
$\frac{3}{8}$			$\frac{21}{64}$		0·3281
	$\frac{7}{16}$			9·40	0·3701
$\frac{7}{16}$				9·70	0·3819
		$\frac{3}{8}$		9·80	0·3858
	$\frac{1}{2}$		$\frac{27}{64}$		0·4219
$\frac{1}{2}$			$\frac{7}{16}$		0·4375
		$\frac{7}{16}$	$\frac{29}{64}$		0·4531
$\frac{9}{16}$			$\frac{1}{2}$		0·5000
		$\frac{1}{2}$	$\frac{33}{64}$		0·5156
	$\frac{5}{8}$		$\frac{17}{32}$		0·5312
$\frac{5}{8}$				14·00	0·5512
		$\frac{9}{16}$	$\frac{37}{64}$		0·5781
	$\frac{3}{4}$		$\frac{21}{32}$		0·6562
		$\frac{5}{8}$	$\frac{41}{64}$		0·640
$\frac{3}{4}$			$\frac{43}{64}$		0·6719
	$\frac{7}{8}$	$\frac{3}{4}$	$\frac{49}{64}$		0·7656
$\frac{7}{8}$				20·00	0·7874
	1		$\frac{7}{8}$		0·8750
		$\frac{7}{8}$	$\frac{57}{64}$		0·8906
			$\frac{29}{32}$		0·9062
		1	$1\frac{1}{64}$		1·0156

BA SCREWS

Size	Diameter (in)	(mm)	Threads per inch	Pitch (in)	(mm)	Hole size Clearance Size	No	Tapping Size	No
0	0·2362	6·0	25·4	0·0394	1·0	0·242	C	0·196	9
1	0·2087	5·3	28·2	0·0354	0·9	0·213	3	0·173	17
2	0·185	4·7	31·4	0·0319	0·81	0·1935	10	0·152	24
3	0·1614	4·1	34·8	0·0287	0·73	0·1695	18	0·128	30
4	0·1417	3·6	38·5	0·026	0·66	0·1495	25	0·116	32
5	0·126	3·2	43·0	0·0232	0·59	0·136	29	0·104	37
6	0·1102	2·8	47·9	0·0209	0·53	0·120	31	0·089	43
7	0·0984	2·5	52·9	0·0189	0·48	0·1065	36	0·081	46
8	0·0866	2·2	59·1	0·0169	0·43	0·0985	42	0·07	50
9	0·0748	1·9	65·1	0·0154	0·39	0·081	46	0·0595	53
	0·0669	1·7	72·6	0·0138	0·35	0·073	49	0·055	54

DIMENSIONS OF BRITISH ASSOCIATION SCREWS, NUTS AND WASHERS SELECTED FROM BS 57 : 1951

BA No	TPI	A dia max mm	A dia max in	B Max	B Tol	C Max	C Tol	D Nom	E Max	E Tol	F rad Max	G Nom	H rad Approx	J Nom	K Max	L Nom
Preferred																
2	31·3	4·7	0·185	0·130	−7	0·052	−8	0·058	0·319	−10	0·015	0·071	0·319	0·036	0·010	0·077
4	38·5	3·6	0·142	0·101	−6	0·040	−6	0·045	0·252	−10	0·010	0·056	0·252	0·031	0·010	0·065
6	47·9	2·8	0·110	0·078	−5	0·033	−6	0·035	0·194	−10	0·010	0·043	0·194	0·024	0·009	0·051
8	59·1	2·2	0·087	0·063	−4	0·030	−6	0·027	0·157	−10	0·010	0·035	0·157	0·021	0·008	0·043
10	72·6	1·7	0·067	0·045	−4	0·024	−5	0·020	0·112	−5	0·007	0·025	0·112	0·016	0·007	0·030
12	90·7	1·3	0·051	0·038	−3	0·020	−5	0·017	0·095	−5	0·005	—	—	0·014	0·006	0·028
Second choice																
0	25·4	6·0	0·236	0·167	−8	0·064	−8	0·075	0·413	−10	0·015	0·092	0·413	0·045	0·010	0·099
1	28·2	5·3	0·209	0·148	−7	0·058	−8	0·066	0·366	−10	0·015	0·081	0·366	0·041	0·010	0·089
3	34·8	4·1	0·161	0·113	−6	0·047	−8	0·051	0·283	−10	0·015	0·062	0·283	0·033	0·010	0·071
5	43·1	3·2	0·126	0·088	−5	0·040	−6	0·040	0·221	−10	0·010	0·048	0·221	0·028	0·010	0·058

Dimensions in inches except where otherwise stated. Tolerance columns given in 0·001 in units.

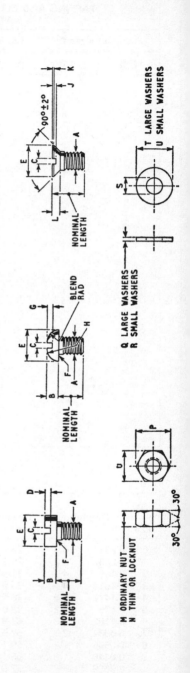

BA No	M Max	M Tol	N Max	N Tol	O Max	O Tol	P Max	Q SWG	Q in	R SWG	R in	S Max	S Tol	T Max	T Tol	U Max	U Tol
Preferred																	
2	0·167	−10	0·123	−10	0·324	−5	0·37	18	0·048	21	0·032	0·202	−5	0·500	−5	0·391	−5
4	0·135	−10	0·094	−10	0·248	−5	0·29	19	0·040	22	0·028	0·157	−5	0·378	−5	0·301	−5
6	0·105	−10	0·073	−10	0·193	−4	0·22	20	0·036	23	0·024	0·123	−5	0·288	−5	0·233	−5
8	0·082	−7	0·058	−7	0·152	−3	0·18	25	0·020	25	0·020	0·099	−5	0·228	−5	0·185	−5
10	0·064	−7	—	—	0·117	−3	0·14	27	0·016	—	—	0·078	−5	0·176	−5	—	—
12	0·049	−5	—	—	0·090	−2	0·10	—	—	—	—	—	—	—	—	—	—
Second choice																	
0	0·213	−10	0·157	−10	0·413	−5	0·48	17	0·056	19	0·040	0·256	−5	0·625	−5	0·500	−5
1	0·188	−10	0·139	−10	0·365	−5	0·42	18	0·048	20	0·036	0·228	−5	0·565	−5	0·443	−5
3	0·153	−10	0·108	−10	0·282	−5	0·33	19	0·040	22	0·028	0·177	−5	0·432	−5	0·341	−5
5	0·120	−10	0·084	−10	0·220	−4	0·25	20	0·036	23	0·024	0·140	−5	0·335	−5	0·268	−5

SOCKET SCREWS

Size	Cap screws D	H	F	L	Set screws G	P
6 BA					0·050	
5 BA					$\frac{1}{16}$	$\frac{3}{16}$–$\frac{3}{4}$
4 BA	0·248	0·142	$\frac{1}{8}$	$\frac{1}{4}$–$\frac{3}{4}$	$\frac{1}{16}$	$\frac{3}{16}$–1
3 BA	0·282	0·161	$\frac{1}{8}$	$\frac{3}{8}$–1	$\frac{5}{64}$	$\frac{3}{16}$–1
2 BA	0·324	0·185	$\frac{5}{32}$	$\frac{3}{8}$–1$\frac{1}{2}$	$\frac{3}{32}$	$\frac{3}{16}$–1$\frac{1}{4}$
1 BA	0·365	0·209	$\frac{3}{16}$	$\frac{3}{8}$–2	$\frac{3}{32}$	$\frac{3}{16}$–1$\frac{1}{4}$
0 BA	0·413	0·236	$\frac{7}{32}$	$\frac{3}{8}$–3	$\frac{1}{8}$	$\frac{3}{16}$–2
$\frac{3}{16}$	$\frac{5}{16}$	$\frac{3}{16}$	$\frac{5}{32}$	$\frac{3}{8}$–2	$\frac{3}{32}$	$\frac{3}{16}$–1$\frac{1}{4}$
$\frac{1}{4}$	$\frac{3}{8}$	$\frac{1}{4}$	$\frac{3}{16}$	$\frac{3}{8}$–3	$\frac{1}{8}$	$\frac{3}{16}$–2

Size	Cap screws D	H	F	L	Set screws G	P	Pipe plugs G	P
$\frac{5}{16}$	$\frac{7}{16}$	$\frac{5}{16}$	$\frac{7}{32}$	$\frac{3}{8}$–3$\frac{1}{2}$	$\frac{5}{32}$	$\frac{1}{4}$–2		
$\frac{3}{8}$	$\frac{9}{16}$	$\frac{3}{8}$	$\frac{5}{16}$	$\frac{1}{2}$–5	$\frac{3}{16}$	$\frac{1}{4}$–2$\frac{1}{2}$	$\frac{3}{16}$	$\frac{3}{8}$
$\frac{7}{16}$ $\frac{3}{8}$ gas	$\frac{5}{8}$	$\frac{7}{16}$	$\frac{5}{16}$	$\frac{1}{2}$–4	$\frac{7}{32}$	$\frac{3}{8}$–2$\frac{1}{2}$		
$\frac{1}{2}$ $\frac{1}{4}$ gas	$\frac{3}{4}$	$\frac{1}{2}$	$\frac{3}{8}$	$\frac{1}{2}$–6	$\frac{1}{4}$	$\frac{3}{8}$–3	$\frac{1}{4}$	$\frac{1}{2}$
$\frac{5}{8}$ $\frac{3}{8}$ gas	$\frac{7}{8}$	$\frac{5}{8}$	$\frac{1}{2}$	1–6	$\frac{5}{16}$	$\frac{1}{2}$–3	$\frac{5}{16}$	$\frac{9}{16}$
$\frac{3}{4}$ $\frac{1}{2}$ gas	1	$\frac{3}{4}$	$\frac{9}{16}$	1$\frac{1}{4}$–6	$\frac{3}{8}$	$\frac{5}{8}$–3	$\frac{3}{8}$	$\frac{9}{16}$
$\frac{7}{8}$ $\frac{3}{4}$ gas	1$\frac{1}{8}$	$\frac{7}{8}$	$\frac{9}{16}$	1$\frac{3}{4}$–6	$\frac{1}{2}$	$\frac{3}{4}$–3	$\frac{9}{16}$	$\frac{5}{8}$
1 1 gas	1$\frac{5}{16}$	1	$\frac{5}{8}$	2–6	$\frac{9}{16}$	1–3	$\frac{5}{8}$	$\frac{3}{4}$

All dimensions in inches

WIRE SIZES

Wire No	SWG (in)	SWG (mm)	AWG (in)	AWG (mm)	BWG (in)	BWG (mm)	Std metric (ref to swg) (mm)
0000	0·40	10·16	0·460	11·68	0·454	11·53	
000	0·372	9·45	0·409	10·41	0·425	10·80	
00	0·348	8·84	0·365	9·27	0·380	9·65	
0	0·324	8·23	0·325	8·25	0·340	8·64	
1	0·300	7·62	0·289	7·35	0·300	7·62	
2	0·276	7·01	0·258	6·54	0·283	7·21	
3	0·252	6·40	0·229	5·83	0·259	6·58	
4	0·232	5·89	0·204	5·19	0·238	6·05	
5	0·212	5·38	0·182	4·62	0·220	5·59	
6	0·192	4·88	0·162	4·11	0·203	5·16	
7	0·176	4·47	0·144	3·66	0·179	4·57	
8	0·160	4·06	0·128	3·26	0·164	4·19	
9	0·144	3·66	0·114	2·90	0·147	3·76	
10	0·128	3·25	0·102	2·59	0·134	3·40	
11	0·116	2·95	0·091	2·30	0·120	3·05	
12	0·104	2·64	0·081	2·05	0·109	2·77	
13	0·092	2·34	0·072	1·83	0·095	2·41	
14	0·081	2·03	0·064	1·63	0·083	2·11	
15	0·072	1·83	0·057	1·45	0·072	1·83	
16	0·064	1·63	0·051	1·29	0·065	1·65	
17	0·056	1·42	0·045	1·15	0·058	1·47	1·5
18	0·048	1·22	0·040	1·02	0·049	1·24	1·25
19	0·040	1·02	0·036	0·91	0·042	1·07	1·00
20	0·036	0·92	0·032	0·81	0·035	0·89	
21	0·032	0·81	0·028	0·72	0·031	0·81	0·8
22	0·028	0·71	0·025	0·64	0·028	0·71	0·71
23	0·024	0·61	0·023	0·57	0·025	0·64	
24	0·023	0·56	0·020	0·51	0·023	0·56	0·56
25	0·020	0·51	0·018	0·45	0·020	0·51	0·5
26	0·018	0·46	0·016	0·40	0·018	0·46	
27	0·016	0·41	0·014	0·36	0·016	0·41	0·4
28	0·014	0·38	0·013	0·32	0·0135	0·356	
29	0·013	0·35	0·011	0·29	0·013	0·33	
30	0·012	0·305	0·010	0·25	0·012	0·305	0·315
31	0·011	0·29	0·009	0·23	0·010	0·254	
32	0·0106	0·27	0·008	0·20	0·009	0·299	
33	0·010	0·254	0·007	0·18	0·008	0·203	0·25
34	0·009	0·229	0·0063	0·16	0·007	0·178	0·224
35	0·008	0·203	0·0056	0·14	0·005	0·127	0·2
36	0·007	0·178	0·0050	0·13	0·004	0·102	
37	0·0067	0·17	0·0044	0·11			
38	0·006	0·15	0·0040	0·10			
39	0·005	0·127	0·0035	0·08			

SWG = Standard wire gauge; AWG = American wire gauge; BWG = Birmingham wire gauge. Diameters in millimetres are derived from original inch sizes.

BRITISH STANDARD COPPER WIRE TABLE

SWG	Diameter (in)	Resistance (a)	Length (b)	Current rating (c)	Turns per linear inch					Turns per square inch					Nearest American wire gauge
					Enamel	Single silk	Double silk	Single cotton	Double cotton	Enamel	Single silk	Double silk	Single cotton	Double cotton	
10	0·128	1·866	6·67	15·442	7·48	—	—	7·35	7·0	56	—	—	54	49	8
12	0·104	2·826	10·23	10·194	9·09	—	—	8·8	8·4	82·6	—	—	77·4	70·6	10
14	0·080	4·776	17·16	6·032	11·78	—	—	11·2	10·5	139	—	—	125·4	110	12
16	0·064	7·463	26·86	3·86	14·8	14·7	14·5	13·9	12·0	219	216	210	193·2	169	14
18	0·048	13·27	47·66	2·1715	19·7	19·8	19·4	18·0	16·8	388	392	376	324	282	17
20	0·036	23·59	85·00	1·2215	26·0	26·0	25·3	23·5	21·0	676	676	640	552	441	19
22	0·028	38·99	140·6	0·73	33·0	33·0	31·9	29·1	25·4	1,089	1,089	1,018	847	645	21
24	0·022	63·16	228·3	0·4561	41·6	42·1	40·0	36·7	31·0	1,731	1,772	1,600	1,347	961	23
26	0·018	94·4	340·0	0·3054	50·2	51·2	48·3	43·0	35·4	2,520	2,621	2,333	1,849	1,253	25
28	0·0148	139·6	503·0	0·2064	61·0	61·7	57·4	50·2	38·6	3,721	3,807	3,295	2,520	1,490	27
30	0·0124	199	716·6	0·1450	72·5	72·4	66·6	57·1	44·4	5,256	5,242	4,436	3,260	1,971	28
32	0·0108	262	943·3	0·1099	82·7	81·9	74·6	62·8	47·8	6,839	6,708	5,565	3,944	2,285	30
34	0·0092	361	1,300	0·0798	97	94·3	84·7	69·9	51·7	9,409	8,892	7,174	4,886	2,673	32
36	0·0076	529	1,903	0·0545	116	111	97·9	85·4	59·9	13,456	12,321	9,584	7,293	3,588	34
38	0·0060	849	3,056	0·0340	145	135	113	99	67·7	21,025	18,225	12,769	9,801	4,583	36
40	0·0048	1,327	4,766	0·0217	178	161	131	112	75·1	31,684	25,921	17,161	12,544	5,640	38

(a) Ohms per 1,000 yards at 60°F; (b) Yards per lb; (c) Amps at 1,200 A/in^2

IMPERIAL/METRIC CABLES AND FLEXIBLES

Imperial Number and size of wire(s) (No/in)	Nominal area (in)	(mm)	Metric Nominal area (mm)	Number and size of wire(s) (No/mm)	Current rating Surface twin and earth (A)	Single core Enclosed (A)	Unenclosed (A)
FIXED CABLE CONDUCTORS—CIRCULAR							
1/0·044	0·0015	1·0	1·0	1/1·13	13	9	12
3/0·029	0·002	1·25					
			1·5	1/1·38	16	11	15
3/0·36	0·003	2·0					
			2·5	1/1·78	23	16	20
7/0·029	0·0045	3·0					
			4·0	7/0·85	30	22	27
7/0·036	0·007	4·5					
			6·0	7/1·04	38	28	34
7/0·044	0·01	6·75					
7/0·052	0·0145	9·5					
			10·0	7/1·35	51	39	46
7/0·064	0·0225	15					
			16·0	7/1·70	68	50	61
19/0·044	0·03	20					
19/0·052	0·04	25	25·0	7/2·14	89	66	80
			35·0	19/1·35	109	80	98
19/0·064	0·06	40					
				19/1·78	175	125	160
FLEXIBLE CORD CONDUCTORS							
14/0·0076	0·0006	0·4					
			0·5	16/0·2	} 3		
			0·5	28/0·15			
23/0·0076	0·001	0·65					
			0·75	24/0·2	} 6		
			0·75	42/0·15			
			1·00	32/0·2			
40/0·0076	0·0017	1·1					
			1·5	30/0·25	15		
70/0·0076	0·003	2·0					
			2·5	50/0·25	20		
110/0·0076	0·0048	3·0					
			4·0	56/0·3	25		
162/0·0076	0·007	4·5					

FUSE WIRE TABLE

Fusing current (A)	Copper Diam (in)	SWG	Tin Diam (in)	SWG	Lead Diam (in)	SWG
1	0·0021	47	0·0072	37	0·0081	35
2	0·0034	43	0·0113	31	0·0128	30
3	0·0044	41	0·0149	28	0·0168	27
4	0·0053	39	0·0181	26	0·0203	25
5	0·0062	38	0·0210	25	0·0236	23
10	0·0098	33	0·0334	21	0·0375	20
15	0·0129	30	0·0437	19	0·0491	18
20	0·0156	28	0·0529	17	0·0595	17

FERRITES

Inductors and transformers

Where cores are used for inductors in tuned circuits, the top end of the frequency range in which a particular grade of ferrite can be used to optimum advantage is the highest frequency for which the value of loss factor is given. It must be noted that the manufacturing conditions particularly affect the higher-frequency behaviour of the ferrites and performance cannot be guaranteed beyond the above-mentioned limits. Performance evaluation on the basis of samples above the specified frequency limits may be very misleading as the losses in this region increase very rapidly and there is no guarantee that another batch of cores will behave in an identical fashion. If a guaranteed value of Q is required, a grade of ferrite should be chosen for which the desired frequency lies within the range of the published loss factors. For example, if the value of Q is to be ensured at 5 MHz grade F14 should not be used, but rather grade F16, the loss factors of which are specified up to 10 MHz.

Where the cores are used in untuned circuits and the value of Q is not the primary consideration, individual grades may be usefully employed well beyond the range of frequency, for which loss factors are specified. This particularly applies to all transformer applications where high permeability makes it possible to reduce the number of turns required for a shunt inductance, thus decreasing the leakage inductance which is usually the limiting factor at the high-frequency end.

In low-power transformers, the core material may, to a close approximation, be regarded as remaining in the Rayleigh region in which the area of the hysterisis loop is very small and the permeability may be considered invariant throughout the cycle of the applied current. Such transformers, which are used at rf and vhf and in pulse circuits, may be tuned or not tuned, depending on the requirements of the particular application. They can be based on a wide variety of core shapes and configurations—open circuit, gapped and toroidal.

If the transformer is to be tuned it is obvious that the choice of ferrite for its core must be determined by the frequency of tuning, ie the material must be so chosen as to provide the optimum (or required) value of Q at the specified frequency. The core configuration depends upon the required value of the inductance of the winding, demand for adjustment facilities, space requirements and expected selectivity, taking into account the loading etc. Typical examples of such transformers occur in radio and television i.f. circuits, and in filter circuits. All these transformers are used to transmit a relatively narrow band of frequencies.

Untuned transformers usually serve to transmit relatively wide bands of frequencies, stretching from low repetition frequency to the high edge-forming frequencies

APPLICATIONS OF SOFT FERRITES

Component	Grade of ferrite
Balun cores	F7, F14, F22
Suppressors	F6, F7, F8, F9
L-cores, E-cores, U-cores and toroids	
Suppression beads	F8, F14
Toroids	All grades
Aerial rods	
—long and medium waves	F11, F14
—short waves	F16
Screw cores, rods, pins and tubes	F8, F14, F16, F22, F25, F29

in the case of pulse transformers. Loss of power, expressed in decibels, is usually the main criterion of quality and it is required that it be as small as possible over very wide frequency spectrum. The lowest frequency at which the loss does not exceed some specified value is determined by the shunt inductance of the winding, ie the value of the inductance measured with the secondary winding open-circuited. The highest frequency that can be tolerated for a given loss depends upon the leakage inductance, ie the value of the inductance with the secondary winding short-circuited. While the shunt inductance is a function of the coil permeability in the magnetic circuit, the leakage inductance is not affected by the core and depends only on the configuration, number of turns and the proximity of the windings.

To obtain a shunt inductance as high as possible for a given number of turns which is specified for a maximum permissible leakage inductance, it is necessary to use a ferrite of the highest permeability and in a configuration ensuring minimum dilution of the permeability, ie in the form of a toroidal core, or, if the winding cost is regarded as unacceptable, in the form of pot cores, E-cores etc. In this context it is often considered that the losses of high-permeability ferrites at the higher frequencies are excessive.

To explain why this is not usually important it is necessary to analyse the nature of the losses occurring in a wide-band transformer. As a first approximation, a transformer can be regarded in the lower-frequency region of its spectrum as an inductance and resistance connected in parallel between the source and the load. The inductance is the shunt inductance of the winding and the resistance is the total loss resistance, ie the dc and ac resistance of the winding, and the resistance representing the losses in the core at the relevant frequency. The loss resistance of the winding equals its reactance multiplied by Q (parallel circuit). To simplify this concept without in any way limiting its general validity, it can be assumed that the source and load impedances are the same, ie the ratio of the transformer is $1:1$. At the low-frequency end of the spectrum the shunt reactance is usually designed to be several times higher than the source or load impedance. Taking the ratio of the shunt reactance to source impedance as m, we have the following values of transformer loss, neglecting at this point the losses due to the resistance of the transformer.

m	Loss (dB)
0·5	3·0
0·75	1·6
0·9	1·17
1·0	0·97
1·1	0·79
1·9	0·29
2·0	0·26
2·1	0·24
3·0	0·12
4·0	0·04
5·0	0·03

Even if the transformer loss of 0·97 dB can be tolerated and easily compensated by additional gain in the system, it is obvious the shunt reactance to circuit impedance ratio of 1 would lead to serious changes in the loss when the permeability of the core (and the shunt reactance) vary with normal tolerances. This is one of the prime reasons for keeping the shunt reactance appreciably higher than the circuit impedance, say three to five times higher, the loss due to the shunt reactance then being so small that the expected changes in this reactance become insignificant from the loss point of view. Another important aspect of transformer design is the transformer loss resistance. At the low-frequency end of the spectrum the value of Q will still be reasonable but in an exaggerated condition it would only be assumed that it is only 3. This would mean that at the frequency for which the shunt reactance is, say, three times as high as the circuit impedance, the loss resistance is nine times as high as this impedance. The losses caused by the presence of the transformer resistance, expressed again by the loss resistance circuit impedance ratio n, are as follows.

n	Loss (dB)
1	3·5
3	1·3
6	0·68
9	0·46
10	0·42
20	0·20
40	0·1

In the case where the loss resistance is nine times higher than the circuit impedance, the loss introduced by it is 0·46 dB and it can be seen that it does not vary greatly with the expected variations of the permeability and Q. At any frequency higher than the bottom limit of the spectrum the ratio of the shunt reactance to the circuit impedance is higher than the value chosen for the lowest frequency as reactance is proportional to frequency, and similarly the ratio of the loss resistance to the circuit impedance is also improving in spite of the rising losses in the ferrite core.

This state of affairs continues until the frequencies are reached where the leakage inductance becomes significant and ultimately the dominant factor. As previously mentioned, the leakage inductance is not affected by the core, neither is the loss associated with it. The value of leakage reactance that equals one half of the circuit impedance causes a loss of 0·26 dB which increases to 2 dB when the leakage reactance is equal to the circuit impedance. The losses caused by the resistance associated with the leakage inductance are not likely to be very significant.

Antenna rods

Antenna rods are manufactured in various grades of ferrite that are most suitable for the wavebands to be covered.

Long and medium-wave bands—grades F11 and F14
Long, medium and short-wave bands—grade F16

The properties of these materials are given in the tables. The measured coil permeability (inductance ratio) depends on the initial permeability of the material, length-to-diameter ratio of the rod and the type and geometry of the winding.

The pick-up sensitivity is a function of the initial permeability of the material length-to-diameter ratio, position of the coil, its number of turns and the loaded value of Q in the circuit.

Antenna rods that generally comply with IEC Publication 223 have diameters of 8 or 10 mm to − 5 per cent. Lengths are up to 160 mm (8 mm diam) and up to 200 mm (10 mm diam) ± 2 per cent.

Small ferrite rods generally complying with IEC Publication 220 have outside diameters of 1·0 to 12·7 mm, lengths 13 to 100 mm (dependant on diameter), in all grades of ferrite.

Ferrite tubes generally complying with IEC Publication 220 have outside diameters of 2·5 to 12·7 mm and inner diameters of 0·6 to 5·0 mm in all grades of ferrite.

Ferrite beads

Screening (suppression) beads are manufactured from relatively high-permeability ferrites, and are threaded on wire leads. At frequencies well beyond the normal range of application, they provide a series impedance, the resistive component of which acts as a fictitious resistor in series with the circuit being protected, while the reactive component serves as a series choke. Beads are used in this manner to prevent high-frequency leakage from screened boxes or parasitic oscillations arising from spurious feedback, and for suppression of interference. This form of protection is possible, because at frequencies far removed from the normal range of application the losses in the ferrites are very high.

A ferrite bead threaded on a lead produces no noticeable direct effect on the operation of the equipment, because at low frequencies the series impedance is very low. Although the bead does not cause a voltage drop at low frequencies, it acts as a suppressor at very high frequencies due to the resistance, representing the losses in the ferrite, being high and the reactance which generally increases with frequency in spite of gradual loss of permeability. This decrease in permeability becomes noticeable at frequencies 10 to 20 times higher than the upper limit of the normal range of application.

Beads made from F8 material give a constant resistance but varying reactance from 50–200 MHz, while with F14 material both components of the impedance are rising with frequency. These measurements were obtained with a 12·7 mm length of 0·9 mm copper wire with a single bead threaded on it.

The series impedance of the wire threaded through the bead is proportional to the length of the bead, or the number of beads used. Alternatively several turns of wire can be wound toroidally on the bead to produce a higher impedance. Suppression beads with six evenly spaced holes in F8 and F14 material are effective from 5 to 150 MHz, length nominally 10 mm and diameter 6·0 mm. The beads are usually wound with $2\frac{1}{2}$ turns (a single wire threaded through five holes) or with $2 \times 1\frac{1}{2}$ turns (both conductors threaded through three holes). The tables show some typical results of impedance measurements on each type of bead, using a Boonton R-X meter type 250A. The resistivity of F14 material is very much higher than that of F8 material. The use of bare wire with F8 suppression beads is not therefore recommended.

SINGLE HOLE FERRITE BEAD

Size (mm) and type of bead		Impedance R + jX		
		50 MHz	100 MHz	200 MHz
4·0 × 1·5 × 9·5	F8	75 + j19	75 + j12	75 + j15
4·0 × 1·5 × 5·0	F19	23 + j19	35 + j30	45 + j34

SIX-HOLE FERRITE BEAD

Frequency (MHz)	Impedance R + jX	
	F14	F8
5	—	160 + j180
12	5 + j135	300 + j160
20	75 + j225	350 + j100
50	270 + j250	370 + j65
100	420 + j275	420 + j40
150	510 + j225	—

Ferrite rings

Ferrite ring cores for toroidal assemblies vary in size from 6·35 mm to 38·1 mm in overall diameter. Inductance of a winding wound on a ring core can be calculated from the formula

$$L = AL. \ n^2 \text{ nanohenrys}$$

where AL is the inductance of one turn in nanohenrys and n is the number of turns

AL is calculated from the initial permeability of the material given in the tables and the dimensional factor $\Sigma(l/a)$

$$AL = \frac{0·4\pi\mu}{\Sigma\frac{l}{A}} \text{nanohenrys}$$

The electrical specification for each ring core diameter is stated in the tables below. The internal diameter is stated on each table heading. Minimum AL values are given for each ring width (both in millimetres)

Ring core (OD = 6·35 mm, i.d. = 3·18 mm)

Width	F7	F8	F9	F14	F25	F29
1·52	379	252	736	37	8·4	2·0
3·96	987	658	1,920	96	21·9	5·2
7·92	1,983	1,322	3,856	193	44·0	10·5

Ring core (OD = 12·7 mm, i.d. = 6·35 mm)

Width	F7	F8	F9	F14	F25	F29
3·18	790	527	1,537	77	17·5	4·2
6·35	1,580	1,054	3,074	154	35·0	8·5
9·52	2,380	1,586	4,627	232	52·8	12·7

Ring core (OD = 19·05 mm, i.d. = 12·7 mm)

Width	F7	F8	F9	F14	F25
3·18	464	309	903	45	10·3
6·35	930	620	1,809	91	20·7
9·52	1,396	930	2,713	136	31·0

Ring core (OD = 25·4 mm, i.d. = 19·05 mm)

Width	F7	F8	F9	F14	F25
4·75	494	329	960	48	10·9
9·52	988	658	1,920	96	21·8
14·30	1,478	985	2,880	144	32·8

Ring core (OD = 38·1 mm, i.d. = 25·4 mm)

Width	F7	F8	F9	F14	F25
6·35	926	618	1,802	90	20
12·70	1,854	1,236	3,604	181	41
19·50	2,790	1,861	5,427	272	62

FERRITE MAGNETIC PROPERTIES (NICKEL-ZINC)

Parameter	Symbol	Standard conditions of test	Unit	F13	F14	F16	F25*	F22	F29*
Initial permeability (±20%)	μi	B→0, 25°C	1 MHz	—	650	220	125	50	19	12
Saturation flux density	B_{sat}	H = 796A/m = 10 Oe, 25°C	mT	320	350	340	—	—	—
Loss factor (maximum)	$\tan \delta_{r+e}$ μi	B→0, 25°C	10^{-6}						
		250 kHz		50					
		500 kHz		65					
		1 MHz		130	40	60	50		
		2 MHz			42		50		
		3 MHz			50		55		
		5 MHz				65	65		
		10 MHz				100	75	300	100
		15 MHz					100		
		20 MHz					125	330	
		40 MHz					300	500	
		100 MHz							200
		200 MHz							1,000
Temperature factor	$\dfrac{\Delta\mu}{\mu i^2 \cdot \Delta T}$	B < 0·25mT, +25°C to +55°C	$10^{-6}/°C$	1·5‡	12–30	20–50	10–15	12–17	50‡
Curie temperature (minimum)	θ_c	B < 0·25mT	°C	180	270	270	450	500	500
Resistivity (typical)	ρ	1 V/cm, 25°C	ohm cm	3×10^4	10^4	10^5	10^5	10^5	10^5

* These are Perminvar ferrites and undergo irreversible changes of characteristics (μ increases and loss factors become much greater especially at higher frequencies) if subjected to strong magnetic fields or mechanical shocks.
‡ Average.

FERRITE MAGNETIC PROPERTIES (MANGANESE–ZINC)

Parameter	Symbol	Standard conditions of test	Unit	F5	F6	F7	F8	F9	F11
Initial permeability (minimum)	μi	B→0, 25°C	—	1,600	1,200	1,800	1,200	3,500	500
			kHz	1	1	100	100	1	100
Saturation flux density	B_{sat}	H = 796A/m = 10Oe, 25°C	mT	480	450	390	380	380	380
Loss factor (maximum)	$\tan \delta_{i+e}$ / μi	B→0, 25°C	10						
			20 kHz	—	—	8	—	—	—
			100 kHz	—	—	—	—	15	20
			250 kHz	—	—	—	30	—	—
			500 kHz	—	—	—	110	—	—
			1 MHz	—	—	—	—	—	47
Temperature factor	$\Delta\mu$ / $\mu i^{2}.\Delta T$	B < 0.25 mT, +25°C + 55°C	10^{-6}/°C	—	—	0–2	0–1	0–2	0.5–2.5
			10 kHz						
Amplitude permeability (minimum)	μ_a	200 mT, 25°C	50 Hz	3,000	3,000	—	—	—	—
		400 mT, 25°C	50 Hz	1,000	1,000	—	—	—	—
		320 mT, 100°C	50 Hz	1,000	1,000	—	—	—	—
Total power loss density (maximum)		200 mT, 25°C	16 kHz	110	150	—	—	—	—
		100°C	16 kHz	120	150	—	—	—	—
Curie temperature (minimum)	θ_c	B < 0.25 mT,	°C	200	190	150	130	135	220
		10 kHz							
Resistivity (typical)	ρ	1 V/cm, 25°C	ohm cm	100	100	100	100	50	500

SI/CGS unit conversions
1A/m = 0·012566 oersted   1Mx = 10^{-8} weber
1Oe = 79·557 ampere/metre   1T = 1Wb/m^2 = 10^4 gauss
1Wb = 1Vs = 10^8 maxwell   1Gs = 0·1 millitesla

BATTERY DATA

Electrochemical system	USA size	Voltage (V)	Type‡	IEC equiv	Length (or diam)	Width	Height	Contacts	Current (mA)	Weight (g)
Zinc carbon	N	1·5	D23	R1	12	—	30·1	Cap and base	1-5	7
	AAA		HP16	R03	10·5	—	45	Cap and base	0-1,000	8·5
	AA		HP7	R6	14·5	—	50·5	Cap and base	0-75	16·5
	AA		C7	R6	14·5	—	50·5	Cap and base	0-75	16·5
	C		SP11	R14	26·2	—	50	Cap and base	20-60	45
	C		HP11	R14	26·2	—	50	Cap and base	0-1,000	45
	C		C11	R14	26·2	—	50	Cap and base	0-5	45
	D		SP2	R20	34·2	—	61·8	Cap and base	25-100	90
	D		HP2	R20	34·2	—	61·8	Cap and base	0-2,000	90
		4·5	AD28	3R25	101·6	34·9	106	Socket	30-300	453·6
			1289	3R12	62	22	67	Flat springs	0-300	113
		6·0	PP8	4-F100-4	65·1	51·6	200·8	Press studs	20-151	1,100
			PJ996	4-R25	67	67	102	Spiral springs	30-300	581
			991		135·7	72·2	125·4	Two screws	30-500	1,470
		9·0	PP3-P	6-F22	26·5	17·5	48·5	Press studs	0-50	39
			PP3-C	6-F22	26·5	17·5	48·5	Press studs	0-50	39
			PP3	6-F22	26·5	17·5	48·5	Press studs	0-10	38
			PP4	6-F20	25·5	—	50	Press studs	0-10	51
			PP6	6-F50-2	36	34·5	70	Press studs	2·5-15	142
			PP7	6-F90	46	46	61·9	Press studs	5-20	198
			PP9	6-F100	66	52	81	Press studs	5-50	425
			PP10	6-F100-3	66	52	226	Socket	15-150	1,250
		15·0	B154	10-F15	16	15	35	End contacts	0·1-0·5	14·2
			B121	10-F20	27	16	37	End contacts	0·1-1·0	21
		22·5	B155	15-F15	16	15	51	End contacts	0·1-0·5	20
			B122	15-F20	27	16	51	End contacts	0·1-1·0	32
Manganese alkaline	ED	1·5	MN1300*	LR20	34·2	—	61·5	Cap and base	0-2,000	12·3
	C		MN1400*	LR14	26·2	—	50	Cap and base	0-1,000	65
	AA		MN1500*	LR6	14·5	—	50·5	Cap and base	0-250	23
	AAA		MN2400*	LR03	10·5	—	44·5	Cap and base	0-100	13
	N		MN9100*	LR1	12	—	30·2	Cap and base	0-100	9·6

BATTERY DATA (continued)

Electrochemical system	USA size	Voltage (V)	Type‡	IEC equiv	Dimensions (mm)			Contacts	Current (mA)	Weight (g)
					Length (or diam)	Width	Height			
Mercuric oxide		1·35/1·4	RM675H	NR07	11·6	—	5·4	Cap and base (button)	—	2·6
			RM625N	MR9	15·6	—	6·2	Cap and base (button)	—	4·3
			RM575H	NR08	11·6	—	3·5	Cap and base (button)	—	1·4
			RM1H	NR50	16·4	—	16·8	Cap and base (button)	—	12·0
Silver oxide		1·5	10L14	5R44	11·56	—	5·33	Cap and base (button)	—	2·2
			10L124	5R43	11·56	—	4·19	Cap and base (button)	—	1·7
			10L123	5R48	7·75	—	5·33	Cap and base (button)	—	1·0
			10L125	5R41	7·75	—	3·58	Cap and base (button)	—	0·8
Nickel cadmium		1·25	NC828	—	See HP7			Button	0·28†	16·5
	AA		NCC60	—	See HP11			Button	0·60†	30·0
	C		NCC200	—	See HP2			Button	2·00†	78·0
	D		NCC400	—				Button	4·00†	170·0
		10·0	NC828/8	—				Button stack	0·28†	126·0
		12·0	10/225DK	—	See PP3			Button stack	0·225†	135·0
		9·0	TR7/8	(DEAC)	See HP7			Press studs	0·07†	45·0
	AA	1·25	501RS	(DEAC)	See HP11			Press studs	0·50†	30·0
	C		RS1·8	(DEAC)				Press studs	1·80†	65·0
	D		RS4	(DEAC)	See HP2			Press studs	4·00†	150·0

† Capacity in ampere hours
‡ BEREC types unless otherwise indicated
* Also Duracell (Mallory)

Part 9

Mathematical tables

LOGARITHMS OF NUMBERS AND PROPORTIONAL PARTS

	0	1	2	3	4	5	6	7	8	9	Proportional Parts 1 2 3 4 5 6 7 8 9
10	0000	0043	0086	0128	0170	0212	0253	0294	0334	0374	4 8 12 17 21 25 29 33 37
11	0414	0453	0492	0531	0569	0607	0645	0682	0719	0755	4 8 11 15 19 23 26 30 34
12	0792	0828	0864	0899	0934	0969	1004	1038	1072	1106	3 7 10 14 17 21 24 28 31
13	1139	1173	1206	1239	1271	1303	1335	1367	1399	1430	3 6 10 13 16 19 23 26 29
14	1461	1492	1523	1553	1584	1614	1644	1673	1703	1732	3 6 9 12 15 18 21 24 27
15	1761	1790	1818	1847	1875	1903	1931	1959	1987	2014	3 6 8 11 14 17 20 22 25
16	2041	2068	2095	2122	2148	2175	2201	2227	2253	2279	3 5 8 11 13 16 18 21 24
17	2304	2330	2355	2380	2405	2430	2455	2480	2504	2529	2 5 7 10 12 15 17 20 22
18	2553	2577	2601	2625	2648	2672	2695	2718	2742	2765	2 5 7 9 12 14 16 19 21
19	2788	2810	2833	2856	2878	2900	2923	2945	2967	2989	2 4 7 9 11 13 16 18 20
20	3010	3032	3054	3075	3096	3118	3139	3160	3181	3201	2 4 6 8 11 13 15 17 19
21	3222	3243	3263	3284	3304	3324	3345	3365	3385	3404	2 4 6 8 10 12 14 16 18
22	3424	3444	3464	3483	3502	3522	3541	3560	3579	3598	2 4 6 8 10 12 14 15 17
23	3617	3636	3655	3674	3692	3711	3729	3747	3766	3784	2 4 6 7 9 11 13 15 17
24	3802	3820	3838	3856	3874	3892	3909	3927	3945	3962	2 4 5 7 9 11 12 14 16
25	3979	3997	4014	4031	4048	4065	4082	4099	4116	4133	2 3 5 7 9 10 12 14 15
26	4150	4166	4183	4200	4216	4232	4249	4265	4281	4298	2 3 5 7 8 10 11 13 15
27	4314	4330	4346	4362	4378	4393	4409	4425	4440	4456	2 3 5 6 8 9 11 13 14
28	4472	4487	4502	4518	4533	4548	4564	4579	4594	4609	2 3 5 6 8 9 11 12 14
29	4624	4639	4654	4669	4683	4698	4713	4728	4742	4757	1 3 4 6 7 9 10 12 13
30	4771	4786	4800	4814	4829	4843	4857	4871	4886	4900	1 3 4 6 7 9 10 11 13
31	4914	4928	4942	4955	4969	4983	4997	5011	5024	5038	1 3 4 6 7 8 10 11 12
32	5051	5065	5079	5092	5105	5119	5132	5145	5159	5172	1 3 4 5 7 8 9 11 12
33	5185	5198	5211	5224	5237	5250	5263	5276	5289	5302	1 3 4 5 6 8 9 10 12
34	5315	5328	5340	5353	5366	5378	5391	5403	5416	5428	1 3 4 5 6 8 9 10 11
35	5441	5453	5465	5478	5490	5502	5514	5527	5539	5551	1 2 4 5 6 7 9 10 10
36	5563	5575	5587	5599	5611	5623	5635	5647	5658	5670	1 2 4 5 6 7 8 10 11
37	5682	5694	5705	5717	5729	5740	5752	5763	5775	5786	1 2 3 5 6 7 8 9 10
38	5798	5809	5821	5832	5843	5855	5866	5877	5888	5899	1 2 3 5 6 7 8 9 11
39	5911	5922	5933	5944	5955	5966	5977	5988	5999	6010	1 2 3 4 5 7 8 9 10
40	6021	6031	6042	6053	6064	6075	6085	6096	6107	6117	1 2 3 4 5 6 8 9 10
41	6128	6138	6149	6160	6170	6180	6191	6201	6212	6222	1 2 3 4 5 6 7 8 9
42	6232	6243	6253	6263	6274	6284	6294	6304	6314	6325	1 2 3 4 5 6 7 8 9
43	6335	6345	6355	6365	6375	6385	6395	6405	6415	6425	1 2 3 4 5 6 7 8 9
44	6435	6444	6454	6464	6474	6484	6493	6503	6513	6522	1 2 3 4 5 6 7 8 9
45	6532	6542	6551	6561	6571	6580	6590	6599	6609	6618	1 2 3 4 5 6 7 8 9
46	6628	6637	6646	6656	6665	6675	6684	6693	6702	6712	1 2 3 4 5 6 7 7 8
47	6721	6730	6739	6749	6758	6767	6776	6785	6794	6803	1 2 3 4 5 5 6 7 8
48	6812	6821	6830	6839	6848	6857	6866	6875	6884	6893	1 2 3 4 4 5 6 7 8
49	6902	6911	6920	6928	6937	6946	6955	6964	6972	6981	1 2 3 4 4 5 6 7 8
50	6990	6998	7007	7016	7024	7033	7042	7050	7059	7067	1 2 3 3 4 5 6 7 8
51	7076	7084	7093	7101	7110	7118	7126	7135	7143	7152	1 2 3 3 4 5 6 7 8
52	7160	7168	7177	7185	7193	7202	7210	7218	7226	7235	1 2 2 3 4 5 6 7 7
53	7243	7251	7259	7267	7275	7284	7292	7300	7308	7316	1 2 2 3 4 5 6 6 7
54	7324	7332	7340	7348	7356	7364	7372	7380	7388	7396	1 2 2 3 4 5 6 6 7

	0	1	2	3	4	5	6	7	8	9	Proportional Parts								
											1	2	3	4	5	6	7	8	9
55	7404	7412	7419	7427	7435	7443	7451	7459	7466	7474	1	2	2	3	4	5	5	6	7
56	7482	7490	7497	7505	7513	7520	7528	7536	7543	7551	1	2	2	3	4	5	5	6	7
57	7559	7566	7574	7582	7589	7597	7604	7612	7619	7627	1	2	2	3	4	5	5	6	7
58	7634	7642	7649	7657	7664	7672	7679	7686	7694	7701	1	1	2	3	4	4	5	6	7
59	7709	7716	7723	7731	7738	7745	7752	7760	7767	7774	1	1	2	3	4	4	5	6	7
60	7782	7789	7796	7803	7810	7818	7825	7832	7839	7846	1	1	2	3	4	4	5	6	6
61	7853	7860	7868	7875	7882	7889	7896	7903	7910	7917	1	1	2	3	4	4	5	6	6
62	7924	7931	7938	7945	7952	7959	7966	7973	7980	7987	1	1	2	3	3	4	5	6	6
63	7993	8000	8007	8014	8021	8028	8035	8041	8048	8055	1	1	2	3	3	4	5	5	6
64	8062	8069	8075	8082	8089	8096	8102	8109	8116	8122	1	1	2	3	3	4	5	5	6
65	8129	8136	8142	8149	8156	8162	8169	8176	8182	8189	1	1	2	3	3	4	5	5	6
66	8195	8202	8209	8215	8222	8228	8235	8241	8248	8254	1	1	2	3	3	4	5	5	6
67	8261	8267	8274	8280	8287	8293	8299	8306	8312	8319	1	1	2	3	3	4	5	5	6
68	8325	8331	8338	8344	8351	8357	8363	8370	8376	8383	1	1	2	3	3	4	4	5	6
69	8388	8395	8401	8407	8414	8420	8426	8432	8439	8445	1	1	2	2	3	4	4	5	6
70	8451	8457	8463	8470	8476	8482	8488	8494	8500	8506	1	1	2	2	3	4	4	5	6
71	8513	8519	8525	8531	8537	8543	8549	8555	8561	8567	1	1	2	2	3	4	4	5	5
72	8573	8579	8585	8591	8597	8603	8609	8615	8621	8627	1	1	2	2	3	4	4	5	5
73	8633	8639	8645	8651	8657	8663	8669	8675	8681	8686	1	1	2	2	3	4	4	5	5
74	8692	8698	8704	8710	8716	8722	8727	8733	8739	8745	1	1	2	2	3	4	4	5	5
75	8751	8756	8762	8768	8774	8779	8785	8791	8797	8802	1	1	2	2	3	3	4	5	5
76	8808	8814	8820	8825	8831	8837	8842	8848	8854	8859	1	1	2	2	3	3	4	5	5
77	8865	8871	8876	8882	8887	8893	8899	8904	8910	8915	1	1	2	2	3	3	4	4	5
78	8921	8927	8932	8938	8943	8949	8954	8960	8965	8971	1	1	2	2	3	3	4	4	5
79	8976	8982	8987	8993	8998	9004	9009	9015	9020	9025	1	1	2	2	3	3	4	4	5
80	9031	9036	9042	9047	9053	9058	9063	9069	9074	9079	1	1	2	2	3	3	4	4	5
81	9085	9090	9096	9101	9106	9112	9117	9122	9128	9133	1	1	2	2	3	3	4	4	5
82	9138	9143	9149	9154	9159	9165	9170	9175	9180	9186	1	1	2	2	3	3	4	4	5
83	9191	9196	9201	9206	9212	9217	9222	9227	9232	9238	1	1	2	2	3	3	4	4	5
84	9243	9248	9253	9258	9263	9269	9274	9279	9284	9289	1	1	2	2	3	3	4	4	5
85	9294	9299	9304	9309	9315	9320	9325	9330	9335	9340	1	1	2	2	3	3	4	4	5
86	9345	9350	9355	9360	9365	9370	9375	9380	9385	9390	1	1	2	2	3	3	4	4	5
87	9395	9400	9405	9410	9415	9420	9425	9430	9435	9440	0	1	1	2	2	3	3	4	4
88	9445	9450	9455	9460	9465	9469	9474	9479	9484	9489	0	1	1	2	2	3	3	4	4
89	9494	9499	9504	9509	9513	9518	9523	9528	9533	9538	0	1	1	2	2	3	3	4	4
90	9542	9547	9552	9557	9562	9566	9571	9576	9581	9586	0	1	1	2	2	3	3	4	4
91	9590	9595	9600	9605	9609	9614	9619	9624	9628	9633	0	1	1	2	2	3	3	4	4
92	9638	9643	9647	9652	9657	9661	9666	9671	9675	9680	0	1	1	2	2	3	3	4	4
93	9685	9689	9694	9699	9703	9708	9713	9717	9722	9727	0	1	1	2	2	3	3	4	4
94	9731	9736	9741	9745	9750	9754	9759	9763	9768	9773	0	1	1	2	2	3	3	4	4
95	9777	9782	9786	9791	9795	9800	9805	9809	9814	9818	0	1	1	2	2	3	3	4	4
96	9823	9827	9832	9836	9841	9845	9850	9854	9859	9863	0	1	1	2	2	3	3	4	4
97	9868	9872	9877	9881	9886	9890	9894	9899	9903	9908	0	1	1	2	2	3	3	4	4
98	9912	9917	9921	9926	9930	9934	9939	9943	9948	9952	0	1	1	2	2	3	3	4	4
99	9956	9961	9965	9969	9974	9978	9983	9987	9991	9996	0	1	1	2	2	3	3	3	4

HYPERBOLIC OR NAPERIAN LOGARITHMS

	0	1	2	3	4	5	6	7	8	9	1 2 3	4 5 6	7 8 9
1·0	0·0000	0099	0198	0296	0392	0488	0583	0677	0770	0862	10 19 29	38 48 57	67 76 86
1·1	0·0953	1044	1133	1222	1310	1398	1484	1570	1655	1740	9 17 26	35 44 52	61 70 78
1·2	0·1823	1906	1989	2070	2151	2231	2311	2390	2469	2546	8 16 24	32 40 48	56 64 72
1·3	0·2624	2700	2776	2852	2927	3001	3075	3148	3221	3293	7 15 22	30 37 44	52 59 67
1·4	0·3365	3436	3507	3577	3646	3716	3784	3853	3920	3988	7 14 21	28 35 41	48 55 62
1·5	0·4055	4121	4187	4253	4318	4383	4447	4511	4574	4637	6 13 19	26 32 39	45 52 58
1·6	0·4700	4762	4824	4886	4947	5008	5068	5128	5188	5247	6 12 18	24 30 36	42 48 55
1·7	0·5306	5365	5423	5481	5539	5596	5653	5710	5766	5822	6 11 17	24 29 34	40 46 51
1·8	0·5878	5933	5988	6043	6098	6152	6206	6259	6313	6366	5 11 16	22 27 32	38 43 49
1·9	0·6419	6471	6523	6575	6627	6678	6729	6780	6831	6881	5 10 15	20 26 31	36 41 46
2·0	0·6931	6981	7031	7080	7129	7178	7227	7275	7324	7372	5 10 15	20 24 29	34 39 44
2·1	0·7419	7467	7514	7561	7608	7655	7701	7747	7793	7839	5 9 14	19 23 28	33 37 42
2·2	0·7885	7930	7975	8020	8065	8109	8154	8198	8242	8286	4 9 13	18 22 27	31 36 40
2·3	0·8329	8372	8416	8459	8502	8544	8587	8629	8671	8713	4 9 13	17 21 26	30 34 38
2·4	0·8755	8796	8838	8879	8920	8961	9002	9042	9083	9123	4 8 12	16 20 24	29 33 37
2·5	0·9163	9203	9243	9282	9322	9361	9400	9439	9478	9517	4 8 12	16 20 24	27 31 35
2·6	0·9555	9594	9632	9670	9708	9746	9783	9821	9858	9895	4 8 11	15 19 23	26 30 34
2·7	0·9933	9969	·0006	0043	0080	0116	0152	0188	0225	0260	4 7 11	15 18 22	25 29 33
2·8	1·0296	0332	0367	0403	0438	0473	0508	0543	0578	0613	4 7 11	14 18 21	25 28 32
2·9	1·0647	0682	0716	0750	0784	0818	0852	0886	0919	0953	3 7 10	14 17 20	24 27 31
3·0	1·0986	1019	1053	1086	1119	1151	1184	1217	1249	1282	3 7 10	13 16 20	23 26 30
3·1	1·1314	1346	1378	1410	1442	1474	1506	1537	1569	1600	3 6 10	13 16 19	22 25 29
3·2	1·1632	1663	1694	1725	1756	1787	1817	1848	1878	1909	3 6 9	12 15 18	22 25 28
3·3	1·1939	1969	2000	2030	2060	2090	2119	2149	2179	2208	3 6 9	12 15 18	21 24 27
3·4	1·2238	2267	2296	2326	2355	2384	2413	2442	2470	2499	3 6 9	12 15 17	20 23 26
3·5	1·2528	2556	2585	2613	2641	2669	2698	2726	2754	2782	3 6 8	11 14 17	20 23 25
3·6	1·2809	2837	2865	2892	2920	2947	2975	3002	3029	3056	3 5 8	11 14 16	19 22 25
3·7	1·3083	3110	3137	3164	3191	3218	3244	3271	3297	3324	3 5 8	11 13 16	19 21 24
3·8	1·3350	3376	3403	3429	3455	3481	3507	3533	3558	3584	3 5 8	10 13 16	18 21 23
3·9	1·3610	3635	3661	3686	3712	3737	3762	3788	3813	3838	3 5 8	10 13 15	18 20 23
4·0	1·3863	3888	3913	3938	3962	3987	4012	4036	4061	4085	2 5 7	10 12 15	17 20 22
4·1	1·4110	4134	4159	4183	4207	4231	4255	4279	4303	4327	2 5 7	10 12 14	17 19 22
4·2	1·4351	4375	4398	4422	4446	4469	4493	4516	4540	4563	2 5 7	9 12 14	16 19 21
4·3	1·4586	4609	4633	4656	4679	4702	4725	4748	4770	4793	2 5 7	9 12 14	16 18 21
4·4	1·4816	4839	4861	4884	4907	4929	4951	4974	4996	5019	2 5 7	9 11 14	16 18 20
4·5	1·5041	5063	5085	5107	5129	5151	5173	5195	5217	5239	2 4 7	9 11 13	15 18 20
4·6	1·5261	5282	5304	5326	5347	5369	5390	5412	5433	5454	2 4 6	9 11 13	15 17 19
4·7	1·5476	5497	5518	5539	5560	5581	5602	5623	5644	5665	2 4 6	8 11 13	15 17 19
4·8	1·5686	5707	5728	5748	5769	5790	5810	5831	5851	5872	2 4 6	8 10 12	14 16 19
4·9	1·5892	5913	5933	5953	5974	5994	6014	6034	6054	6074	2 4 6	8 10 12	14 16 18
5·0	1·6094	6114	6134	6154	6174	6194	6214	6233	6253	6273	2 4 6	8 10 12	14 16 18
5·1	1·6292	6312	6332	6351	6371	6390	6409	6429	6448	6467	2 4 6	8 10 12	14 16 18
5·2	1·6487	6506	6525	6544	6563	6582	6601	6620	6639	6658	2 4 6	8 10 11	13 15 17
5·3	1·6677	6696	6715	6734	6752	6771	6790	6808	6827	6845	2 4 6	7 9 11	13 15 17
5·4	1·6864	6882	6901	6919	6938	6956	6974	6993	7011	7029	2 4 5	7 9 11	13 15 17

Hyperbolic or Naperian Logarithms of 10^{+n}

n	1	2	3	4	5	6	7	8	9
$\log_e 10^n$	2·3026	4·6052	6·9078	9·2103	11·5129	13·8155	16·1181	18·4207	20·7233

	0	1	2	3	4	5	6	7	8	9	Mean Differences 1 2 3	4 5 6	7 8 9
5·5	1·7047	7066 7084 7102	7120 7138 7156	7174 7192 7210	2 4 5	7 9 11	13 14 16						
5·6	1·7228	7246 7263 7281	7299 7317 7334	7352 7370 7387	2 4 5	7 9 11	12 14 16						
5·7	1·7405	7422 7440 7457	7475 7492 7509	7527 7544 7561	2 3 5	7 9 10	12 14 16						
5·8	1·7579	7596 7613 7630	7647 7664 7681	7699 7716 7733	2 3 5	7 9 10	12 14 15						
5·9	1·7750	7766 7783 7800	7817 7834 7851	7867 7884 7901	2 3 5	7 8 10	12 13 15						
6·0	1·7918	7934 7951 7967	7984 8001 8017	8034 8050 8066	2 3 5	7 8 10	12 13 15						
6·1	1·8083	8099 8116 8132	8148 8165 8181	8197 8213 8229	2 3 5	6 8 10	11 13 15						
6·2	1·8245	8262 8278 8294	8310 8326 8342	8358 8374 8390	2 3 5	6 8 10	11 13 14						
6·3	1·8405	8421 8437 8453	8469 8485 8500	8516 8532 8547	2 3 5	6 8 9	11 13 14						
6·4	1·8563	8579 8594 8610	8625 8641 8656	8672 8687 8703	2 3 5	6 8 9	11 12 14						
6·5	1·8718	8733 8749 8764	8779 8795 8810	8825 8840 8856	2 3 5	6 8 9	11 12 14						
6·6	1·8871	8886 8901 8916	8931 8946 8961	8976 8991 9006	2 3 5	6 8 9	11 12 14						
6·7	1·9021	9036 9051 9066	9081 9095 9110	9125 9140 9155	1 3 4	6 7 9	10 12 13						
6·8	1·9169	9184 9199 9213	9228 9242 9257	9272 9286 9301	1 3 4	6 7 9	10 12 13						
6·9	1·9315	9330 9344 9359	9373 9387 9402	9416 9430 9445	1 3 4	6 7 9	10 12 13						
7·0	1·9459	9473 9488 9502	9516 9530 9544	9559 9573 9587	1 3 4	6 7 9	10 11 13						
7·1	1·9601	9615 9629 9643	9657 9671 9685	9699 9713 9727	1 3 4	6 7 8	10 11 13						
7·2	1·9741	9755 9769 9782	9796 9810 9824	9838 9851 9865	1 3 4	6 7 8	10 11 12						
7·3	1·9879	9892 9906 9920	9933 9947 9961	9974 9988 ·0001	1 3 4	5 7 8	10 11 12						
7·4	2·0015	0028 0042 0055	0069 0082 0096	0109 0122 0136	1 3 4	5 7 8	9 11 12						
7·5	2·0149	0162 0176 0189	0202 0215 0229	0242 0255 0268	1 3 4	5 7 8	9 11 12						
7·6	2·0281	0295 0308 0321	0334 0347 0360	0375 0386 0399	1 3 4	5 7 8	9 10 12						
7·7	2·0412	0425 0438 0451	0464 0477 0490	0503 0516 0528	1 3 4	5 6 8	9 10 12						
7·8	2·0541	0554 0567 0580	0592 0605 0618	0631 0643 0656	1 3 4	5 6 8	9 10 11						
7·9	2·0669	0681 0694 0707	0719 0732 0744	0757 0769 0782	1 3 4	5 6 8	9 10 11						
8·0	2·0794	0807 0819 0832	0844 0857 0869	0882 0894 0906	1 3 4	5 6 7	9 10 11						
8·1	2·0919	0931 0943 0956	0968 0980 0992	1005 1017 1029	1 2 4	5 6 7	9 10 11						
8·2	2·1041	1054 1066 1078	1090 1102 1114	1126 1138 1150	1 2 4	5 6 7	9 10 11						
8·3	2·1163	1175 1187 1199	1211 1223 1235	1247 1258 1270	1 2 4	5 6 7	8 10 11						
8·4	2·1282	1294 1306 1318	1330 1342 1353	1365 1377 1389	1 2 4	5 6 7	8 9 11						
8·5	2·1401	1412 1424 1436	1448 1459 1471	1483 1494 1506	1 2 4	5 6 7	8 9 11						
8·6	2·1518	1529 1541 1552	1564 1576 1587	1599 1610 1622	1 2 3	5 6 7	8 9 10						
8·7	2·1633	1645 1656 1668	1679 1691 1702	1713 1725 1736	1 2 3	5 6 7	8 9 10						
8·8	2·1748	1759 1770 1782	1793 1804 1815	1827 1838 1849	1 2 3	4 6 7	8 9 10						
8·9	2·1861	1872 1883 1894	1905 1917 1928	1939 1950 1961	1 2 3	4 6 7	8 9 10						
9·0	2·1972	1983 1994 2006	2017 2028 2039	2050 2061 2072	1 2 3	4 6 7	8 9 10						
9·1	2·2083	2094 2105 2116	2127 2138 2148	2159 2170 2181	1 2 3	4 5 6	8 9 10						
9·2	2·2192	2203 2214 2225	2235 2246 2257	2268 2279 2289	1 2 3	4 5 6	8 9 10						
9·3	2·2300	2311 2322 2332	2343 2354 2364	2375 2386 2396	1 2 3	4 5 6	7 9 10						
9·4	2·2407	2418 2428 2439	2450 2460 2471	2481 2492 2502	1 2 3	4 5 6	7 8 10						
9·5	2·2513	2523 2534 2544	2555 2565 2576	2586 2597 2607	1 2 3	4 5 6	7 8 9						
9·6	2·2618	2628 2638 2649	2659 2670 2680	2690 2701 2711	1 2 3	4 5 6	7 8 9						
9·7	2·2721	2732 2742 2752	2762 2773 2783	2793 2803 2814	1 2 3	4 5 6	7 8 9						
9·8	2·2824	2834 2844 2854	2865 2875 2885	2895 2905 2915	1 2 3	4 5 6	7 8 9						
9·9	2·2925	2935 2946 2956	2966 2976 2986	2996 3006 3016	1 2 3	4 5 6	7 8 9						
10·0	2·3026												

Hyperbolic or Naperian Logarithms of 10⁻ⁿ

n	1	2	3	4	5	6	7	8	9
$\log_e 10^{-n}$	3·6974	5·3948	7·0922	10·7897	12·4871	14·1845	17·8819	19·5793	21·2767

NATURAL SINES, TANGENETS AND COSINES
To Ten Minutes of Arc

° '	Sine	Tan.	Cotan.	Cosine	'	° °	'	Sine	Tan.	Cotan.	Cosine	'	°
0 0	0·0000	0·0000	Infinite	1·0000	0	90 11	0	0·1908	0·1944	5·1446	0·9816	0	79
10	0·0029	0·0029	343·7737	1·0000	50		10	0·1937	0·1974	5·0658	0·9811	50	
20	0·0058	0·0058	171·8854	1·0000	40		20	0·1965	0·2004	4·9894	0·9805	40	
30	0·0087	0·0087	114·5887	1·0000	30		30	0·1994	0·2035	4·9152	0·9799	30	
40	0·0116	0·0116	85·9398	0·9999	20		40	0·2022	0·2065	4·8430	0·9793	20	
50	0·0145	0·0145	68·7501	0·9999	10		50	0·2051	0·2095	4·7729	0·9787	10	
1 0	0·0175	0·0175	57·2900	0·9998	0	89 12	0	0·2079	0·2126	4·7046	0·9781	0	78
10	0·0204	0·0204	49·1039	0·9998	50		10	0·2108	0·2156	4·6382	0·9775	50	
20	0·0233	0·0233	42·9641	0·9997	40		20	0·2136	0·2186	4·5736	0·9769	40	
30	0·0262	0·0262	38·1885	0:9997	30		30	0·2164	0·2217	4·5107	0·9763	30	
40	0·0291	0·0291	34·3678	0·9996	20		40	0·2193	0·2247	4·4494	0·9757	20	
50	0·0320	0·0320	31·2416	0·9995	10		50	0·2221	0·2278	4·3897	0·9750	10	
2 0	0·0349	0·0349	28·6363	0·9994	0	88 13	0	0·2250	0·2309	4·3315	0·9744	0	77
10	0·0378	0·0378	26·4316	0·9993	50		10	0·2278	0·2339	4·2747	0·9737	50	
20	0·0407	0·0407	24·5418	0·9992	40		20	0·2306	0·2370	4·2193	0·9730	40	
30	0·0436	0·0437	22·9038	0·9990	30		30	0·2334	0·2401	4·1653	0·9724	30	
40	0·0465	0·0466	21·4704	0·9989	20		40	0·2363	0·2432	4·1126	0·9717	20	
50	0·0494	0·0495	20·2056	0·9988	10		50	0·2391	0·2462	4·0611	0·9710	10	
0	0·0523	0·0524	19·0811	0·9986	0	87 14	0	0·2419	0·2493	4·0108	0·9703	0	76
10	0·0552	0·0553	18·0750	0·9985	50		10	0·2447	0·2524	3·9617	0·9696	50	
20	0·0581	0·0582	17·1693	0·9983	40		20	0·2476	0·2555	3·9136	0·9689	40	
30	0·0610	0·0612	16·3499	0·9981	30		30	0·2504	0·2586	3·8667	0·9681	30	
40	0·0640	0·0641	15·6048	0·9980	20		40	0·2532	0·2617	3·8208	0·9674	20	
50	0·0669	0·0670	14·9244	0·9978	10		50	0·2560	0·2648	3·7760	0·9667	10	
4 0	0·0698	0·0699	14·3007	0·9976	0	86 15	0	0·2588	0·2679	3·7321	0·9659	0	75
10	0·0727	0·0729	13·7267	0·9974	50		10	0·2616	0·2711	3·6891	0·9652	50	
20	0·0756	0·0758	13·1969	0·9971	40		20	0·2644	0·2742	3·6470	0·9644	40	
30	0·0785	0·0787	12·7062	0·9969	30		30	0·2672	0·2773	3·6059	0·9636	30	
40	0·0814	0·0816	12·2505	0·9967	20		40	0·2700	0·2805	3·5656	0·9628	20	
50	0·0843	0·0846	11·8262	0·9964	10		50	0·2728	0·2836	3·5261	0·9621	10	
5 0	0·0872	0·0875	11·4301	0·9962	0	85 16	0	0·2756	0·2867	3·4874	0·9613	0	74
10	0·0901	0·0904	11·0594	0·9959	50		10	0·2784	0·2899	3·4495	0·9605	50	
20	0·0929	0·0934	10·7119	0·9957	40		20	0·2812	0·2931	3·4124	0·9596	40	
30	0·0958	0·0963	10·3854	0·9954	30		30	0·2840	0·2962	3·3759	0·9588	30	
40	0·0987	0·0992	10·0780	0·9951	20		40	0·2868	0·2994	3·3402	0·9580	20	
50	0·1016	0·1022	9·7882	0·9948	10		50	0·2896	0·3026	3·3052	0·9572	10	
6 0	0·1045	0·1051	9·5144	0·9945	0	84 17	0	0·2924	0·3057	3·2709	0·9563	0	73
10	0·1074	0·1080	9·2553	0·9942	50		10	0·2952	0·3089	3·2371	0·9555	50	
20	0·1103	0·1110	9·0098	0·9939	40		20	0·2979	0·3121	3·2041	0·9546	40	
30	0·1132	0·1139	8·7769	0·9936	30		30	0·3007	0·3153	3·1716	0·9537	30	
40	0·1161	0·1169	8·5555	0·9932	20		40	0·3035	0·3185	3·1397	0·9528	20	
50	0·1190	0·1198	8·3450	0·9929	10		50	0·3062	0·3217	3·1084	0·9520	10	
7 0	0·1219	0·1228	8·1443	0·9925	0	83 18	0	0·3090	0·3249	3·0777	0·9511	0	72
10	0·1248	0·1257	7·9530	0·9922	50		10	0·3118	0·3281	3·0475	0·9502	50	
20	0·1276	0·1287	7·7704	0·9918	40		20	0·3145	0·3314	3·0178	0·9492	40	
30	0·1305	0·1317	7·5958	0·9914	30		30	0·3173	0·3346	2·9887	0·9483	30	
40	0·1334	0·1346	7·4287	0·9911	20		40	0·3201	0·3378	2·9600	0·9474	20	
50	0·1363	0·1376	7·2687	0·9907	10		50	0·3228	0·3411	2·9319	0·9465	10	
8 0	0·1392	0·1405	7·1154	0·9903	0	82 19	0	0·3256	0·3443	2·9042	0·9455	0	71
10	0·1421	0·1435	6·9682	0·9899	50		10	0·3283	0·3476	2·8770	0·9446	50	
20	0·1449	0·1465	6·8269	0·9894	40		20	0·3311	0·3508	2·8502	0·9436	40	
30	0·1478	0·1495	6·6912	0·9890	30		30	0·3338	0·3541	2·8239	0·9426	30	
40	0·1507	0·1524	6·5606	0·9886	20		40	0·3365	0·3574	2·7980	0·9417	20	
50	0·1536	0·1554	6·4348	0·9881	10		50	0·3393	0·3607	2·7725	0·9407	10	
9 0	0·1564	0·1584	6·3138	0·9877	0	81 20	0	0·3420	0·3640	2·7475	0·9397	0	70
10	0·1593	0·1614	6·1970	0·9872	50		10	0·3448	0·3673	2·7228	0·9387	50	
20	0·1622	0·1644	6·0844	0·9868	40		20	0·3475	0·3706	2·6985	0·9377	40	
30	0·1650	0·1673	5·9758	0·9863	30		30	0·3502	0·3739	2·6746	0·9367	30	
40	0·1679	0·1703	5·8708	0·9858	20		40	0·3529	0·3772	2·6511	0·9356	20	
50	0·1708	0·1733	5·7694	0·9853	10		50	0·3557	0·3805	2·6279	0·9346	10	
10 0	0·1736	0·1763	5·6713	0·9848	0	80 21	0	0·3584	0·3839	2·6051	0·9336	0	69
10	0·1765	0·1793	5·5764	0·9843	50		10	0·3611	0·3872	2·5826	0·9325	50	
20	0·1794	0·1823	5·4845	0·9838	40		20	0·3638	0·3906	2·5605	0·9315	40	
30	0·1822	0·1853	5·3955	0·9833	30		30	0·3665	0·3939	2·5386	0·9304	30	
40	0·1851	0·1883	5·3093	0·9827	20		40	0·3692	0·3973	2·5172	0·9293	20	
50	0·1880	0·1914	5·2257	0·9822	10		50	0·3719	0·4006	2·4960	0·9283	10	
° '	Cosine	Cotan.	Tan.	Sine	'	° °	'	Cosine	Cotan.	Tan.	Sine	'	

°	'	Sine	Tan.	Cotan.	Cosine	'	°
22	0	0·3746	0·4040	2·4751	0·9272	0	68
	10	0·3773	0·4074	2·4545	0·9261	50	
	20	0·3800	0·4108	2·4342	0·9250	40	
	30	0·3827	0·4142	2·4142	0·9239	30	
	40	0·3854	0·4176	2·3945	0·9228	20	
	50	0·3881	0·4210	2·3750	0·9216	10	
23	0	0·3907	0·4245	2·3559	0·9205	0	67
	10	0·3934	0·4279	2·3369	0·9194	50	
	20	0·3961	0·4314	2·3183	0·9182	40	
	30	0·3987	0·4348	2·2998	0·9171	30	
	40	0·4014	0·4383	2·2817	0·9159	20	
	50	0·4041	0·4417	2·2637	0·9147	10	
24	0	0·4067	0·4452	2·2460	0·9135	0	66
	10	0·4094	0·4487	2·2286	0·9124	50	
	20	0·4120	0·4522	2·2113	0·9112	40	
	30	0·4147	0·4557	2·1943	0·9100	30	
	40	0·4173	0·4592	2·1775	0·9088	20	
	50	0·4200	0·4628	2·1609	0·9075	10	
25	0	0·4226	0·4663	2·1445	0·9063	0	65
	10	0·4253	0·4699	2·1283	0·9051	50	
	20	0·4279	0·4734	2·1123	0·9038	40	
	30	0·4305	0·4770	2·0965	0·9026	30	
	40	0·4331	0·4806	2·0809	0·9013	20	
	50	0·4358	0·4841	2·0655	0·9001	10	
26	0	0·4384	0·4877	2·0503	0·8988	0	64
	10	0·4410	0·4913	2·0353	0·8975	50	
	20	0·4436	0·4950	2·0204	0·8962	40	
	30	0·4462	0·4986	2·0057	0·8949	30	
	40	0·4488	0·5022	1·9912	0·8936	20	
	50	0·4514	0·5059	1·9768	0·8923	10	
27	0	0·4540	0·5095	1·9626	0·8910	0	63
	10	0·4566	0·5132	1·9486	0·8897	50	
	20	0·4592	0·5169	1·9347	0·8884	40	
	30	0·4617	0·5206	1·9210	0·8870	30	
	40	0·4643	0·5243	1·9074	0·8857	20	
	50	0·4669	0·5280	1·8940	0·8843	10	
28	0	0·4695	0·5317	1·8807	0·8829	0	62
	10	0·4720	0·5354	1·8676	0·8816	50	
	20	0·4746	0·5392	1·8546	0·8802	40	
	30	0·4772	0·5430	1·8418	0·8788	30	
	40	0·4797	0·5467	1·8291	0·8774	20	
	50	0·4823	0·5505	1·8165	0·8760	10	
29	0	0·4848	0·5543	1·8040	0·8746	0	61
	10	0·4874	0·5581	1·7917	0·8732	50	
	20	0·4899	0·5619	1·7796	0·8718	40	
	30	0·4924	0·5658	1·7675	0·8704	30	
	40	0·4950	0·5696	1·7556	0·8689	20	
	50	0·4974	0·5735	1·7437	0·8675	10	
30	0	0·5000	0·5774	1·7321	0·8660	0	60
	10	0·5025	0·5812	1·7205	0·8646	50	
	20	0·5050	0·5851	1·7090	0·8631	40	
	30	0·5075	0·5890	1·6977	0·8616	30	
	40	0·5100	0·5930	1·6864	0·8601	20	
	50	0·5125	0·5969	1·6753	0·8587	10	
31	0	0·5150	0·6009	1·6643	0·8572	0	59
	10	0·5175	0·6048	1·6534	0·8557	50	
	20	0·5200	0·6088	1·6426	0·8542	40	
	30	0·5225	0·6128	1·6319	0·8526	30	
	40	0·5250	0·6168	1·6212	0·8511	20	
	50	0·5275	0·6208	1·6107	0·8496	10	
32	0	0·5299	0·6249	1·6003	0·8480	0	58
	10	0·5324	0·6289	1·5900	0·8465	50	
	20	0·5348	0·6330	1·5798	0·8450	40	
	30	0·5373	0·6371	1·5697	0·8434	30	
	40	0·5398	0·6412	1·5597	0·8418	20	
	50	0·5422	0·6453	1·5497	0·8403	10	
33	0	0·5446	0·6494	1·5399	0·8387	0	57
	10	0·5471	0·6536	1·5301	0·8371	50	
	20	0·5495	0·6577	1·5204	0·8355	40	

°	'	Sine	Tan.	Cotan.	Cosine	'	°
	30	0·5519	0·6619	1·5108	0·8339	30	
	40	0·5544	0·6661	1·5013	0·8323	20	
	50	0·5568	0·6703	1·4919	0·8307	10	
34	0	0·5592	0·6745	1·4826	0·8290	0	56
	10	0·5616	0·6787	1·4733	0·8274	50	
	20	0·5640	0·6830	1·4641	0·8258	40	
	30	0·5664	0·6873	1·4550	0·8241	30	
	40	0·5688	0·6916	1·4460	0·8225	20	
	50	0·5712	0·6959	1·4370	0·8208	10	
35	0	0·5736	0·7002	1·4281	0·8192	0	55
	10	0·5760	0·7046	1·4193	0·8175	50	
	20	0·5783	0·7089	1·4106	0·8158	40	
	30	0·5807	0·7133	1·4019	0·8141	30	
	40	0·5831	0·7177	1·3934	0·8124	20	
	50	0·5854	0·7221	1·3848	0·8107	10	
36	0	0·5878	0·7265	1·3764	0·8090	0	54
	10	0·5901	0·7310	1·3680	0·8073	50	
	20	0·5925	0·7355	1·3597	0·8056	40	
	30	0·5948	0·7400	1·3514	0·8039	30	
	40	0·5972	0·7445	1·3432	0·8021	20	
	50	0·5995	0·7490	1·3351	0·8004	10	
37	0	0·6018	0·7536	1·3270	0·7986	0	53
	10	0·6041	0·7581	1·3190	0·7969	50	
	20	0·6065	0·7627	1·3111	0·7951	40	
	30	0·6088	0·7673	1·3032	0·7934	30	
	40	0·6111	0·7720	1·2954	0·7916	20	
	50	0·6134	0·7766	1·2876	0·7898	10	
38	0	0·6157	0·7813	1·2799	0·7880	0	52
	10	0·6180	0·7860	1·2723	0·7862	50	
	20	0·6202	0·7907	1·2647	0·7844	40	
	30	0·6225	0·7954	1·2572	0·7826	30	
	40	0·6248	0·8002	1·2497	0·7808	20	
	50	0·6271	0·8050	1·2423	0·7790	10	
39	0	0·6293	0·8098	1·2349	0·7771	0	51
	10	0·6316	0·8146	1·2276	0·7753	50	
	20	0·6338	0·8195	1·2203	0·7735	40	
	30	0·6361	0·8243	1·2131	0·7716	30	
	40	0·6383	0·8292	1·2059	0·7698	20	
	50	0·6406	0·8342	1·1988	0·7679	10	
40	0	0·6428	0·8391	1·1918	0·7660	0	50
	10	0·6450	0·8441	1·1847	0·7642	50	
	20	0·6472	0·8491	1·1778	0·7623	40	
	30	0·6494	0·8541	1·1708	0·7604	30	
	40	0·6517	0·8591	1·1640	0·7585	20	
	50	0·6539	0·8642	1·1571	0·7566	10	
41	0	0·6561	0·8693	1·1504	0·7547	0	49
	10	0·6583	0·8744	1·1436	0·7528	50	
	20	0·6604	0·8796	1·1369	0·7509	40	
	30	0·6626	0·8847	1·1303	0·7490	30	
	40	0·6648	0·8899	1·1237	0·7470	20	
	50	0·6670	0·8952	1·1171	0·7451	10	
42	0	0·6691	0·9004	1·1106	0·7431	0	48
	10	0·6713	0·9057	1·1041	0·7412	50	
	20	0·6734	0·9110	1·0977	0·7392	40	
	30	0·6756	0·9163	1·0913	0·7373	30	
	40	0·6777	0·9217	1·0850	0·7353	20	
	50	0·6799	0·9271	1·0786	0·7333	10	
43	0	0·6820	0·9325	1·0724	0·7314	0	47
	10	0·6841	0·9380	1·0661	0·7294	50	
	20	0·6862	0·9435	1·0599	0·7274	40	
	30	0·6884	0·9490	1·0538	0·7254	30	
	40	0·6905	0·9545	1·0477	0·7234	20	
	50	0·6926	0·9601	1·0416	0·7214	10	
44	0	0·6947	0·9657	1·0355	0·7193	0	46
	10	0·6967	0·9713	1·0295	0·7173	50	
	20	0·6988	0·9770	1·0235	0·7153	40	
	30	0·7009	0·9827	1·0176	0·7133	30	
	40	0·7030	0·9884	1·0117	0·7112	20	
	50	0·7050	0·9942	1·0058	0·7092	10	
45	0	0·7071	1·0000	1·0000	0·7071	0	45

| ° | ' | Cosine | Cotan. | Tan. | Sine | ' | ° |

DEGREES OF RADIANS

Degrees	0' 0°·0	6' 0°·1	12' 0°·2	18' 0°·3	24' 0°·4	30' 0°·5	36' 0°·6	42' 0°·7	48' 0°·8	54' 0°·9	Mean Differences				
											1	2	3	4	5
0	0·0000	0017	0035	0052	0070	0087	0105	0122	0140	0157	3	6	9	12	15
1	0·0175	0192	0209	0227	0244	0262	0279	0297	0314	0332	3	6	9	12	15
2	0·0349	0367	0384	0401	0419	0436	0454	0471	0489	0506	3	6	9	12	15
3	0·0524	0541	0559	0576	0593	0611	0628	0646	0663	0681	3	6	9	12	15
4	0·0698	0716	0733	0750	0768	0785	0803	0820	0838	0855	3	6	9	12	15
5	0·0873	0890	0908	0925	0942	0960	0977	0995	1012	1030	3	6	9	12	15
6	0·1047	1065	1082	1100	1117	1134	1152	1169	1187	1204	3	6	9	12	15
7	0·1222	1239	1257	1274	1292	1309	1326	1344	1361	1379	3	6	9	12	15
8	0·1396	1414	1431	1449	1466	1484	1501	1518	1536	1553	3	6	9	12	15
9	0·1571	1588	1606	1623	1641	1658	1676	1693	1710	1728	3	6	9	12	15
10	0·1745	1763	1780	1798	1815	1833	1850	1868	1885	1902	3	6	9	12	15
11	0·1920	1937	1955	1972	1990	2007	2025	2042	2060	2077	3	6	9	12	15
12	0·2094	2112	2129	2147	2164	2182	2199	2217	2234	2251	3	6	9	12	15
13	0·2269	2286	2304	2321	2339	2356	2374	2391	2409	2426	3	6	9	12	15
14	0·2443	2461	2478	2496	2513	2531	2548	2566	2583	2601	3	6	9	12	15
15	0·2618	2635	2653	2670	2688	2705	2723	2740	2758	2775	3	6	9	12	15
16	0·2793	2810	2827	2845	2862	2880	2897	2915	2932	2950	3	6	9	12	15
17	0·2967	2985	3002	3019	3037	3054	3072	3089	3107	3124	3	6	9	12	15
18	0·3142	3159	3176	3194	3211	3229	3246	3264	3281	3299	3	6	9	12	15
19	0·3316	3334	3351	3368	3386	3403	3421	3438	3456	3473	3	6	9	12	15
20	0·3491	3508	3526	3543	3560	3578	3595	3613	3630	3648	3	6	9	12	15
21	0·3665	3683	3700	3718	3735	3752	3770	3787	3805	3822	3	6	9	12	15
22	0·3840	3857	3875	3892	3910	3927	3944	3962	3979	3997	3	6	9	12	15
23	0·4014	4032	4049	4067	4084	4102	4119	4136	4154	4171	3	6	9	12	15
24	0·4189	4206	4224	4241	4259	4276	4294	4311	4328	4346	3	6	9	12	15
25	0·4363	4381	4398	4416	4433	4451	4468	4485	4503	4520	3	6	9	12	15
26	0·4538	4555	4573	4590	4608	4625	4643	4660	4677	4695	3	6	9	12	15
27	0·4712	4730	4747	4765	4782	4800	4817	4835	4852	4869	3	6	9	12	15
28	0·4887	4904	4922	4939	4957	4974	4992	5009	5027	5044	3	6	9	12	15
29	0·5061	5079	5096	5114	5131	5149	5166	5184	5201	5219	3	6	9	12	15
30	0·5236	5253	5271	5288	5306	5323	5341	5358	5376	5393	3	6	9	12	15
31	0·5411	5428	5445	5463	5480	5498	5515	5533	5550	5568	3	6	9	12	15
32	0·5585	5603	5620	5637	5655	5672	5690	5707	5725	5742	3	6	9	12	15
33	0·5760	5777	5794	5812	5829	5847	5864	5882	5899	5917	3	6	9	12	15
34	0·5934	5952	5969	5986	6004	6021	6039	6056	6074	6091	3	6	9	12	15
35	0·6109	6126	6144	6161	6178	6196	6213	6231	6248	6266	3	6	9	12	15
36	0·6283	6301	6318	6336	6353	6370	6388	6405	6423	6440	3	6	9	12	15
37	0·6458	6475	6493	6510	6528	6545	6562	6580	6597	6615	3	6	9	12	15
38	0·6632	6650	6667	6685	6702	6720	6737	6754	6772	6789	3	6	9	12	15
39	0·6807	6824	6842	6859	6877	6894	6912	6929	6946	6964	3	6	9	12	15
40	0·6981	6999	7016	7034	7051	7069	7086	7103	7121	7138	3	6	9	12	15
41	0·7156	7173	7191	7208	7226	7243	7261	7278	7295	7313	3	6	9	12	15
42	0·7330	7348	7365	7383	7400	7418	7435	7453	7470	7487	3	6	9	12	15
43	0·7505	7522	7540	7557	7575	7592	7610	7627	7645	7662	3	6	9	12	15
44	0·7679	7697	7714	7732	7749	7767	7784	7802	7819	7837	3	6	9	12	15

Degrees	0′ 0°·0	6′ 0°·1	12′ 0°·2	18′ 0°·3	24′ 0°·4	30′ 0°·5	36′ 0°·6	42′ 0°·7	48′ 0°·8	54′ 0°·9	Mean Differences 1	2	3	4	5
45	0·7854	7871	7889	7906	7924	7941	7959	7976	7994	8011	3	6	9	12	15
46	0·8029	8046	8063	8081	8098	8116	8133	8151	8168	8186	3	6	9	12	15
47	0·8203	8221	8238	8255	8273	8290	8308	8325	8343	8360	3	6	9	12	15
48	0·8378	8395	8412	8430	8447	8465	8482	8500	8517	8535	3	6	9	12	15
49	0·8552	8570	8587	8604	8622	8639	8657	8674	8692	8709	3	6	9	12	15
50	0·8727	8744	8762	8779	8796	8814	8831	8849	8866	8884	3	6	9	12	15
51	0·8901	8919	8936	8954	8971	8988	9006	9023	9041	9058	3	6	9	12	15
52	0·9076	9093	9111	9128	9146	9163	9180	9198	9215	9233	3	6	9	12	15
53	0·9250	9268	9285	9303	9320	9338	9355	9372	9390	9407	3	6	9	12	15
54	0·9425	9442	9460	9477	9495	9512	9529	9547	9564	9582	3	6	9	12	15
55	0·9599	9617	9634	9652	9669	9687	9704	9721	9739	9756	3	6	9	12	15
56	0·9774	9791	9809	9826	9844	9861	9879	9896	9913	9931	3	6	9	12	15
57	0·9948	9966	9983	1·0001	1·0018	1·0036	1·0053	1·0071	1·0088	1·0105	3	6	9	12	15
58	1·0123	0140	0158	0175	0193	0210	0228	0245	0263	0280	3	6	9	12	15
59	1·0297	0315	0332	0350	0367	0385	0402	0420	0437	0455	3	6	9	12	15
60	1·0472	0489	0507	0524	0542	0559	0577	0594	0612	0629	3	6	9	12	15
61	1·0647	0664	0681	0699	0716	0734	0751	0769	0786	0804	3	6	9	12	15
62	1·0821	0838	0856	0873	0891	0908	0926	0943	0961	0978	3	6	9	12	15
63	1·0996	1013	1030	1048	1065	1083	1100	1118	1135	1153	3	6	9	12	15
64	1·1170	1188	1205	1222	1240	1257	1275	1292	1310	1327	3	6	9	12	15
65	1·1345	1362	1380	1397	1414	1432	1449	1467	1484	1502	3	6	9	12	15
66	1·1519	1537	1554	1572	1589	1606	1624	1641	1659	1676	3	6	9	12	15
67	1·1694	1711	1729	1746	1764	1781	1798	1816	1833	1851	3	6	9	12	15
68	1·1868	1886	1903	1921	1938	1956	1973	1990	2008	2025	3	6	9	12	15
69	1·2043	2060	2078	2095	2113	2130	2147	2165	2182	2200	3	6	9	12	15
70	1·2217	2235	2252	2270	2287	2305	2322	2339	2357	2374	3	6	9	12	15
71	1·2392	2409	2427	2444	2462	2479	2497	2514	2531	2549	3	6	9	12	15
72	1·2566	2584	2601	2619	2636	2654	2671	2689	2706	2723	3	6	9	12	15
73	1·2741	2758	2776	2793	2811	2828	2846	2863	2881	2898	3	6	9	12	15
74	1·2915	2933	2950	2968	2985	3003	3020	3038	3055	3073	3	6	9	12	15
75	1·3090	3107	3125	3142	3160	3177	3195	3212	3230	3247	3	6	9	12	15
76	1·3265	3282	3299	3317	3334	3352	3369	3387	3404	3422	3	6	9	12	15
77	1·3439	3456	3474	3491	3509	3526	3544	3561	3579	3596	3	6	9	12	15
78	1·3614	3631	3648	3666	3683	3701	3718	3736	3753	3771	3	6	9	12	15
79	1·3788	3806	3823	3840	3858	3875	3893	3910	3928	3945	3	6	9	12	15
80	1·3963	3980	3998	4015	4032	4050	4067	4085	4102	4120	3	6	9	12	15
81	1·4137	4155	4172	4190	4207	4224	4242	4259	4277	4294	3	6	9	12	15
82	1·4312	4329	4347	4364	4382	4399	4416	4434	4451	4469	3	6	9	12	15
83	1·4486	4504	4521	4539	4556	4573	4591	4608	4626	4643	3	6	9	12	15
84	1·4661	4678	4696	4713	4731	4748	4765	4783	4800	4818	3	6	9	12	15
85	1·4835	4853	4870	4888	4905	4923	4940	4957	4975	4992	3	6	9	12	15
86	1·5010	5027	5045	5062	5080	5097	5115	5132	5149	5167	3	6	9	12	15
87	1·5184	5202	5219	5237	5254	5272	5289	5307	5324	5341	3	6	9	12	15
88	1·5359	5376	5394	5411	5429	5446	5464	5481	5499	5516	3	6	9	12	15
89	1·5533	5551	5568	5586	5603	5621	5638	5656	5673	5691	3	6	9	12	15

Index